Crisis and Conflict in Han China
104 BC to AD 9

By the same author

Imperial China (George Allen & Unwin)
Everyday Life in Early Imperial China (Batsford)
Records of Han Administration (Cambridge University Press)

Jade suit used in special burials (see p. 125).

CRISIS AND CONFLICT IN HAN CHINA

104 BC to AD 9

Michael Loewe

Lecturer in Chinese Studies, University of Cambridge

London   George Allen & Unwin Ltd
Ruskin House Museum Street

ISBN 0 04 951021 5

Printed in Great Britain
by W & J Mackay Limited, Chatham

FOR
PASTUREWOOD
AND ITS
MOST PRECIOUS GIFT

Contents

Illustrations

Preface

The historical developments of China during the Western Han dynasty (202 BC–AD 9) can best be understood in terms of two attitudes or convictions which characterised intellectual, religious and political change alike. The one attitude, which is denoted in these pages by the term 'Modernist', struck the keynote for the first of the two centuries in question. It informed the policies which were being promoted with growing intensity and vigour during the reign of Wu ti (141–87 BC), and its most successful point was symbolised by certain acts of state during 104. The reigns of Chao ti (87–74), and more particularly Hsüan ti (74–49), formed a transitional stage until the second attitude, which is known here as 'Reformist', took root. This came to characterise the second of the two centuries, and from about 70 BC onwards it gathered sufficient strength to form a dominant influence at court. The Reformist attitude may be discerned conspicuously in the policies adopted under Yüan ti (49–33) and Ch'eng ti (33–7), and it formed the ideological support on which Wang Mang relied and by which he claimed the right to rule the empire.

The Modernists were concerned with directing the efforts of statesmen to the problems of the contemporary world; the Reformists wished to eliminate the political and social abuses of the day by a return to conditions which they believed to have existed in the remote past. The Modernists derived their tradition from Ch'in and its unification of the world under a single rule, and the occult forces which they worshipped had been served by the kings and then the emperors of Ch'in. The Reformists harked back to a tradition which they traced to the kings and ethical ideas of Chou; and they worshipped Heaven, as the kings of Chou had done before them. The Modernists tried to shape imperial policies so that they could control human endeavour, utilise human strength and exploit natural resources in order to enrich and strengthen the state. The Reformists found it repugnant to exercise more controls on the population than were absolutely necessary, and in place of the obedience to official orders which the Modernists demanded, the Reformists looked to the people of China to follow the example and moral lead given by the Emperor. The Modernists saw useful purposes being served by lavish expenditure designed to display the strength, wealth and dignity of the throne. The Reformists preferred to eliminate unnecessary extravagance in the interests of devoting public resources to the benefit of the people of China.

In practice these divergences led to different policies regarding the behaviour expected of the Emperor and the palace; the structure of government and the functions of the senior officials of state; religious observances and the attention paid to omens; the sponsorship of literature; land-ownership; the exploitation of the mines; and foreign policy. To Modernists the Emperor stood at the apex of the State and administrative duties were delegated according to a strictly prescribed scheme of senior and junior officials. The Reformists saw the Emperor first and foremost as an instrument for conferring bounties on mankind and believed that the most senior statesmen should share the supreme responsibility for government from positions that were of equal status. The Modernists took little count of omens or of signs of a supernatural force. They advocated the observance of the state cults at sites which lay at some distance from Ch'ang-an and which were thus removed from the centre of the administration, and they believed that the Emperor and officials should take part in the rites so as to secure temporal blessings and prosperity. The Reformists believed as an article of faith that a beneficent Heaven would issue warnings to mankind by means of strange phenomena which could be seen in the skies or on earth and that the Emperor's purpose in worshipping Heaven lay in fostering the correct relationship between Heaven, Earth and Man. Eventually the Reformists succeeded in having the scene of the state cults moved to the outskirts of Ch'ang-an.

Modernists and Reformists differed over the authenticity of certain versions of ancient texts and over the choice of books for inclusion in the 'Canon': the Modernists sponsored the cause of the recently discovered copies written in contemporary script (*chin wen*), while the Reformists favoured those that were written in the obsolete seal script (*ku wen*). Modernists liked, for example, the

Kung yang commentary to the *Spring and Autumn Annals*, while the Reformists introduced first the *Ku Liang* commentary and later the *Tso chuan*. Modernists saw the growth of a prosperous economy by way of unrestricted ownership of land and the imposition of a state monopoly of the iron and salt mines. The Reformists thought that the material lot of the Chinese would be improved by regulating the extent of land holdings so as to prevent the growth of large estates, and by leaving the mines open for private enterprise. Finally, Modernist foreign policy was directed towards expansion and that of the Reformists towards retrenchment. These and other issues were grievously complicated by the affiliations of different parties at court and by the rivalries of an emperor's several consorts and their ambitious relatives.

The pattern whereby the Reformists came to supplant the Modernist view stands revealed in a number of incidents and crises and in the arguments which were put forward in support or criticism of certain decisions of state. The process may be traced in the conscious adoption of symbolic changes in 105 and 104 BC which mark the adoption of new attitudes and the intensification of the Modernists' policies (see Chapter 1); in the dynastic events which gave rise to Huo Kuang's political dominance and which ended in the eclipse of the family of Huo (91 to 66 BC; see Chapters 2 and 4); in the grand debate on state policies in 81 (see Chapter 3); in the religious reformation of 31 and its precedents (see Chapter 5); in the establishment (*c.* 114), curtailment (from *c.* 70) and the abolition (7 BC) of the Office of Music (see Chapter 6); in the government's reaction to a threat of involvement in central Asia (36; see Chapter 7); in the attitudes and destinies of certain statesmen during the short reign of Ai ti (7 to 1 BC; see Chapter 8); and in the response of officials and statesmen to the claims put forward by Wang Mang (see Chapter 9).

By no means all the incidents which are crucial to these changes are described in this book, which is mainly concerned with the second of the two centuries of Western Han. Equally important events such as the review of literary authorities of 51 BC, or the visit of a Hsiung-nu leader to the Han court in the same year, do not feature here, as they will be treated in some detail in a later study.

I am grateful to the editorial boards of *Asia Major* and the *Bulletin of the School of Oriental and African Studies* for permission to reprint articles that have appeared in those journals. These form Chapters 2, 5 and 6, and I have taken the opportunity to make certain corrections.

Dates are expressed in the usual way, with the numbers of years corresponding to those adopted for the western calendar. Due allowance should therefore be made for those periods of the year in which the correspondence is not exact. For rendering Han titles, I am using a new set of equivalent terms, on an experimental basis; the terms that were coined by Dubs and which have been used subsequently are given in the footnotes, on the basis of the list published by R. de Crespigny (*Official Titles of the Former Han Dynasty*, Canberra, 1967). For convenience, a brief account of the structure of Han government is given in the Appendix.

Tables 1–3 show the relationship of certain persons mentioned in the text; they are not intended to present all the available information regarding the particular families. Figure 3 shows places mentioned in Chapter 7—identification should be regarded as approximate.

Abbreviations

The following abbreviations are used in the footnotes:

Aristocratic Ranks M. Loewe, 'The orders of aristocratic rank of Han China', *T'oung Pao* XLVIII, 1–3 (1960), pp. 97–174.

Everyday Life M. Loewe, *Everyday Life in Early Imperial China during the Han period 202 BC–AD 220* (Batsford, London and Putnam, New York, 1968).

Fujikawa Fujikawa Masakazu, *Kan dai ni okeru rei gaku no kenkyū* (Kazama shobō, Tokyo, 1968).

HFHD H. H. Dubs, *History of the Former Han Dynasty*, vol. I–III (Baltimore, 1938–55).

HHS Hou Han-shu and *Hsü Han-shu*; references are to Wang Hsien-ch'ien's edition (Ch'ang-sha, 1915).

HS Han-shu; references are to Wang Hsien-ch'ien's edition (Ch'ang-sha, 1900).

Hulsewé A. F. P. Hulsewé, *Remnants of Han Law* (Leiden, 1955).

MH E. Chavannes, *Les Mémoires Historiques de Se-ma Ts'ien* (E. Leroux, Paris, 1895–1905; republished, Adrien Maisonneuve, Paris, 1967).

RHA M. Loewe, *Records of Han Administration* (Cambridge, 1967).

SC Shih-chi. References are to *Shiki kaichū kōshō*, edited by Takigawa Kametarō (first published by Tōhō bunka gakuin, Tokyo, 1932–34).

Swann N. L. Swann, *Food and Money in Ancient China* (Princeton, 1950).

Wang Wang Yü-ch'üan, An outline of the Central Government of the Former Han Dynasty, *Harvard Journal of Asiatic Studies* (1949), vol. 12, pp. 134–87; reprinted in *Studies of Governmental Institutions in Chinese History* (Harvard, 1968).

YTL Yen-t'ieh lun; references are to the number of the section (*p'ien*) followed in parenthesis by the page number in Wang Li-ch'i, *Yen-t'ieh lun chiao-chu* (Shanghai, 1958).

CHAPTER 1

The Grand Beginning – 104 BC

According to the laconic record of the *Han-shu*, on the first day of the eleventh month of the first year of T'ai-ch'u, the day of the winter solstice, the Emperor made sacrifice to the Supreme Power in the Hall of Spirits.[1] The day corresponds with what would have been 25 December 105 BC had the western calendar been in use, and the economy of expression whereby the event is described may be paralleled by a famous entry in the *Court Circular of St James* (London) for 12 May 1937. This entry told the reader that 'The coronation of the King and Queen took place in the Abbey Church of Westminster this day'. The entry had hardly been composed with a view to describing the intense emotion of the occasion, in which a sense of national pride and loyalty was intermingled with profound solemnity and a spontaneous outburst of rejoicing. Implications of a similar nature were almost certainly involved both in the act of worship which took place near Mount T'ai at the end of 105 BC and in the symbolical and institutional changes which were introduced six months later. These implications derived from the intellectual outlook of the period and reveal the religious attitude of the state and the dynasty's sense of purpose and imperial achievement.

Members of the court who attended that ceremony in 105 BC and who were aged forty or fifty years would have been glad to be alive, and thankful that they had survived so long, to an age that lay beyond that of most men and women. Had they looked

---

[1] *HS* 6.31a (*HFHD*, II, p. 98).

to the past, on that day of the winter solstice, shivering in the sharp winds that swept in from the north, they might well have recalled with gratitude the progress that had been made in the last thirty years; progress in bringing stability to the Han court, safety to the cities and farms of north China, and a satisfying, convincing belief that the temporal order of which they formed a part was prospering under the benediction of cosmic powers.

There were men there, in all probability, who could recall the accession of the present emperor, in 141 BC, at the tender age of sixteen. For some years afterwards the court had been subject to the Empress Dowager with her passionate belief in the natural way of the world and of mankind.[2] Only on her death, in 135 BC,[3] had it been possible to detect a change of emphasis in state affairs, an access of vigour in determining the policies of state and a resolute will to organise the empire so that it would develop to the greatest strength and wealth that it could reach. As the years went by, not a great deal was known about the new Emperor. Rumour had it that he was subject to the influence of a few magicians, some of whom had been shown to be unscrupulous charlatans,[4] as they had failed dismally to substantiate their claims that they could bring the dead back to life, that they knew where to procure the drugs that would assure immortality, or that they possessed the secret of manufacturing gold. But this did not detract from the Emperor's virtues. He paid a lot of attention to performing the cults of state, and he was manfully doing his best to raise a family of successors—four sons had been born by 105 BC, and one of these had carried the proud title of Heir Apparent for nearly eighteen years.

Intellectuals had found it an interesting thirty years since the emperor's accession. The court had patronised the poet Ssu-ma Hsiang-ju, who had come back from the south-west with strange tales of the uncouth peoples there. He had written a lot of poetry in the newly developing *fu* form of versification

[2] *HS* 97A.8a.   [3] *HS* 6.4a (*HFHD*, II, p. 34).   [4] *HS* 25A.24a, *et seq.*

which was utterly different from the centuries' old 'Songs' that had always been so highly esteemed. Ssu-ma Hsiang-ju's works told a story, describing the deeds, lives and circumstances of sovereigns, which stirred the imagination and which could be verified in the things that one saw round about the palace. At the same time Ssu-ma Ch'ien, who had succeeded his father as Director of Records,[5] was in the last stages of the great history of mankind on which he and his father had been engaged for years. The book had started as a private venture, but it appeared that the author could call on the state archives when he needed first-hand evidence, and, by all accounts, the chapters would make far better reading than the other historical records such as the dry-as-dust *Spring and Autumn Annals*. They had the further advantage of being written in contemporary language, which any man of letters could understand.

There were other signs of the intellectual activity of these decades. Only some ten years previously the Office of Music had been founded to collect songs and to organise musical performances on state occasions. In addition, it seemed that some of the prominent men of the day were taking account of Tung Chung-shu, now either dead or on the point of death, who had done much to mould official opinion. He was a deep thinker, rather 'touched', as some said, for he heard the warning voice of Heaven everywhere, in a clap of thunder, or in the floods that burst out in east China all too often. But for all his insistence and his voice of doom, Tung Chung-shu may well have been right about a number of things, as he seemed to be able to explain where man's place lay in relation to Heaven and Earth. Naturally enough he had never made much of a career in the public service, for the professional civil servants, those staid and highly efficient members of the administration, always made sure that people with a wide imagination or high intelligence were denied the highest honours or positions, in case they became too dangerous.

[5] *T'ai-shih ling*; Dubs—Prefect Grand Clerk.

It was odd, perhaps, that the people who had been most admired in the last twenty years had not necessarily been those who held the highest positions of state, or those who had promoted the schemes of government. Kung-sun Hung, who had died in office as Chancellor[6] in 127, had been one of the most respected of statesmen, but he had been somewhat old-fashioned in his views, not always in keeping with the vigorous ideas of the world in which he lived. He used to insist on the value of traditional morality, and he had had some difficulty in keeping his career going.[7] Pu Shih had been a man of kindred spirit, who openly criticised the way in which the government was trying to organise the resources of China, and he had been dismissed from the post of Imperial Counsellor,[8] the second most responsible position in the empire. That had been in 110.[9]

Some of the decisions which really affected people's lives were being taken in the department of the Superintendent of Agriculture.[10] The men there included a genius called Sang Hung-yang, who had been a mathematical prodigy in his youth and had gained considerable experience in business in his father's counting house in Lo-yang.[11] Sang Hung-yang had been quick to apply commercial methods to the art of government, and it had been largely due to his influence that the state had established its monopolies in the mines some fifteen years previously. Naturally enough the private salt and iron magnates had loathed the scheme. They had seen the state take over the enterprises and manufactures that they and their fathers had built up over many years and had operated by their own efforts, and they had seen the civil servants take over the plant and work it with corvée labour. Huo Kuang was another member of the government who may have been behind that scheme,

[6] *Ch'eng-hsiang*: Dubs—Lieutenant Chancellor.   [7] *HS* 58.1a, *et seq.*
[8] *Yü-shih ta-fu*: Dubs—Imperial Clerk Grandee, or Grandee Secretary
[9] *HS* 58.8b, *et seq.*
[10] *Ta-ssu-nung*: Dubs—Grand Minister of Agriculture.
[11] *HS* 24B.12a (Swann, p. 272).

but it was difficult to say for certain. He was a terribly shrewd man, but as he was not given to careless talk it was difficult to ascertain where his opinions lay. Possibly he felt that he had to be particularly careful as he was related to the Empress, and if he had got himself disliked or distrusted he might have found himself in grave danger from his rivals.

The service had expanded considerably during the last thirty years and all sorts of persons were now gaining admission and making their careers in the offices of the central, provincial or local government. Ever since the death of the Empress Dowager in 135 the government had been actively trying to attract good men to join the profession, so that there would be a sufficient number of civil servants, of whom a few would rise to become statesmen. The authorities had stipulated that candidates for the service should be honest and reasonably intelligent. They must have a good educational grounding in the right sort of texts, i.e. those with a feeling for the humanities and for moral values, and not those pragmatic books on which the previous dynasty had depended for its ruthless outlook,[12] and which had been out of favour since the beginning of the reign. The provincial authorities had responded by sending up quite a number of candidates, and some of these had been accepted for training.

But in addition there was a considerable proportion of riff-raff in the service; there were a number of men whom the government had been forced to reward with official titles, for the brave way in which they had fought on the field of battle, and they were hardly fitted for public administration, by any standards.[13] Hardship arose when such people found themselves in a position of authority to collect taxes. Such a task gave them an excellent chance of oppression and of filling their own pockets, and they would never think of sparing a household, however severely it had been hit by the quirks of nature—floods one year, droughts the next, or if a good harvest was

[12] *HS* 6.1b (*HFHD*, II, p. 28).   [13] *HS* 24B.9a (Swann, pp. 253f.)

sprouting, sure enough swarms of locusts would descend and leave the earth brown and the tree-trunks bare as leafless stumps. As it happened, this very year, the first of T'ai-ch'u, the locusts started spreading from the east in the summer, and had even reached as far as Tun-huang.[14]

Those who were really rich were all right; they could own as much land as they liked, and they could let some of it to the peasantry to till. But the peasants were the people who suffered acutely, with their high rents, and the continual demands to serve in the army, not to speak of the regular month's hard labour that they had to put in each year for the local authorities. Others, who had managed to hold on to their small plots of land or their few possessions, found themselves subject to all sorts of taxes, not only the land tax and the poll tax, which were bad enough, but also the dues raised on property such as waggons, boats or domestic animals, and the tax on sale and purchase which the supervisors of the markets levied.

It was quite understandable that the government needed money. Ever since one could remember there had been a war to fight, as those savage horsemen from the north were always waiting for a chance to gallop south into the farms and fields and to seize what they could find; it must have been worse under the old emperors who had no strength with which to resist them and had had to buy them off with precious presents of silk. Then Chang Ch'ien had come back after a terrible but exciting journey in the northwest. This had been about twenty years earlier, and he had told a tale of the riches you could get for the asking. He had actually seen some of the products of south China on sale over in northern India. He was convinced that better routes could be found to get there on the northern side, and he was quite sure that the Chinese could beat the Hsiung-nu, even in that dreadful desert with its blistering heat of summer and its deathly cold of winter. The government had been right to try and settle with these barbarians, cost what it

[14] *HS* 6.31b (*HFHD*, II, p. 100).

might with the expense of fitting out expeditions with horses, clothing and weapons. They had been clever enough to call on foreign troops, particularly horsemen, to help the Chinese conscripts, but it was they, the peasants, who had borne the main brunt and burden of the day.

Unfortunately there was no end to this problem. Even when the enemy had been thrown back defeated, as they had been fifteen years earlier, the Chinese still had to keep up the pressure, or the Hsiung-nu would have returned. So the government had launched one campaign after another, partly to prevent the enemy extending his influence, partly to expand Chinese influence. In this way, troops had been sent into Mongolia, or across the sea to Korea, and they had also been sent south into Vietnam or westwards towards Burma. Very often the local labour forces had been obliged to build roads for the troops or to repair bridges. If an official's post was planted in these remote spots, he needed quarters that were suited to his dignity, and the men had to set to work to build the Governor's lodge or villa. Some of the officials who found themselves serving in these strange places liked it well enough. They were quite on their own and could expect little interference from other authorities; but, at the same time they were fully responsible if anything went wrong, for example if the natives broke out in revolt, and it would take a very long time to get a call for help back to the centre. There was also another disadvantage, with quite soon began to tell on a man who was posted to these places. There would hardly be a civilized person to talk to, other than his own staff, for months on end, and this could become very soul-destroying. The same sacrifice, the deprivation of company, was required of those young imperial princesses who had had to do their duty by accepting marriage with the uncouth leaders of central Asia. Only recently arrangements had been made to cement an alliance with far-away Wu-sun by this means.[15]

[15] *HS* 96B.3b.

In the north the government had had to restore the old line of earthworks built by the Ch'in dynasty. It had been considerably extended, so that there was now a chain of forts and lookout towers which stretched across the hills and deserts as far as Tun-huang. These lines were guarded by conscripts who came from all parts of China, and who were also busy keeping watch for any enemy movement, sending messages and signals up and down the line, building and repairing barracks and fortifications, gathering wood and vegetables, conserving the precious water of the streams and ponds, and working the farms that were intended to grow the troops' corn. Naturally this meant a drain on the government's budget, and people sometimes wished that the statesmen had not been quite as ambitious or extravagant.

However, all in all, the state of the Empire must have seemed bright on that winter's morning at the end of 105. Officials who saw something of public affairs must have felt that the Han Empire was achieving its purposes, and they must have felt part and parcel of the state. The standard of law and order was reasonably high—higher than it had been in the past —so that people felt reasonably free from robbers. There were ways and means of getting out of the worst demands made on a man for labour service. Even though the laws were fairly harsh and complicated, there were ways of buying one's way out of punishment if one was brought up on a charge. Now that the government had taken control of minting coins and had banned private individuals from doing so, the cash piece was fairly trustworthy, and there was only one form of it in circulation.[16] If some of the officials, especially those in the provinces, had shown signs of practising extortion or oppression, the new system of regional inspectors, not yet a year old,[17] should help to stamp out the worst abuses. Three years previously the government had actually completed a project for containing

[16] *HS* 24B.16a (Swann, pp. 293 and 377f.).
[17] *HS* 6.30a (*HFHD*, II, p. 96).

the Yellow River.[18] This had been causing trouble for years, and repairs to the dykes had been delayed—to suit the pockets of some of the senior statesmen, it was said. But now the Emperor had taken a hand and had gone in person to see that the work had been properly done. He had even written a poem to celebrate the success of the venture.

There was no doubt about it, the central government, appointed by the Emperor, held a firm grasp on the Empire. Fifty years had passed since that dangerous revolt of the Emperor's own kinsmen. This could easily have brought the Empire to ruin, but in fact it had left the central government in a far stronger position than it had ever been before. Since then there had only been one rebellion, which had been started by the misguided King of Huai-nan in 122. It was he who had assembled all those experts in Taoist thought and natural science, whose writings were beginning to circulate. But the king had paid the price of an unsuccessful rebellion, and once more the government was victorious. Not long ago—seven years to be precise—the government had made another deliberate break with the past in order to display its authority. They had found a pretext to degrade to commoner status all but a handful of those nobles who had any pretension to a background,[19] i.e. the men who had inherited their family honours in a direct line that could be traced back for almost a hundred years. But those links with the past did not suit the current regime; the government preferred to guard the privilege of bestowing honours jealously, and only to give them to those who had themselves rendered meritorious service; and for this reason the old established nobility had fallen a victim to contemporary trends.

At court there was an obvious feeling of affluence. Outside the western walls of Ch'ang-an a vast new summer palace had been laid out, with halls, lodges and pavilions stretched out one

[18] *HS* 6.26b (*HFHD*, II, p. 90) and *HS* 29.9a.
[19] *HS* 6.22a (*HFHD*, II, p. 80).

after another. They were situated in the Shang-lin Park, beautiful enough itself with its exotic plants and the animals that had been brought from strange climes. Inside these buildings, very little was spared by way of adornment. You could see precious pearls, gems and horns from the south, and the imperial stables were filled with the most splendid mounts.[20] All this was very different from what it had been some sixty or seventy years previously, in the days of the Emperor's grandfather (Wen ti). Money had been very tight then, to be sure, but had it really been necessary to have been so miserly? Wen ti had never approved expenditure for brightening the palace or for his own personal comforts. He had even stopped a new terrace from being completed, when he found out how much it was likely to cost—the traces left by the workmen could still be seen a century after the event, exactly as they had left them.[21]

Admittedly, Wen ti had suffered badly from the Hsiung-nu, and now it was certainly true that they had been unable to attack China for fifteen years, and some of their leaders had even settled inside China. Wen ti had had to send out valuable consignments of silk to keep the enemy appeased, but nowadays it was a very different story. The government was regularly despatching trading caravans, over ten a year, manned by several hundred men;[22] they would bring back all sorts of riches and delights for China, such as the most precious pieces of raw jade, and silky furs. The old guard grumbled that these goods were of no material use to the Chinese people. However, they certainly served to enrich the Empire—the old guard were always ready to criticise new policies. They complained about the government's foreign policy, saying that there was no need for territorial expansion in a well-ordered community, and that there could be no justification in spending

[20] *HS* 96B.37a.
[21] *HS* 4.21a, b (*HFHD*, I, pp. 272f.) and *HS* 75.19b.
[22] *SC* 123.24f.

Chinese money, in risking Chinese lives and in wasting Chinese labour in order to lay hold of more and more foreign possessions and lands. But, really all the Government had done was to plant outposts at the boundaries and make it easier for the natives to join the Empire and for the Chinese to exploit local products for the benefit of China. It was quite an achievement to have founded no less than fifteen new commanderies in the last twenty-one years, twelve of them since 111 BC. At the same time there was plenty for the foreign leaders, many of whom came from very distant parts, to see in Ch'ang-an. The way of life there was very different from that to which they were accustomed in the steppes or out on the lines of oases, and these men can only have been deeply impressed by the grandeur and the sophisticated standard of living that they saw around them. The court had arranged some marvellous spectacles for their entertainment—ballet, musical performances and sports—and everyone in Ch'ang-an, Chinese or not, had been glad of a chance to watch.[23]

The Emperor was steady enough, now that he had reached his mature fifties, and things seemed stable enough inside the palace. Not everyone could know exactly what went on behind the scenes, but if the imperial consorts and their families were jostling for position, they did not seem to be upsetting the equilibrium of government or the smooth flow of orders for the conduct of the administration. If anyone did wonder how far favours counted in getting an appointment, there was considerable evidence to show that these were distributed fairly evenly. Wei Ch'ing, the highly successful general who had died a year earlier,[24] had been a brother of the Empress, and his comrade in arms Huo Ch'ü-ping had been a half brother. The other family which had enjoyed imperial favours, the Li family, had not missed out either. The Lady Li was one of those women

[23] *HS* 96B.38a.

[24] *HS* 6.30a (*HFHD*, II, p. 96). (For doubts regarding the date of Wei Ch'ing's death, see Chapter 2, note 49.)

who had enjoyed the Emperor's attentions for some years. One of her brothers held a prominent position in court as an expert musician and composer,[25] and it was said that another brother, Li Kuang-li, was shortly to be promoted to a high-ranking military command, though he certainly had had no military training or experience.

The Emperor himself knew where his duty lay. After all he was not dubbed Son of Heaven for nothing, and he had certainly been doing his best to get the powers that be to bless the dynasty. In the last ten years he had inaugurated state cults of worship to the Grand Unity and the Earth Queen, and as well as actually taking part in these ceremonies he had performed the sacrifices to the Five Powers, of Yellow, Green, White, Red and Black.[26] This was a very old cult indeed; four of the Powers had been held in honour for centuries, and Kao tsu, founding emperor of Han, had insisted that the fifth Power, of Black, should be included. The present Emperor obviously took all these rites very seriously. Before his time there had only been two occasions when a Han emperor had attended them in person, and now he was going to one of the three almost every year. To cap it all he had performed very solemn ceremonies at Mount T'ai six years previously, in the very year after he had been busy holding a splendid review of troops in the north.[27] Nobody knew exactly what had occurred at the summit of the mountain, as the ceremony had been conducted in the strictest secrecy, but there was no doubt that it had formed the climax to a whole series of imperial progresses and sacred rites and that the emperor had been in contact with the supreme powers of the universe. Nor were signs lacking that the spiritual powers were responding to these devotions, and the hymns which accompanied the state services gave thanks for what had been clear indications of the goodwill of the spirits—events such as

[25] i.e. Li Yen-nien, see Chapter 2, below, p. 53; see also *HS* 93.4a.
[26] See Chapter 5, p. 167.
[27] *HS* 6.25b (*HFHD*, II, p. 86); *HS* 6.24a (*HFHD*, II, p. 84).

the discovery of the holy tripods in 112, the growth of the magical plant of immortality (109) or the capture of the white magical Lin animal (122).

There had been argument enough in the learned world about the Hall of Spirits before it had been built, mainly about the plan of the building and its purpose, for there were a number of very old-fashioned scholars who could claim to be heard in discussion when these matters were concerned and who seemed to think that they knew exactly what such a building had looked like centuries before.[28] Eventually the government had been given a painting of what the hall was supposed to have been like and this had probably been used by the state artisans when they had been ordered to start work. It had therefore been designed as a single hall with four open sides; the roof was thatched and a moat ran around the perimeter of the site; and there was a covered way, surmounted by a tower, which provided access from the south-west. At last the building had been completed, at the foot of Mount T'ai,[29] in 109, and it was going to be used for state occasions. The Emperor would probably sacrifice there to the soul of his early ancestor who had founded the dynasty. Sometimes he would receive reports there from the provinces, and he intended to make good use of the solemn atmosphere of the hall to see that the officials and kings did not rise above their stations.[30] But the winter solstice of 105 BC was the first time when the Hall of Spirits had been used to offer worship to the Supreme Power.

There was one puzzling feature of court life. The Emperor's attendants were regularly clothed in black,[31] which was the colour of Water, and it seemed strange that the Han dynasty had still kept Water as its patron element. It had been the patron of the old kings of Ch'in, and then of the Ch'in emperors, and the first of the Han emperors had inherited it, along with many

[28] *HS* 25B.2b; SC 28.82 (*MH*, III, p. 511).
[29] *HS* 6.27a (*HFHD*, II, p. 91).
[30] *HS* 6.34b, 36a (*HFHD*, II, pp. 107, 111).   [31] *HS* 98.15a.

other characteristics of the Ch'in institutions.[32] But it was odd that Water was still held in high honour. Sixty years previously Chia I, who had seemed to be set on a brilliant career but had come to a tragic end so young, had thought the time ripe for a change. He had wanted to show that Han was not the simple inheritor of the Ch'in authority but that it had won its supreme position legitimately, by conquest. So he had suggested that the dynasty should make a symbolic change, by adopting Earth as the patron element in place of Water; for Earth always conquers Water, but he had failed dismally to convince Wen ti's statesmen of the need for a change.[33]

In the meantime, however, public affairs had been transformed, almost radically; for a new spirit of adventure and a power of decision had gripped the statesmen and civil servants of the Empire. To those who stood around on that day of the winter solstice in 105, it must surely have seemed that the government of man had never before been so successful or so secure. For all its arrogance and boasting the Ch'in Empire had not lasted for more than fifteen years and two emperors. But Han had been founded a century ago and had already seen four complete reigns, not counting the eight years of the Empress Lü and the thirty-six years since the present Emperor's accession. And had the attendant courtiers known it on that day, the government was soon to announce very significant changes which would show that they were fully aware of their destiny and that they could afford to be bolder than their predecessors of some sixty years back. Only six months need pass before those statesmen who believed that China was on the verge of a new era would have their way, and the faith they reposed in their age was to be displayed by solemn and symbolic acts of state.[34]

Perhaps the most important change was the very one that

[32] SC 6.20, 35 (MH, III, pp. 429, 449).
[33] HS 48.1b; SC 10.32 (MH, II, p. 479).
[34] HS 6.31b (HFHD, II, p. 99); HS 25B.23b.

Chia I had recommended. It was decided to abandon the patron element of Water and to adopt Earth instead; and by this change the Han government avowed its moral faith, its belief that the dynasty reigned legitimately and justifiably as the conquering successor of Ch'in. The change involved a few immediate alterations in the life of the court and in government offices. Yellow became the favoured colour in place of black, and five the favourite number in place of six. This last provision could affect the style of inscription on an official's seal, but this was a minor change, when compared with the introduction of a whole host of new titles for some of the offices of state which were announced at the same time. Nearly all the terms were quite new, and they had been chosen with good care to avoid any association with the institutions of China's past. However, the change was more formal than practical, for the duties of, say, the new *Ta-hung-lu* were no different from those of the former *Tien-k'o* or *Ta-hsing-ling*[35] as he had been called since 144. It was always the same office which made arrangements for receiving foreign dignitaries and provided for their entertainment in a suitable form. Still, the new expressions lent a new sense of purpose to the departments of state and reflected the new attitude to the world.

Secondly, a new expression was introduced for counting the years. Such a change was nothing new, as there had already been a total of six regnal titles in use during the Emperor's reign, each of six years' duration. So far, however, the terms had been chosen to commemorate an historical incident or a state occasion, such as the foundation of a new commandery in the north (128) or the performance of the religious ceremonies on Mount T'ai (110). The difference in 104 lay in the choice of an expression which had much more panache about it, and which looked to the future rather than to the past. T'ai-ch'u— the Grand Beginning—marked the start of a new dispensation,

---

[35] i.e. Superintendent of State Visits: Dubs—Director of Guests, Prefect Grand Usher, Grand Herald.

which was to enjoy the blessing of the newly adopted patron element of Earth.

This symbolic step could not escape the notice of any official who was carrying out the routine work of dating a document. In addition, the message of T'ai-ch'u was re-iterated when he came to fill in the month and day in question. The adoption of the new element and the new regnal title was accompanied by a further change, the introduction of a new calendar, which had been calculated more accurately than its predecessor, and, whereas previously the calendar year had started on the first day of the tenth month, it was now ordained that it would begin on the first day of the first month.

So hopes ran high in 104 BC, at a time when the Emperor's government had reached the highest point of its achievement. But the manner whereby these successes had been accomplished and the assumptions that lay behind the state policies were by no means universally approved. There were those who distrusted the whole idea of a new era, who had no wish to break away from the past, and who thought poorly of the Grand Beginning. They took the view that the work of government had become too complex, and that it was improper to direct it to the materialist objective of enriching and strengthening the state. They preferred a less intensive type of government, which put less pressure on the people and interfered less assiduously in their occupations. They thought that government should do its best to keep the Emperor's subjects contented, to see that the way of running the Empire was in full accord with the principles of Heaven, and to ensure that human affairs were regulated in such a way that they kept in step with the rhythms of nature. It would be a long time, as much as fifty years, before these protestant voices would be heard to effect and before they would carry enough conviction to affect the choice of state policies. But quite soon a number of developments were to take place which would show that these men were not simply false prophets of doom, and which made it quite clear that the heyday of imperial success was now past.

In the same year that the title T'ai-ch'u was adopted, the government embarked on what was perhaps its most ambitious military enterprise yet. Li Kuang-li, as had been expected, was appointed to a high command, perhaps because the Emperor wanted to please his favourite consort who was Li Kuang-li's sister.[36] His orders were to lead a campaign against the King of Ta-yüan, which lay far away to the west of the Taklamakan Desert, one hardly knew exactly where. It was General Li's business to search out the enemy and to see to it that some of their excellent horses would be brought back to China. But he found the going more difficult than had been expected. The small communities which lay in his path resisted his advance, and he was in acute difficulties over supplies. Eventually he had to turn back, without reaching his objective, making his way back to Tun-huang in some ignominy, hoping to pick up some reinforcements from that base. The government was furious. Was this pusillanimous show the way to start the Grand Beginning? The Emperor gave orders that the gates of Tun-huang were to be barred against General Li, to show his anger at such cowardice; and eventually Li Kuang-li was forced to set out again, in a second attempt to fulfil his mission.

There were other indications that Han power and Han prestige were on the wane. Some of the new lines of forts were overrun,[37] and when Li Kuang-li eventually found his way back to Ch'ang-an, with some successes to his credit, he had staggeringly high casualties to report. In 103 BC and again in 98 the Hsiung-nu felt able to start raiding Chinese territory again.[38] A brave Chinese officer, fighting with infantry against superior forces, was obliged to surrender in 99,[39] and Li Kuang-li himself suffered a similar disgrace after a defeat in the field in 90.[40]

[36] *HS* 61.9b.
[37] *HS* 6.32b (*HFHD*, II, p. 102); *HS* 94A.23a.
[38] *HS* 6.34b (*HFHD*, II, p. 107); *HS* 94A.23b.
[39] *HS* 54.9a, *et seq.*   [40] *HS* 6.37b (*HFHD*, II, p. 116).

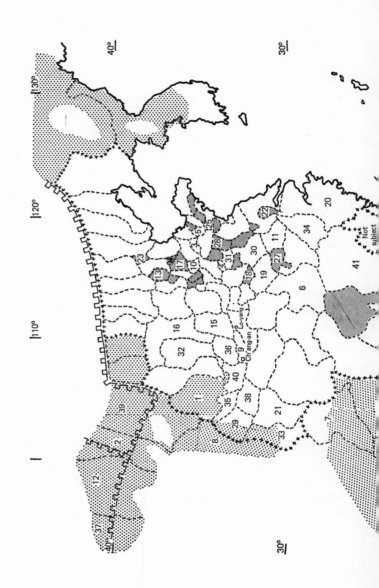

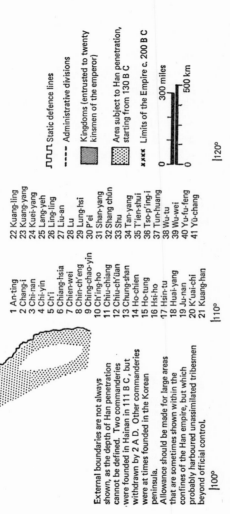

20°

20°

External boundaries are not always shown, as the depth of Han penetration cannot be defined. Two commanderies were founded in Hainan in 111 B C, but withdrawn by 2 A D. Other commanderies were at times founded in the Korean peninsula.

Allowance should be made for large areas that are sometimes shown within the confines of the Han empire, but which probably harboured unassimilated tribesmen beyond official control.

|100°

|110°

1 An-ting
2 Chang-i
3 Chi-nan
4 Chi-yin
5 Ch'i
6 Chiang-hsia
7 Chien-wei
8 Chin-ch'eng
9 Ching-chao-yin
10 Ch'ing-ho
11 Chiu-chiang
12 Chiu-ch'üan
13 Chung-shan
14 Ho-chien
15 Ho-tung
16 Hsi-ho
17 Hsin-tu
18 Huai-yang
19 Ju-nan
20 K'uai-chi
21 Kuang-han

22 Kuang-ling
23 Kuang-yang
24 Kuei-yang
25 Lang-yeh
26 Ling-ling
27 Liu-an
28 Lu
29 Lung-hsi
30 P'ei
31 Shan-yang
32 Shang chün
33 Shu
34 Tan-yang
35 T'ien-shui
36 Tso-p'ing-i
37 Tun-huang
38 Wu-tu
39 Wu-wei
40 Yu-fu-feng
41 Yü-chang

ᒋᒍᒪ Static defence lines

----- Administrative divisions

▨ Kingdoms (entrusted to twenty kinsmen of the emperor)

▨ Area subject to Han penetration, starting from 130 B C

xxx Limits of the Empire c. 200 B C

0   300 miles
0   500 km

|120°

Fig. 1. The extent of the Han Empire and the administrative units at AD 2. Figures 1–41 refer to the more important commanderies and kingdoms that are mentioned in the text.

The following kingdoms no longer existed in AD 2: Ch'ang-i —in the commandery of Shan-yang 97–74; Chiang-tu—comprising the later commanderies of K'uai-chi and Tan-yang; Heng-shan—comprising the later commanderies of Chiang-hsia and kingdom of Liu-an; Huai-nan—ended in 122, com-

prising the commanderies of Chiu-chiang and Yü-chang; Kuang-ch'uan—in the kingdom of Hsin-tu 155–151; Ting-t'ao—in the commandery of Chi-yin 25–5; Yen—the later commandery of Kuang-yang.

Meanwhile there were other signs of internal unrest in the Empire. In the thickly populated regions of east China, robber bands had been seizing control of cities and mountain passes, and the roads were no longer safe. In 99 the government found it necessary to send out special armed commissioners with orders to restore the authority of the government by force and even intimidation;[41] and in 91 BC the palace and government, and Ch'ang-an city itself, were rent asunder in violence and bloodshed that had arisen from the marital jealousies of the Emperor's consorts and the political rivalries of their families.[42] It was a far cry from that happy moment of inauguration of the new era in 104, to the open fighting which broke out in Ch'ang-an in September 91, and which left the Empire bereft of an empress and an heir-apparent, the government subject to weakness and suspicion, and the Chinese people a prey to insecurity and bewilderment.

[41] *HS* 6.34a (*HFHD*, II, p. 106).   [42] See Chapter 2, pp. 37f.

The Case of Witchcraft in 91 BC

Stirring events took place in Ch'ang-an, city of Eternal Tranquillity, during the years 92–90 BC. Some of the highest in the land, including chief dignitaries of state and members of the imperial family, were executed or forced to suicide. Fears of witchcraft, possibly of an hysterical nature, resulted in the deaths of many who were suspected of such practices, and large numbers were killed in the open fighting that broke out in the city. In the name of justice men and women were sentenced to severe punishments, and senior officials tried in vain to persuade the Emperor to relax and rule with a greater measure of clemency. It was a time of acute danger for the Han dynasty; the survival of the imperial house was threatened by the problem of the imperial succession; there was dissatisfaction expressed against the authority of the government and acts of rebellion had taken place; and the heavy expenditure of the previous years had depleted the Han treasuries. Some measure of stability followed the death of Wu ti in 87 and his succession by an infant son. At the same time there was an institutional change of no small significance. Three senior officials were appointed to act as members of a regency, and took all important decisions of state, to the exclusion of the responsibility vested hitherto in the Chancellor, the most senior official of duly established government.

These incidents formed more than a part of a sordid and unimportant political intrigue. They sprang from dynastic causes and possibly affected the choice of policies of state; they demonstrate the strength of the contemporary reaction to witchcraft and the political and social instability of the time; and while shedding some light on a series of dynastic plots and political intrigues that took place from time to time until 74 BC they explain the selection of the candidates who became emperors of Han China in 87 and, on two occasions, in 74. Above all, the incidents demonstrate that whatever lip-service was paid in edict or official pronouncement to the superior virtues of 'Confucian' values, decisions of state were frequently dictated by ambition, jealousy or fear. In addition the incidents show how the formal provisions of Han institutions could be invoked as a means of carrying through decisions of a personal nature.

In November to December 92 BC, the Emperor ordered cavalrymen to carry out a search of the Shang-lin Park, a large pleasure ground including ornamental waterways, shrines for the worship of various spirits and a hunting park.[1] The object of the search is not specified, and it may have included articles used in witchcraft as well as individuals such as traitors, criminals or practisers of sorcery. To prevent the escape of such persons the gates of Ch'ang-an were closed, and it was only after ten days that the search was brought to an end. The *Han-shu* continues immediately with the information that the witch-craft case arose, and it seems likely, if not certain, that the search was intended to disclose evidence of just such practices.

In February 91 two of the most senior officials of government were thrown into prison and died.[2] These were Kung-sun Ho and his son Kung-sun Ching-sheng. Since 103 Ho had held the office of *ch'eng-hsiang* or Chancellor. This was the highest ranking office of state, and he held supreme respon-

[1] *HS* 6:36b; *HFHD*, II, 113. For a similar search, in 99, in which it is possible that Sang Hung-yang and members of the imperial family were involved, see *HS* 6.34a (*HFHD*, vol. II, p. 105), *HS* 60.2b, and Chapter 7, note 100. A search had also taken place in 100 (*HS* 6.33a, *HFHD*, vol. II, p. 103).

[2] *HS* 6:36b, *HFHD*, II, 114; *HS* 63:1b; *HS* 66:1a, *et seq.*

sibility, below the Emperor, for the conduct of government. On his appointment to that office his son Ching-sheng had succeeded him as *t'ai-pu*, or Superintendent of Transport,[3] and had thus become one of the nine ministers of state who ranked below the Chancellor and carried direct responsibility for one of the specialist tasks of government. The high status and power enjoyed by these men was enhanced by their relationship to Wu ti's principal consort the Empress Wei; for Kungsun Ho, the Chancellor, was married to one of her sisters.

The fall of these two highly placed officials involved other members of the Empress's family, and, in addition, it was linked with the question of witchcraft. Kung-sun Ching-sheng had been accused of embezzling a large sum of money from funds allocated to the northern army of Ch'ang-an. In the course of the case a man who had been imprisoned for acting with scant respect to the provisions of government sent in a written accusation. Kung-sun Ching-sheng was alleged to have had illicit sexual relations with the Princess Yang-shih, who was a daughter of Wu ti and the Empress Wei and thus his own cousin. In addition he was accused of having shamans offer prayers and express curses against the Emperor, and of having manikins buried with similar intent near the road at Kanch'üan, where Wu ti had a summer retreat.[4]

The case was proved and both men met their deaths. On a day corresponding with 14 April 91 BC,[5] Liu Ch'u-li was appointed Chancellor in place of Kung-sun Ho. The intention had evidently been to follow an earlier precedent of Han

[3] Dubs—Grand Coachman.   [4] *HS* 66:1b, *et seq.*

[5] There is some doubt about the exact date. *HS* 19B:25b dates Kungsun Ho's death in prison on the day *jen-shen* of the fourth month, which however did not include that day, and Liu's appointment as Chancellor on the day *ting-ssu* in the fifth month (13 June). *HS* 6:36b (*HFHD*, II, 114) dates Ho's death in the first month, and *HS* 66:2a gives Liu's appointment in the spring. *HS* 15A:58b and *SC* 22:28 give *ting-ssu* in the third month (14 April) for Liu's appointment and the conferment on him of a nobility.

government by dividing this high office between two men, so as to avoid reposing excessive authority in a single individual. For this reason Liu was nominated Chancellor of the Left, but there is in fact no record of the simultaneous appointment of a Chancellor of the Right. Liu Ch'u-li was a nephew of Wu ti, and, as will be shown later, he was related to another imperial consort, rival to the Empress Wei.

The family of the Empress Wei suffered a further blow in the intercalary month, i.e. June to July 91.[6] The Princess Yang-shih, with whom Kung-sun Ho's name had been linked, was impeached for practising witchcraft and put to death; the same fate overtook her sister the Princess Chu-i.[7]

During the summer Wu ti, now aged sixty-six, duly travelled to Kan-ch'üan, where he fell ill, and one of the chief actors of the drama, Chiang Ch'ung, makes his entry.[8] Earlier in his career he had exposed a case of immorality and incest and brought about the death of a distant relative of the Emperor.[9] At court he had impressed Wu ti as being a man of character, and at his own request he had been sent on a mission to the Hsiung-nu. On return he had been put in charge of the suppression of banditry and the investigation of extravagant living in the metropolitan area. The rigorous and impartial way in which he had brought forward cases that involved men of high status or relatives of the imperial family had commended itself to the Emperor, and Wu ti was convinced that Chiang Ch'ung was

[6] *HS* 6:37a, *HFHD*, II, 114; *HS* 45:13a; *HS* 63:1b.

[7] *HS* 63:2a states that Wei K'ang suffered a similar fate, but Wang Hsien-ch'ien shows that this was not so. See *HS* 18:8a.

[8] *HS* 45:11a.

[9] This was the case of Liu P'eng-tsu king of Chao, in April–May 92. A half-brother of Wu ti, he had been nominated king of Kuang-ch'uan in 155, being moved to Chao four years later. At his death in 92 he had thus successfully held a kingdom for sixty-three years. His son Tan, who was heir apparent to the kingdom, had been accused by Chiang Ch'ung of incest and immorality and had been brought to trial and put to death; see *HS* 6:36b, *HFHD*, II, 113; *HS* 45:11a.

completely loyal, law-abiding and incorruptible. In 93 BC he had been appointed to the post of *shui-heng tu-wei* which carried financial responsibilities and which ranked just below the nine chief ministers of state. In addition, the office was responsible for the Shang-lin Park,[10] and it is therefore possible that Chiang Ch'ung had been concerned with the search conducted in 92. It seems clear that he was a man of some power who was able to protect his clients from the processes of the law.

In an earlier incident Chiang Ch'ung had aroused the enmity of the Empress Wei's family. He had found a servant of the Heir Apparent, i.e. the son of the Empress, infringing the rules that governed the use of the imperial highway, and he had duly brought the case to the notice of the emperor. Seeing Wu ti lying ill at Kan-ch'üan, Chiang Ch'ung realised that the Heir Apparent would probably exact reprisals for this incident once he had acceded as Emperor. Chiang now submitted to Wu ti that his illness had been brought about by witchcraft, and, as he had probably expected, he was put in charge of an investigation. In the work of this tribunal he was assisted by Han Yüeh, who held the post of *kuang-lu-hsün*, or Superintendent of the Palace.[11] This ranked as one of the nine chief ministers, and the incumbent controlled certain guards units. Chiang Ch'ung was also helped by Chang Kan and Su Wen.

Events now moved towards a climax. Chiang Ch'ung had foreign shamans, probably from central Asia, dig the ground to look for manikins, and a variety of steps were taken to prove that witchcraft had been practised.[12] As yet it seems that Chiang Ch'ung was not directing his efforts so as to involve the Heir Apparent, but to engender an atmosphere of fear and distrust; in this endeavour he was eminently successful. Members of the population were accusing each other of witchcraft, and officials immediately had them brought up on charges of *ta-ni*

[10] *HS* 19A: 20a.
[11] Dubs—Superintendent of the Imperial Household.
[12] *HS* 45:13b; *HS* 63:2a. For the actual steps taken see pp. 86f.

wu-tao, or gross immorality;[13] and before the incident was over, people had been put to death in large numbers, by the ten thousand according to the *Han-shu*. The victims included the famous Generals Kung-sun Ao (no relative of Kung-sun Ho) and Chao P'o-nu, as well as the family of Li Kuang-li, who will feature below.[14]

Chiang Ch'ung was now able to exploit the situation to the detriment of the Wei family. Wu ti, old and impressionable, suspected all around him of witchcraft and imprecation, and none dared protest that a man was innocent. Realising where Wu ti's thoughts lay, Chiang Ch'ung had it reported that there had been an emanation of witchcraft inside the palace, and he proceeded to investigate the situation there. He started by examining those of the palace women folk whose charms had all but lost their attraction for the Emperor; by stages he reached the Empress, and he then had men dig for evidence of witch-craft in the Heir Apparent's palace, and human images in wood were duly found.[15]

Wu ti was still away from Ch'ang-an. Fearing that he could not clear himself of suspicion, the Heir Apparent consulted Shih Te a member of his staff, who advised him to take immediate action. So he had the necessary documents drawn up and sent a commission to arrest Chiang Ch'ung and his associates. Han Yüeh, who doubted whether the commission possessed the requisite authority to arrest him, was killed but Chang Kan managed to escape to Kan-ch'üan, wounded. The Heir Apparent then informed his mother, the Empress, of the situation, so that guards could be called out and weapons issued from the armouries of the palace. He gave out to officials that

---

[13] See Hulsewé, pp. 156f. where the term is rendered, more precisely, as great refractoriness (*ta-ni*) and impiety (*pu-tao*).

[14] *HS* 55:18b; *HS* 55:20a; *HS* 94A:25b. For the possibility that K'ung An-kuo or his family were involved, with a subsequent effect on scholastic history, see *HS* 36:33a and 88:14b.

[15] *HS* 45:13b; *HS* 63:2a.

Chiang Ch'ung had staged a revolt, and on 1 September he had him executed, attending the scene in person and reviling him for his conduct in the past. He also had the shamans burnt to death in the Shang-lin Park.

Open fighting now broke out in Ch'ang-an between the Heir Apparent and the Emperor.[16] At the death of Chiang Ch'ung, some of the Heir Apparent's forces had made their way into the Chancellor's office. Liu Ch'u-li had managed to escape, alone, and bereft of the insignia of his office. His assistant rode post-haste to Kan-ch'üan to give the Emperor the news, and Wu ti expostulated at the Chancellor's feeble behaviour. Sending orders for the arrest of the rebels, the avoidance of bloodshed and the closure of the city gates so as to prevent the escape of the Heir, Wu ti soon arrived back at Ch'ang-an. From the Chien-chang palace, which lay beyond the western wall of the city, he had troops called up from the neighbouring counties of the metropolitan area and put under the command of the senior officials of state. For his part the Heir Apparent, who lacked the authority to do so, had an amnesty proclaimed for criminals and convicts in Ch'ang-an. Arms were issued to them from the state armouries and they were put under the command of Shih Te and Chang Kuang. The Heir Apparent also tried to call out a force of central Asian cavalry from local garrisons, but the attempt was foiled by Ma T'ung, who took charge of the force and brought it into the city to support the Emperor. Ma T'ung also secured the loyalty of Shang-ch'iu Ch'eng, one of the nine chief ministers who held the post of *ta-hung-lu* or Superintendent of State Visits.[17]

A further incident occurred at this time in which the historian Ssu-ma Ch'ien may have been concerned. The Heir Apparent tried to persuade Jen An, inspector of the northern armies in Ch'ang-an, to send out troops in his support. Jen An firmly closed the gates of the barracks, refusing to comply with the

[16] *HS* 6:37a, *HFHD*, II, 114; *HS* 63:3a; *HS* 66:3a.
[17] Dubs—Grand Herald.

request. Nonetheless he was later to be accused by Wu ti of waiting on events and duplicity, and he was executed at the Emperor's orders.[18] The Heir Apparent withdrew after this rebuff and rounded up support from the city.

Five days of fighting followed; according to the *Han-shu*[19] the dead were numbered by the ten thousand, and the gutters of Ch'ang-an's streets flowed with blood; and as the forces of the Chancellor, who fought for Wu ti, grew in strength, those of the Heir Apparent were overcome. On 9 September, nine days after Chiang Ch'ung had been put to death by the Heir Apparent, Wu ti had officers sent to take custody of the Empress Wei's insignia and she took her life. On the same day the Heir Apparent contrived to escape from Ch'ang-an and to lie up in hiding. But before long his presence was revealed, and on 30 September he followed his mother's example. His three sons and one daughter also died; there survived one grandson, still a babe in arms, who was in due course to become the Emperor Hsüan ti.[20]

There was a further casualty at this time of some importance. The Chancellor's assistant, who had been responsible for closing the city gates, had been accused of negligence, thereby allowing the Heir Apparent to escape. The Chancellor had decided to have him executed, but was persuaded to release him, pending official permission to do so. Pao Sheng-chih, who had stayed the Chancellor's hand, held the office of *yü-shih ta-fu* or Imperial Counsellor,[21] which was second in importance only to that of the Chancellor. On Wu ti's fury that an officer who had indulged the rebels had not been punished, Pao Sheng-chih committed suicide.

[18] *HS* 66:4a; for the exchange of correspondence between Jen An and Ssu-ma Chi'en and the difficulties of dating the letters, see *MH*, vol. I, xlii, *et seq.*; and Burton Watson, *Ssu-ma Ch'ien Grand Historian of China* (New York, 1958), pp. 194f.

[19] *HS* 6:37a, *HFHD*, II, 114; *HS* 63:4b; *HS* 97A:12b.

[20] *HS* 8:1a, *HFHD*, II, 199; *HS* 63:5b.

[21] Dubs—Imperial Clerk Grandee, or Grandee Secretary.

Between February and the end of September 91 BC, the Wei Empress and her family had thus suffered virtual extinction. At court the atmosphere must surely have been charged with uncertainty and distrust, as, for the first time since 122, there was no duly nominated heir to succeed the Emperor. The next development, which was to bring about the execution of a Chancellor, started in April to May 90.[22]

The Chancellor was married to a daughter of Li Kuang-li, brother of a former deeply beloved concubine of Wu ti. Li Kuang-li had served with some distinction, if not complete success, in the army, leading campaigns that had penetrated deeply into central Asia.[23] In the third month of 90 (April to May) he was sent off on a further expedition, in which Ma T'ung and Shang-ch'iu Ch'eng also held commands. According to custom, the Chancellor, i.e. Li Kuang-li's son-in-law, accompanied the troops as far as the bridge over the Wei river, to wish the expedition every success. Li Kuang-li took the opportunity to suggest that his own nephew, i.e. Liu Po, son of the Lady Li and cousin of the Chancellor's wife, should be nominated as Heir Apparent. The Chancellor fell in with the suggestion. We are not informed of what steps, if any, were taken, or whether news of this arrangement leaked out, but the *Han-shu* points out that the witchcraft scandal was then at its height. It was now reported that the Chancellor's wife had arranged for shamans to curse the Emperor, and Li Kuang-li was involved in a charge of attempting to establish his nephew as Emperor. The case came up for trial, and a charge of gross immorality (*ta-ni pu-tao*) was proved. On 18 July, Liu Ch'u-li was executed publicly, and his wife's and children's heads were displayed in one of Ch'ang-an's streets. Li Kuang-li's family were taken into custody, and Li Kuang-li himself, now on campaign, surrendered to the Hsiung-nu.

[22] *HS* 66:4b.

[23] e.g. the campaigns against Ta-yüan of 104–101 (see pp. 54 and 218 below), and the expeditions against the Hsiung-nu of 99, 97.

This event marks a reaction in favour of the Wei family which can actually be traced further back.[24] As early as September 91 BC, before the death of the Heir Apparent, a minor local dignitary named Ling-hu Mao[25] submitted a statement to the Emperor, suggesting that the motives for the Heir Apparent's murder of Chiang Ch'ung had been fear rather than disloyalty, and alluding, somewhat pointedly, to the previous occasion when Chiang Ch'ung's machinations had resulted in the accusation and death of an heir to a kingdom.[26] After the Heir Apparent's suicide, on 30 September 91, rewards were duly bestowed on those who had taken part in that incident: but we then read[27] 'Some time later many cases of witchcraft were failing to gain credence. The Emperor realised that his heir had been frightened and that he had not harboured treacherous intentions'.

At this juncture T'ien Ch'ien-ch'iu submitted a memorial to the Throne seeking to demonstrate the innocence of the Heir Apparent.[28] Wu ti was clearly impressed, and showed his change of heart by appointing T'ien to be Superintendent of State Visits (*ta-hung-lu*). This appointment was dated sometime in 90; it was quite exceptional, in so far as T'ien had not served in any other official capacity, and he now, suddenly, found himself one of the nine chief ministers of state. Furthermore on 27 July 89, T'ien was promoted to the post of Chancellor, that had been vacant since the execution of Liu Ch'u-li on 18 July 90.[29] The family of Chiang Ch'ung was punished for his actions, together with Su Wen and those men who had taken part in encompassing the death of the heir. Wu ti's remorse was further shown by his erection of the Ssu-tzu palace, so named as the palace wherein he would think of his son and pray for the return of his spirit, and a terrace was built with the same intention. The final act in the re-instatement of the Wei family

[24] *HS* 63:3a.   [25] For this name see the note in *HS* 63:3a.
[26] See note 9 to p. 40 above.   [27] *HS* 63:5a.
[28] *HS* 66:5a. T'ien's surname was originally Chü.   [29] *HS* 19B:26a.

took place after the accession of Hsüan ti, their sole survivor, in 74 BC. Members of the family who had succumbed during the troubles were reburied in positions of honour, with a full provision of plantations, an establishment of retainers and revenue, to ensure that the proper services were paid to their souls.

In the meantime events had affected other leading men of the day. It will be recalled that before the fighting actually broke out in Ch'ang-an, two officers, Ma T'ung and Shang-ch'iu Ch'eng had shown themselves loyal to Wu ti and against the Heir Apparent. On 12 September, when the fight was over, they were duly ennobled as a reward for their services. For Shang-ch'iu Ch'eng the citation read[30] 'In his capacity of Superinten-dent of State Visits (*ta-hung-lu*) he attacked the Heir Apparent of the Wei family and fought valiantly without harbouring thoughts of treason'. Ma T'ung, whose nobility was consider-ably larger than that of Shang-ch'iu Ch'eng,[31] received his award because 'as a courtier in attendance at the palace he brought out troops to attack the rebel Ju Hou'.[32]

In October–November 91 BC Shang-ch'iu Ch'eng was appointed to the post of Imperial Counsellor, which had become vacant on the suicide of Pao Sheng-chih.[33] In the following April–May he and Ma T'ung held commands in the expedition that was sent into central Asia under the supreme command of Li Kuang-li, and in the course of the campaign they were both more successful than Li Kuang-li himself, who, it will be re-called, surrendered to the enemy.[34] Unlike Li Kuang-li, both Shang-ch'iu Ch'eng and Ma T'ung survived the reaction that

[30] *HS* 17:23b.

[31] Shang-ch'iu Ch'eng's nobility allowed him to collect taxation from 2120 households, whereas that given to Ma T'ung allowed him to do so for 4870 households.

[32] *HS* 17:24a. For Ju Hou's part in supporting the heir apparent, see *HS* 66:4a.   [33] *HS* 19B:25b.

[34] *HS* 6:37b, *HFHD*, II, 116; *HS* 17:23a; *HS* 61:14a; *HS* 94A:25a; *HS* 96B:30a.

set in in favour of the Wei family and which is marked by the execution of Liu Ch'u-li on 18 July 90. But by the time of Wu ti's death, early in 87, both had met a violent end.

There are two accounts of the death of Shang-ch'iu Ch'eng in the *Han-shu*. According to the entry which records the history of his nobility,[35] in 87 he was brought up on a charge that, as *chan-shih*, he had been in attendance at the ancestral shrine of Wen ti, and being drunk in the ceremonial hall had given voice to a highly unsuitable song: charged with *pu-ching* or irreverence[36] he committed suicide. This is somewhat puzzling. The *chan-shih*, sometimes rendered Supplier, was an officer attached to the household of the Heir Apparent, but, as we know, there was no nominated heir at this time, and there is no reference to Shang-ch'iu Ch'eng's appointment to the post. According to the second account, which is perhaps a little more convincing, he was charged as Imperial Counsellor with the crime of cursing the Emperor, and he duly committed suicide.[37] It may be noted that he was replaced as Imperial Counsellor by the famous statesman Sang Hung-yang, whose appointment was dated on 17 March 87—precisely ten days before Wu ti's death.[38]

Shang-ch'iu Ch'eng's suicide is dated[39] in July–August 88, and at just this time Ma T'ung and his brother Ma Ho-luo staged an unsuccessful attempt to murder the Emperor, who was once more at Kan-ch'üan. Ma Ho-luo had been on terms of friendship with Chiang Ch'ung; and the Ma brothers were now frightened that they would be penalised as a result of the turn of fortune against Chiang and in favour of the late Heir Apparent. In the event the plot was foiled and both brothers were executed, sometime in 88.[40]

---

[35] *HS* 17:23b.

[36] See Hulsewé, pp. 156f., where *pu-ching* is rendered as *nefas*.

[37] *HS* 19B:25b.   [38] *HS* 19B:26b.   [39] *HS* 6:38b, *HFHD*, II, 118.

[40] *HS* 6:38b, *HFHD*, II, 118. According to this passage the brothers were executed in 88 sixth month (i.e. July–August). *HS* 17:24a gives 87.

The events of 92–90 BC and later show in high relief the contrast between the ideal of government by Confucian precept and moral principle and the practice of political and dynastic manoeuvre, based on motives of ambition and jealousy. The compiler of the *Han-shu*[41] affirms by way of comment that the causes of the witchcraft case lay far deeper than the machinations of a single individual, Chiang Ch'ung. The compiler points out that the whole life of the Heir Apparent had been passed in an atmosphere coloured by warfare, and he takes note of the dangers of instability and violence that are attendant on an habitual resort to fighting. He also commends the action of T'ien Ch'ien-ch'iu, who was not a man of outstanding intelligence, in clarifying the witchcraft issue and vindicating the late Heir Apparent; by this action he had realised the value of eliminating evil and of damming the source of instability.

These events had considerable repercussions on the imperial succession, and it is not altogether impossible that the plot of the Ma brothers in 88 was part of a further attempt to restore the fortunes of the Li family at the expense of those who were associated with the now defunct Wei family. To understand these implications fully, it is necessary to review the whole situation at Wu ti's palaces together with the rivalries that existed between the families of different consorts.

The institutions of the Han imperial house provided for the nomination of one of the Emperor's consorts as Empress, i.e. *huang-hou* and one of his sons as Heir Apparent, i.e. *t'ai-tzu*. Apart from such cases the term *hou* was used only in titles given to the Emperor's mother or grandmother. In the same way as an empress or heir apparent could be nominated, so could they also be removed from their exalted positions by the Emperor's personal decree; and although there was no institutional necessity which demanded that one of the Emperor's consorts

[41] *HS* 63:22b.

should be nominated as Empress, it was clearly in the interests of dynastic stability that there should be one, and that her son should be duly recognised as the successor to the throne. For the imperial palaces housed a large establishment of consorts or concubines. In general these were termed *fu-jen*, but particular ones could be, and often were, distinguished by a further title which conveyed a mark of status. Thus, by the end of the western Han period there were no less than fourteen types of consort, and the *Han-shu* provides a set of equivalent symbols, i.e. titles in the civil service and titles in the hierarchic scale of orders of rank, whereby the position of the women could be assessed.[42] Except for the title *chao-i* which was introduced under Yüan ti (48–33 BC), the other titles were all in use by Wu ti's time. Nominations of women as empresses or of sons as heirs apparent formed occasions of congratulation and rejoicing in Ch'ang-an, and were often marked by imperial bounties and a general conferment of *chüeh* or orders of aristocratic rank to certain members of the population.[43]

In this situation rivalries and jealousies could be expected to flourish at a court where supreme authority for government and the conduct of justice was imposed by Heaven in the Emperor. Different balances of power could easily develop, according to the age of the emperor, the strength of character of his women-folk or the political agility of their relatives. An infant emperor could be controlled by other parties, as happened during the eastern Han period on several notorious occasions; an emperor might wish to reward a favourite consort by conferring high-ranking civil or military office on her next of kin; alternatively, a statesman whose protegée had successfully won the Emperor's heart might expect to enhance his family's position and wealth accordingly, and to ensure their safety under the dispensation of the next Emperor.

These situations had arisen before Wu ti's time and became

[42] *HS* 97A:2a. See *Aristocratic Ranks*, p. 162.
[43] *Ibid.*, p. 116f.

conspicuous again at the close of the western Han period. For Wu ti's reign, account must be taken of six principal consorts and five sons.[44] (See Table 2, facing p. 64.)

(1) Wu ti's first Empress, whose surname was Ch'en,[45] had become his wife while he was still heir apparent, and she was duly nominated Empress in 141 BC. Having failed to bear Wu ti a son, and being highly jealous of the success of the Wei family's consort in this respect, she did her best to remedy her deficiency by various artifices. In 130 one of her daughters was charged with practising witchcraft on her behalf and of having curses uttered. The Empress was dismissed from her position and a total of 300 persons who were involved in the case were executed.[46]

(2) Wei Tzu-fu, who was a professional singer, was presented to Wu ti several years after his accession, when he still had no son.[47] She bore him three daughters, and, in 128 when he was twenty-nine years old, a son who was named Chü. After this event Wei Tzu-fu was proclaimed Empress; her brother Wei Ch'ing had been summoned for service, and from 129 onwards he commanded a series of expeditions against the Hsiung-nu, culminating in the victorious campaigns of 119. He had been granted a nobility in 127, and in 124 his three sons were similarly honoured, as a mark of their father's achievements.[48]

Huo Ch'ü-ping was another relative of the Empress Wei whose position was advanced thanks to the relationship. He was her nephew, and half-brother of Huo Kuang who features prominently in Han history towards the end of Wu ti's reign and afterwards. Like Wei Ch'ing, Huo Ch'ü-ping was appointed to a high military command and fought successfully against

---

[44] It is not possible to compile a complete list of the women who enjoyed the favours of Wu ti (e.g. see stray references such as that to Yin Chieh-yü in *HS* 97A:12a and *SC* 49:27).

[45] *HS* 97A:10b.   [46] *HS* 59:2a.   [47] *HS* 97A:11a.

[48] *HS* 18:8a.

the Hsiung-nu and in the north-west. He received his nobility in 123 BC. In the following year, on a day corresponding with 31 May 122, the Empress' son Chü was proclaimed Heir Apparent, and Chü's own first son was born in 113. The strength of the family may have been somewhat impaired by the deaths of Huo Ch'ü-ping in 116 and Wei Ch'ing ten years later,[49] although Huo Kuang was at this time steadily gathering influence at the capital.

Reference has been made above to a further relative of the Empress Wei who played a prominent part in Han history. Kung-sun Ho, whose family came from the north-west, was married to a sister of Wei Tzu-fu. As early as 135 he had been appointed *t'ai-p'u*, or Superintendent of Transport, and he held this position for thirty-three years until his promotion as Chancellor. He saw active service in the campaigns of 133, 129, 124, 123 and 119, and was ennobled in 124. In 112 he was deprived of that honour together with a large number of his peers, but he received a nobility for the second time on his appointment as Chancellor in 103.[50]

It has been noted that after the virtual elimination of the Wei family in 91–90 BC, their re-instatement came about only after the accession of Hsüan-ti in 74.[51] Hsüan-ti was himself the grandson of the Heir Apparent Chü, who had committed suicide in 91, and it was only by good luck and human kindness that he survived the troubles and scandals of those years. He was a few months old when the witchcraft hunt broke out, but was nonetheless charged with complicity and thrown into prison. Thanks to the humanity of Ping Chi, who was in charge of part of the official investigation, he was saved from death and brought up privately, out of harm's way.[52]

---

[49] *HS* 6:30a, *HFHD*, II, 96 and *HS* 19B:22a give this in 106, but according to the succession of the nobility in HS 18:8a, Wei Ch'ing died in 104.

[50] *HS* 17:2b.   [51] *HS* 97A:12b.

[52] *HS* 74:7a; *HS* 94A:19b. For Ping Chi, see Chapter 4, pp. 121–2.

(3) Li Fu-jen or the Lady Li[53] was brought to Wu ti's attention as an entertainer and younger sister of Li Yen-nien. The latter was an expert musician and composer who had suffered the punishment of castration after some involvement with the laws. Serving as a eunuch in the palace he pleased the Emperor with the musical compositions that he made for religious ceremonies. In due course his sister bore Wu ti a son, named Po; Li Yen-nien was given an official post and achieved a position of affection and personal influence over Wu ti. However, after being concerned with disturbances among the eunuchs he lost this advantage, and after the death of his sister both he and his younger brother were put to death. In the meantime Li Fu-jen's son had been created King of Ch'ang-i in 100. The precise date of her death is not given, but we are told that Wu ti was heart-broken. He had her portrait on display at Kan-ch'üan, and the *Han-shu* carries the famous story of a magician's attempt to have her ghost appear before him. The *Han-shu* also includes[54] the text of a *fu* which Wu ti is said to have composed to express the intensity of his grief.

Reference has been made above to an attempt made by Liu Ch'u-li and Li Kuang-li to have Liu Po, king of Ch'ang-i, nominated as Heir Apparent, some time between May and July 90 BC. Liu Po himself died soon afterwards, either in 88 or 86,[55] and was succeeded by his son Ho; it will be shown later that Ho, a descendant of the Lady Li, was actually put on the throne as Emperor for twenty-seven days in 74.

In the meantime one member at least of Lady Li's family had received material advantage from the hold that her affections had gained on the Emperor. Her brother Li Kuang-li was given

---

[53] *HS* 14:21a; *HS* 93:4a; *HS* 97A:12b.   [54] *HS* 97A:14a.

[55] *HS* 6:38b, *HFHD*, II, 118, records his death for the first month of hou-yüan, first year, i.e. January to February 88. However, *HS* 14:21a and *HS* 63:17b write that he died eleven years after his accession in 97, i.e. in 86, and they specify 86 as the year of Liu Ho's accession. From (4) below, it would seem that *HS* 97A:16b implies that Liu Po died in 88.

a nobility in 101, after successful service in the field. In 104 he had been nominated to lead the most ambitious expedition yet launched under Wu ti, which was to attack Ta-yüan (Ferghana); in the event he was successful, but not before he had had to retire to Tun-huang to collect reinforcements. In connection with this incident the author of the *Han-shu* permits himself a comment of a biased or at least a subjective nature.[56] Li's appointment to command the expedition is described as being due to Wu ti's wish to bestow noble rank on the family of his favourite concubine Li, and it is noticeable that similar remarks, with an implication that military skill was a matter of secondary importance, are not recorded in connection with the appointments of Wei Ch'ing or Huo Ch'ü-ping. Wu ti's anger at Li Kuang-li's failure to reach his objective immediately[57] may conceivably have been coloured by the feeling that his favourite had let him down. It will be recalled that Liu Ch'u-li, who held the office of Chancellor from April 91 to July 90 BC, when the Wei family was in eclipse, was the son-in-law of Li Kuang-li.

After Wu ti's death the Lady Li was posthumously given the title of Hsiao Wu huang-hou, Empress of the Pious Wu. This title was given after the succession problem had been solved and a descendant of neither the Wei nor the Li family had acually become Emperor. The move may perhaps be explained as part of Huo Kuang's highly circumspect policy, which was intended to preserve a façade of unity and to prevent the further outbreak of jealousies.

(4) The third and last consort of Wu ti to receive the title *huang-hou* was named Chao,[58] and, as with Lady Li, the title was given posthumously. During her lifetime, and when she was Wu ti's favourite, she had borne the title *chieh-yü*, which ranked at that time at the head of the titles of concubines. Nothing is told of her forebears, other than the fact that her father

[56] *HS* 61:9b.   [57] *HS* 61:10a.
[58] *HS* 7:1a, *HFHD*, II, 151; *HS* 97A:16a.

had been indicted for an offence and castrated by way of punishment, and that he had then served at court as a eunuch. A son who was born to Miss Chao in 94 BC was being considered for the succession when he was five or six years old, i.e. 89–88. At this time the Heir Apparent of the Wei family had recently met his death and the king of Ch'ang-i had also, in all probability, died, and it was evidently recognised that two other sons of Wu ti, who will be mentioned shortly, were not to be considered as candidates. The boy, who was called Fu-ling, was actually made Heir Apparent after the death of his mother. He was then aged eight, and simultaneously with his nomination, Huo Kuang was promoted by the grant of the title *ta-ssu-ma-ta-chiang-chün* or Marshall of State and General, and given a valedictory decree from Wu ti ordering him to assume the regency. Within two days Wu ti was dead, and Fu-ling, better known under his posthumous title of Chao ti, acceded. A nobility was posthumously conferred on the late grandfather of the new Emperor, and gifts were bestowed on other relatives of the Chao family. However, no member of the family is known to have risen to prominence in dynastic or political affairs.

(5) The origins of Wang Fu-jen or the Lady Wang, are untraced.[59] She bore Wu ti a son, Hung, who was created king of Ch'i in 117, dying eight years later without a successor. There do not appear to have been any family connections affecting dynastic or political developments.

(6) A second favourite of Wu ti whose surname was Li is distinguished from Li Fu-jen, the Lady Li, by the title *i*.[60] She bore Wu ti two sons, called Tan and Hsü, who were created king of Yen and king of Kuang-ling respectively in 117. According to a statement which appears twice in the *Han-shu*,[61] they had been behaving in a somewhat abandoned way by the time the succession problem arose in 91–90 BC.

[59] *HS* 14:20; *HS* 63:7.   [60] *HS* 63:8b; *HS* 68:1b; *HS* 97A:16b.
[61] *HS* 68:1b and *HS* 97A:16b.

Table 1. Table of Dates of Emperors of the Western Han Dynasty

Name	Title	Acceded	Died
Liu Pang	Kao tsu	202	195
Liu Ying	Hui ti	195	188
(The empress Lü)*		188	180
Liu Heng	Wen ti	180	157
Liu Ch'i	Ching ti	157	141
Liu Ch'e	Wu ti	141	87
Liu Fu-ling	Chao ti	87	74
Liu Ho	—	74 (reigned for twenty-seven days only)	
Liu Ping-i	Hsüan ti	74	49
Liu Shih	Yüan ti	49	33
Liu Ao	Ch'eng ti	33	7
Liu Hsin	Ai ti	7	1 BC
Liu Chi-tzu	P'ing ti	AD 1	6
Liu Ying†			

* During this time two infants successively held the formal title of Emperor (*HFHD* vol II, pp. 191, 198).

† Named to be Emperor following P'ing ti's death and during the time of Wang Mang's regency (*HFHD*, vol. III, pp. 217f.).

The *Han-shu* does not provide supporting evidence for this judgment of Tan's character, but tells a long tale of Tan's misplaced and abortive hopes for the succession; of his hints that he should be considered as a candidate; and, finally, of two plots in which he tried to attain this objective. On the death of Hung, king of Ch'i, in 110BC. Tan had taken steps to indicate to Wu ti that he should become his successor, but Wu ti had rejected the overture. The incident is a little puzzling, as by now Prince Chü had been nominated as heir for a dozen years. Nothing is recorded of Tan's actions or reactions during the scandals of 91–90, but in 87 he was evidently dissatisfied with the circumstances of Wu ti's death and Chao ti's accession. His enquiries proved fruitless, but he submitted a memorial to the Throne, praising Wu ti's achievements and suggesting the establishment of shrines in his honour in the commanderies of the Empire. In this way he was doubtless insinuating that he possessed superior feelings of duty towards the late Emperor as compared with those of Chao ti, and it is noteworthy that on a later occasion he went so far as to allege that Chao ti was no son of Wu ti.[62] By this time Huo Kuang was in sole charge of the Government. He rejected the memorial but offered Tan a gift of thirty million cash and a large nobility. Furious at the insult, Tan re-iterated that he possessed the true qualifications to be Emperor, and now proceeded to scheme for Chao ti's replacement. This was the first of two plots in which Tan was involved, and on this occasion he succeeded in evading responsibility and fastening this on Liu Tse.[63] He claimed that he had received special authority from Wu ti to take military precautions against any eventuality, and he immediately took such steps as summoning dissident elements, collecting revenue,

[62] *HS* 63:10a.

[63] *HS* 63:9a. Liu Tse was the great-grandson of one of Kao tsu's sons who had been created king of Ch'i in 201. This line died out in 126 and the kingdom of Ch'i was re-created for Wu ti's son Hung in 117; *HS* 14:6a and *HS* 14:20a.

manufacturing arms and armour from metals,[64] reviewing infantry, and cavalry and raising his own military banners. Such steps were tantamount to a declaration of rebellion, and fifteen officials who dared to remonstrate with Tan were put to death. However, news of the plot leaked out and Liu Tse was executed in September 86.[65] In Tan's second plot, which was staged in 80, he was forced to suicide.[66] (See p. 75.)

Hsü, the other son of the concubine Li, was not effectively involved in dynastic intrigues or political disturbances during the reign of Wu ti or Chao ti, but died eventually by his own hand in 54.[67] He is said to have been addicted to amusements and to have been capable of feats of strength. As his behaviour was unprincipled, he failed to qualify as a candidate to succeed Wu ti,[68] and although he was the sole surviving son of Wu ti at the time of Chao ti's death in 74, again he could not be considered.[69] We shall meet Hsü again in connection with the utterance of curses against the Emperor.

An attempt may now be made to summarise the foregoing somewhat tangled web of incident, treason and plot. Between February and September 91 BC, all the leading personalities of the Wei family had been put to death, except for Huo Kuang. There had been a series of events which included the exploitation of public fear of witchcraft, and bloody fighting in Ch'ang-an between forces supporting the Emperor and those collected by the Heir Apparent. During this process two members of the Li family rose to prominence, but the attempt in May 90 to have their own nominee declared Heir Apparent was foiled. By July 90 a reaction had set in and the most powerful member of the Li family group was executed. In 88 an unsuccessful

---

[64] At this time the iron industry was under the control of state monopoly; hence independent manufacture of such goods was not authorised.

[65] *HS* 7:3a, *HFHD*, II, 155.

[66] *HS* 7:6b, *HFHD*, II, 164; *HS* 63:14a.

[67] *HS* 63:14b.   [68] *HS* 63:15a.   [69] *HS* 68:4b.

attempt was made on Wu ti's life by officers who had stood by him in the fighting of 91 and who could not countenance the restoration of some honour, albeit posthumously, to the Wei family. In March 87, when Wu ti lay near to death, an infant who was of neither the Wei nor the Li family was declared Heir Apparent and succeeded two days later as Chao ti, with Huo Kuang acting as the head of a regency. In 86 Tan, King of Yen, entered into the first of two plots to take the place of Chao ti.

Partly as a result of these events, government was now conducted not by the recognised devolution of authority from the Emperor and the Chancellor, but directly by a triumvirate led by Huo Kuang. The critical years under consideration had at the same time seen the abandonment of some of the policies of expansion that had been adopted for up to four decades previously. It is therefore necessary to consider how far the growth of rivalries in the palace, the affiliations of leading officials, and the rise and fall of statesmen may be associated with such changes of policy, that affected both foreign and domestic matters. Subsequent events that are linked with these questions and which will be examined in due course include the debate on state policies that was arranged in 81; the second plot and the suicide of Tan, together with the execution of San Hung-yang in 80; and the accession of two emperors in 74, of whom one lasted for only twenty-seven days, to be replaced by a descendant of the Empress Wei. Before proceeding to such questions, attention should be drawn to the state of government prevailing in China during the last decade of Wu ti's reign.

The period of fifty years preceding the incidents of 91 BC was one of the most formative in Han history. Until *c.* 140 the key-note of imperial policy had been defence and consolidation; thereafter, for nearly a century, initiative and expansion characterised many of the government's decisions. The change can be seen in the new arrangements evolved for administering the Empire and enforcing the will of government; in deliberate

measures to increase China's wealth and to organise the production and distribution of resources; and in the extension of
Chinese influence more widely in the northern and southern
perimeters of the Empire. By 91 the cumulative effect of these
changes had left its mark on Han institutions and society.
Whatever measures had been taken to promote the study of
Confucian texts or to practise teachings traditionally ascribed
to Confucian thought,[70] statesmen such as Chia I and, more
particularly, Ch'ao Ts'o enjoined the acceptance of strikingly
different concepts; and in the sphere of practical government,
decisions rested on realist principles that are associated with
some of the legalist writers rather than on the traditional ethical
precepts that were ascribed to the saintly kings of old.

Internally the grip of Han government had been noticeably
tightened during this half century. The revolt of the Kings of
Huai-nan and Heng-shan in 122 and its suppression marked in
effect the final stage in a struggle between the central government and the *chu-hou-wang* or kings. These were the blood
relatives of the Emperor whose forebears had received titles
and administrative authority over large areas from Kao tsu.
Thereafter, Han governments had successively curtailed their
powers, and after the abortive revolt of 122 the kings could no
more threaten the central government's authority. This was
now extended ever more widely, as the territories that had
been made over to the Kings were incorporated as commanderies (*chün*) directly under the control of the central
Government.

At the same time steps were being taken to reduce the size
of some of the larger administrative units and thus to prevent
the exercise of unduly powerful responsibilities by a single
provincial official. Thus in 135 BC the highly important metropolitan area was divided into two units, and one of these was
further sub-divided in 104.[71] Further north, Shang chün was

[70] See Dubs in *HFHD*, II, pp. 20f.

[71] According to the 'original' notes in *HS* 28A1:19b, 24b, and 30b, the

split by the creation of Hsi-ho commandery in 125, and at the perimeter, Lung-hsi was reduced in size by the foundation of T'ien-shui and An-ting in 114; and Kuei-yang and Kuang-han were reduced by the foundation of Ling-ling and Wu-tu in 111. A further measure designed to increase the scope of the central government's supervision of the provinces is seen in the establishment of the posts of *tz'u-shih* or circuit inspector in 106.

Fuller administration needed the services of more officials, and the decree of 135 calling for the recommendation of individuals for service marks the government's realisation of this need.[72] A further measure of positive government which was based on the principles of Shang Yang and which illustrates the purposeful character of Wu ti's governments may be noted in the exploitation of the system of aristocratic ranks. These carried some material advantages and some legal privileges and were utilised to encourage service and to reward merit. Whereas at certain times of Han history these ranks were bestowed on a widespread basis as an act of imperial bounty, under Wu ti's dispensation such bestowals were very rare.[73] Instead the ranks were given in direct return for services rendered to the state, and thus formed an instrument of government that is described in the *Han-fei-tzu*. This deliberate use of rewards is seen again in the introduction (123) of a further series of orders which were given for military success or became available for the contribution of funds to a depleted treasury.[74]

In addition, the government's use of the highest of these orders, i.e. the *ch'e-hou* or nobilities, demonstrates clearly a

---

area under the *nei-shih* was put under the control of two officials, the *nei-shih* of the left and the right, in 135; but in *HS* 19A:20b this change is dated in 155. The balance of the evidence, as seen in the appointments listed in *HS* 19B, is in favour of 135. For the subdivision of the area under the *yu nei-shih* and the adoption of new titles for the metropolitan officials in that year see *HS* 28A1 as cited.

[72] See Dubs, in *HFHD*, II, 20.   [73] See *Aristocratic Ranks*, pp. 137f.
[74] See *Aristocratic Ranks*, pp. 132f.

realistic means of exploiting the system in order to consolidate central government, and there is ample evidence of this practice in the decades before 91 BC. The conferment of nobilities on the sons of the Kings was an important instrument of reducing their power, and this was used no less than 178 times during Wu ti's reign, mostly before 116.[75] Alternatively, the gift of a nobility was used as a means of retaining the loyalties of surrendered enemy leaders, and it is noticeable that of the seventy-five nobilities given directly for services rendered to the state under Wu ti, no less than forty-one were given to foreigners of that type. By contrast, Wu ti's government was also capable of withdrawing these honours as a means of punishment or, possibly, for political purposes; and the most obvious example of a wholesale reduction of rank is seen in the purge of the nobilities of 112.[76]

Further evidence of the increasing force of government during Wu ti's reign may be seen in connection with economic matters. State monopolies for salt and iron were introduced *c.* 119 BC; within the next five years attempts were made to regulate the transport of staple goods and to standardise prices; and from 112 the State eventually established a firm control over the minting of coins to the government's specification. As a direct measure to encourage greater agricultural production, the Government was sponsoring the promotion of Chao Kuo's new technique for sowing crops, and we know that this technique, which was capable of altering China's agriculture radically, was being practised in the State's colonies of the north-west by 90–80 BC.[77] Even more revealing of the new

[75] Altogether 406 nobilities were given to the sons of kings during western Han. Of the 178 given in Wu ti's reign, at least 160 were dated in the short period 130–116. Apart from Wu ti's reign, the most frequent bestowals were made during the reigns of Hsüan ti (74–49; 63 instances); Yüan ti (49–33; 48 instances); and Ch'eng ti (33–7; 43 instances).

[76] See Dubs in *HFHD*, II, 126f.

[77] For these changes and topics see Swann, 57, 61, 377f.; for Chao Kuo's change, see *RHA*, *I*, 70, and *Everyday Life*, fig. 75 and pp. 168f.

attitude towards the positive conduct of government was the appointment *c.* 120 of two rich men, whose fortunes derived from salt and iron workings, to senior offices which collected state revenue. This was at the time when Sang Hung-yang, son of a rich merchant of Lo-yang, was first earning a reputation for shrewd business sense in government finances.[78]

Above all, the positive policies adopted under Wu ti are shown very significantly in connection with foreign relations. Up to 141, Han China had in general been forced to accept terms from its neighbours; *c.* 139 Chang Ch'ien was first sent on a mission of exploration into central Asia. From now Han took the initiative, and the numerous campaigns fought against the Hsiung-nu culminated in the Han victories of 119. These were followed by the penetration of Chinese officials and soldiers in the south, south-east and south-west and into the Korean peninsula (112–108); and diplomatic ventures in the north-west were followed by military expeditions (from 104) which were intended to complete the expulsion of the Hsiung-nu or to provide a line of communication with central Asia. These steps resulted in the foundation of some twenty-four commanderies during Wu ti's reign; state-sponsored caravans plied the routes into Asia; static defence lines were extended as far as Tun-huang and manned by conscripts; and there were hopes of using river communications from the south-west to the sea coast. In these ventures it is to be observed that Han statesmen were capable of taking strategic considerations into mind and of trying to avoid dissipation of their resources. Unfortunately the tactical implementation of these plans did not always avoid such errors, with the result that from 99 onwards Han resources had been spent, and we hear of Han reverses on the field and of large-scale military losses.

Sustained efforts of this sort cost the Han treasury large sums. If we may believe sample figures that are given for certain campaigns, but which may well be somewhat rhetorical,

[78] *HS* 24B:12a and 14a; Swann, 271, 285.

expenses amounted to 200000 units of gold in the campaigns of 124–3 BC, to 500000 for those of 119, and 40000 in 101.[79] Similar sums must have been needed for the expeditions led by Li Kuang-li, Kung-sun Ao and Li Ling in 99, and by other officers in 97.

In commenting on the extension of Han influence in the western regions of central Asia at this time, the author of the *Han-shu* drew attention to the drain of money and the increased taxation involved. He continued:[80] 'The strength of the people was spent and resources were exhausted, and there followed some years of poor harvests. Robbers and thieves rose up everywhere and the roads were impassable. For the first time commissioners appointed directly by the Emperor were sent out, clothed in embroidered silk and bearing axes, to exterminate the bandits in the commanderies and the kingdoms, and only then was the danger overcome. For these reasons, in his latter days [Wu ti] abandoned the lands of Lun-t'ai and proclaimed a decree expressing anguish and sorrow.'

The text of the decree is duly carried in the *Han-shu*,[81] and although it is not dated precisely, it was probably proclaimed sometime after 18 July 90.[82] In addition to rejecting the latest proposals for expansion in the north-west on the grounds of the popular hardship that would ensue, the text refers to the contemporary failure to keep the static defence lines in a state of efficiency, the poor discipline of the officers serving there and the bad morale of the troops. Pan Ku's statement of the growth of banditry and the measures taken to suppress it is supported

---

[79] *HS* 24B:8a and 12b, Swann, 251 and 274; *HS* 61:14a and *SC* 123:42. These figures are difficult to interpret in a full economic context, in the absence of further information. The accepted value of gold was 10000 copper cash to one unit (i.e. *chin* 244 grams).

[80] *HS* 96B:38b.   [81] *HS* 96B:17a, *et seq*.

[82] The preamble to Sang Hung-yang's memorial which preceded the decree refers to Li Kuang-li's surrender (*HS* 96B:15b), and the decree itself mentions his defeat (*ibid.*, 19a, b). Dubs (*HFHD*, II, 116, note 37.5) dates the defeat after Liu Ch'u-li's execution on 18 July 90.

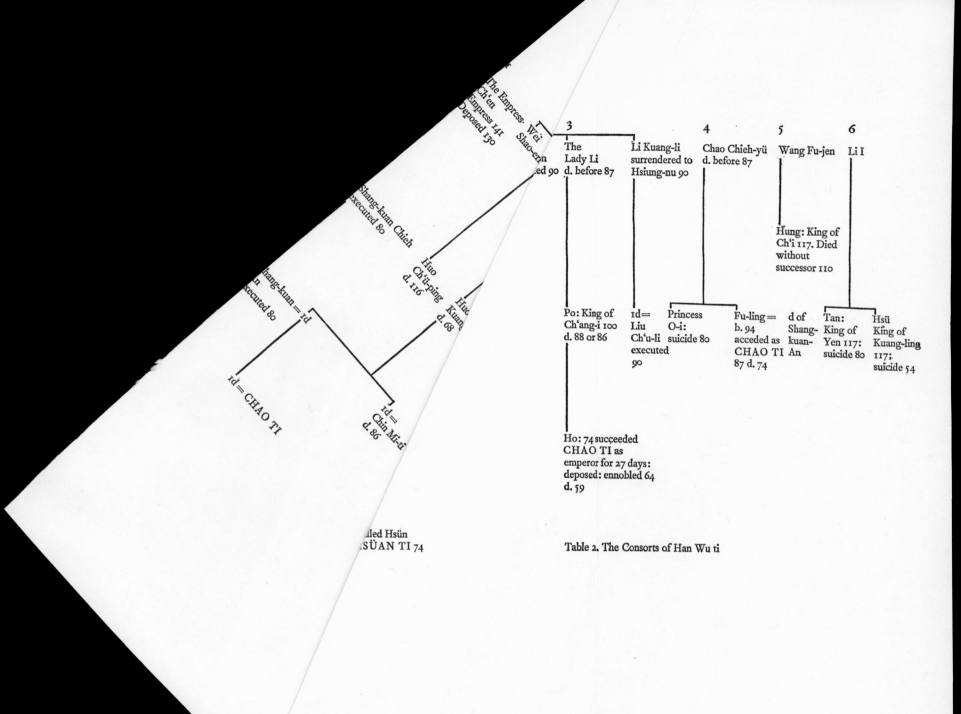

The Empress: Wei
Ch'en
Empress 141
Deposed 130

Shao-ern
...ed 90

Shang-kuan Chieh
executed 80

Huo
Ch'ü-ping
d. 116

Huo
Kuan...
d. 68

...hang-kuan = 1d
n
...executed 80

1d = 1d

1d = CHAO TI

1d =
Chin Mi-ti
d. 86

...lled Hsün
...SÜAN TI 74

3
The
Lady Li
d. before 87

Po: King of
Ch'ang-i 100
d. 88 or 86

Ho: 74 succeeded
CHAO TI as
emperor for 27 days:
deposed: ennobled 64
d. 59

Li Kuang-li
surrendered to
Hsiung-nu 90

1d =
Liu
Ch'u-li
executed
90

4
Chao Chieh-yü
d. before 87

Princess
O-i:
suicide 80

Fu-ling =
b. 94
acceded as
CHAO TI
87 d. 74

5
Wang Fu-jen

Hung: King of
Ch'i 117. Died
without
successor 110

d of
Shang-
kuan-
An

6
Li I

Tan:
King of
Yen 117:
suicide 80

Hsü
King of
Kuang-ling
117:
suicide 54

Table 2. The Consorts of Han Wu ti

elsewhere in the *Han-shu* in respect of two men who have been encountered already; both Chiang Ch'ung and Pao Sheng-chih had served as special commissioners appointed to the task.[83]

From these considerations it seems that by the end of Wu ti's reign the force of the Chinese expansionist effort had been spent, and that at a time when civilian morale was deteriorating Wu ti or his advisers had realised the need for retrenchment. Probably this appreciation may be dated between the despatch of the last of Wu ti's expeditions into central Asia, i.e. April or May 90 BC, and the decree refusing Sang Hung-yang's proposal, i.e. late July 90; and the change of policy is certainly seen in the choice of the title *Fu-min* 'enrichment of the people' for the nobility that was conferred on T'ien Ch'ien-ch'iu on 27 July 89.[84]

There is not sufficient information in the *Han-shu* to assess how far changes of policy can be associated directly with the rise and fall of particular imperial favourites or by the turn of fortune that affected so many high-ranking officials during these critical years. But the *Tzu-chih-t'ung-chien* includes a suggestive paragraph in this connection.[85] The passage draws a contrast between Wu ti's rigorous implementation of the laws and the clemency exhibited by the Heir Apparent. The difference was conspicuous at times when Wu ti was away from Ch'ang-an, and affairs of state were left to the direction of the Empress and the Heir Apparent. As a result, the Heir Apparent is said to have acquired a popular following, while those statesmen who relied on the application of the laws were far from pleased. They did their best to calumniate the Heir, while those officials who were of a more liberal frame of mind

[83] *HS* 45:12b; *HS* 66:7b; *HS* 71:1a. Pao Sheng-chih's work in this respect was started in 99 (*HS* 6:34a, *HFHD*, II, 106).

[84] *HS* 18:11a; *HS* 24:17a, Swann, 184.

[85] Punctuated edition, Peking, 1956, p. 727. I have been unable to trace the source of the passage.

attached themselves to his cause; but in the event there were few to praise and many to criticise the Heir Apparent. The death of Wei Ch'ing in 106 denied to some interested parties their means of access to high places, and there followed considerable competition to cultivate the Heir's friendship.

The rise of Huo Kuang to a position of virtual dictatorship in Han China forms a remarkable episode in Chinese political history. His achievement followed a long preparatory period in which his behaviour had been beyond reproach, and in his long climb to eminence he made use of some institutional changes and doubtless relied on his relationship with the Empress Wei, his aunt.

It has been observed[86] that during Wu ti's reign the position of the *ch'eng-hsiang* or Chancellor had been gradually outmoded and that the Emperor conducted government by means of his private secretariat, the *shang-shu* or so-called masters of writing. However far this process had actually been taken, it seems clear that even by the end of Wu ti's reign the posts of Chancellor and Imperial Counsellor still counted for much. Indeed, their significance may be measured, somewhat cynically, by the dangers attendant on tenure of the posts, and the series of holders may be recapitulated as follows.

Chancellor	Imperial Counsellor
Kung-sun Ho, 103–February 91, executed.	Pao Sheng-chih, 94–October 91; suicide.
Liu Ch'u-li, April 91–July 90, executed.	Shang-ch'iu Ch'eng, October 91–87, suicide.
Unfilled, July 90 – July 89.	Sang Hung-yang, March 87–80, executed.
T'ien Ch'ien-ch'iu, July 89–February 77, died naturally.	

The post of Chancellor was thus left vacant just at the time

[86] Dubs, in *HFHD*, II, 10.

when the reaction in favour of the late Heir Apparent was setting in, and it is to be noted that for part of the twelve months in question Shang-ch'iu Ch'eng the Imperial Counsellor was away from Ch'ang-an on a campaign. We are not informed which authority was responsible for government during that crucial period; it may be guessed, but not proved, that effectively it was Huo Kuang.

Wu ti's final illness and death proved to be the occasion when Huo Kuang was able to establish himself in a position of dominance.[87] When he tactfully raised the question of the succession to the Throne, Wu ti indicated the need for a regency and made three appointments. Huo Kuang was nominated *ta-ssu-ma ta-chiang-chün*, Marshal of State and General; Chin Mi-ti, General of Cavalry and Superintendent of Transport (*chü-ch'i chiang-chün, t'ai-p'u*); Shang-kuan Chieh, General of the Left (*tso chiang-chün*); and at the same time Sang Hung-yang became Imperial Counsellor.[88] As Sang's appointment took effect from 17 March 87 BC, it is likely that the other nominations were dated on that day.

These officers were given a valedictory decree which ordered them to assist the young Emperor, and according to the *Han-shu* all decisions were actually taken by Huo Kuang.[89] Huo, Chin and Shang-kuan were also awarded nobilities for the services they had rendered in suppressing the revolt of the Ma brothers in 88, and the citations for these awards date them at *ien-yin* in the first month, i.e. New Year's day in the second year of Shih-yüan. This corresponded with 22 February 85.[90]

Fu-ling was nominated as Wu ti's Heir Apparent on 27

---

[87] *HS* 68:2b. A translation of many of the parts of the *Han-shu* which concern Huo Kuang, together with maps, tables and some annotation, was published in 1930 by Ardid Jongchell, under the title *Huo Kuang och Hans Tid* (Göteborg).

[88] *HS* 19B:26b.   [89] *HS* 7:1a, *HFHD*, II, 151.

[90] *HS* 7:3a, *HFHD*, II, 156; *HS* 18:11a, 11b. There is some doubt regarding the time for Chin Mi-ti's ennoblement (*HS* 17:26a, notes, and *HS* 68:20a).

March 87 BC and Wu ti died two days later. At the time the validity of Wu ti's last decree was questioned by the son of Wang Mang, who was Superintendent of the Guards (*wei-wei*)[91] and thus one of the nine chief ministers. He claimed to have been present during Wu ti's last days and accused the triumvirate of taking arbitrary steps to ennoble themselves. The allegation was rejected and Wang Mang had his son poisoned.[92]

In the meantime T'ien Ch'ien-ch'iu had been appointed as Chancellor. He is described in the *Han-shu*[93] as 'a man of no particular abilities or talents and with no record of proven achievements; one single utterance drew attention to him and brought him senior statesman's office and a nobility.' The single utterance was presumably the memorial that T'ien submitted in favour of the Heir Apparent.[94] Although the leader of the Hsiung-nu was apparently unable to comprehend why the Han Empire had been entrusted to the care of such a man, there are obvious reasons why the appointment suited Huo Kuang very well. Huo made a point of deferring to T'ien's opinion and consulting him at the meetings held at court, and T'ien would reply by handing over responsibility to Huo. By this piece of play acting Huo's actions were duly validated, in so far as they had been agreed by the highest ranking dignitary in the service of the Emperor.

Chin Mi-ti came from a leading family of the Hsiung-nu.[95] His father had been the Hsiung-nu king of Hsiu-t'u and had been put to death by one of the other kings. Following the Han victories of 121 BC, Chin Mi-ti, who was then aged fourteen, had been taken into service in the palace where he caught the eye of Wu ti. He served in various capacities, leading finally to

[91] Dubs—Commandant of the Palace Guard.

[92] *HS* 68:2a. The text of the *Han-shu* notes, but does not attempt to explain, the delay between the suppression of the revolt in 88 and the ennoblement of the three men.

[93] *HS* 66:5b.   [94] See p. 46.   [95] *HS* 68:18b.

that of *kuang-lu ta-fu* or Counsellor of the Palace.[96] His behaviour was impeccable, and he was greatly loved and rewarded by Wu ti, to the jealousy of the court, who resented a
situation in which an alien should receive special favours. It is
said that he suspected that Ma Ho-luo and Ma T'ung were
plotting to murder the Emperor, and that it was only by his
personal intervention that Wu ti's life was saved. This incident,
coupled with his refusal to accept privileges, endeared him
even further to Wu ti and increased the latter's respect for his
integrity. Chin Mi-ti died after assisting in the regency for one
year only, on 29 September 86.

Very little is known about the antecedents of Shang-kuan
Chieh, who is to be distinguished from a man of the same name
who served in Li Kuang-li's campaign in central Asia of 104–
101 and was appointed Superintendent of the Lesser Treasury
(*shao-fu*) in 102.[97] The statesman of this name came from the
west; he served as one of the gentlemen of the court (*lang*), and
after an incident in which he won Wu ti's confidence he was
appointed Superintendent of Transport, probably in 88.[98] His
son Shang-kuan An was married to one of Huo Kuang's
daughters. After Chao ti's accession, if Huo Kuang was on
leave from his duties, Shang-kuan Chieh acted as his substitute,
taking all the necessary decisions. In 83 Shang-kuan An's
daughter, then aged six, was nominated as Chao ti's empress
despite Huo Kuang's opposition on the grounds of the parties'
youth.[99] The quarrel between the two statesmen came to a
head in 80, as will be shown below.

In the meantime the triumvirate had been strengthened by a
further matrimonial tie, as another daughter of Huo Kuang had
been married to Chin Mi-ti.[100] Clearly the enthronement of

[96] Dubs—Imperial Household Grandee.

[97] *HS* 19B:23a; *HS* 61:12a, 13a. Dubs renders *Shao-fu* as Privy
Treasurer.

[98] *HS* 7:3a, *HFHD*, II, 156; *HS* 19B:26b, *HS* 97A:17a.

[99] *HS* 7:3b, *HFHD*, II, 157; *HS* 97A:18a.   [100] *HS* 68:20a.

Fu-ling in 87 had worked very well to the advantage of Huo Kuang. Descended from neither the Wei nor the Li family the infant could be accepted as a neutral party in the principal rivalries of the palace; and those who had previously supported the Wei or the Li family could offer their loyalty to the young Emperor without loss of face and without apprehension. As yet Fu-ling was not encumbered by having relatives who were highly placed in the official hierarchy and might question Huo Kuang's position; and not for the last time in Han history did ambitious men see advantage in establishing an infant emperor whose will they could manipulate. The *Han-shu* remarks[101] that Wu ti hesitated long before deciding to nominate Fu-ling as his heir, as he was well aware of the dangers that might beset the dynasty with an infant emperor and a young mother. The statement, which was presumably written by a member of the Pan family in the first century AD, may have been coloured by wisdom acquired after similar occurrences. However, in the passage appended to *Shih-chi*, Chapter 49, by Ch'u Shao-sun (fl.*c.*55 BC)[102] it is hinted that Wu ti encompassed the death of Fu-ling's mother, Miss Chao, before nominating him as Heir Apparent. According to Ch'u Shao-sun, Wu ti explained this as being due to the need to eliminate the obvious danger, and cited the case of the Empress Lü as a warning.

Chao ti's reign was punctuated by a number of incidents which involved the issues that had come to the fore previously. In 82 BC, four years after the first plot of Tan, King of Yen, a man called Chang Yen-nien drove up to the palace gates with his carriage horses, banners and clothing all dressed in yellow.[103] This was the colour reserved for the imperial family, and Chang claimed to be the Heir Apparent of the Wei family. Senior

[101] *HS* 97A:16b.

[102] *SC* 49:30f. For Ch'u Shao-sun's additions to the *Shih-chi*, see Burton Watson, *ibid.*, 226 note 9.

[103] *HS* 7:4a, *HFHD*, II, 158; *HS* 71:2a.

officials, including those who had known the Heir, were ordered to see if they could recognise him; large crowds gathered in Ch'ang-an to observe the spectacle, and as a precautionary measure the General of the Right posted troops at the palace. Neither the Chancellor nor his junior colleagues dared to express an opinion, until Chüan Pu-i, superintendent of one of the three metropolitan districts, ordered the arrest of the man, asserting roundly that he was a criminal impostor.

There are several interesting features in the *Han-shu's* account of this incident, which occurred at a time when no heir had been nominated. Not only did it create a stir in Ch'ang-an; but apparently, even nine years after the former Heir Apparent's death, there were officials who were either ready to be persuaded by the claim or unwilling to come out in the open against the Wei family. Huo Kuang is not reported to have played any part and his evasion of the issue may be an example of that circumspect behaviour whereby he had reached his exalted position. He is said to have congratulated Chüan once the imposture had been exposed, and to have offered him one of his daughters in marriage.

The next notable incident was the famous debate held at court in 81. The disputants were given general terms of reference, 'to discuss the sufferings of the common people':[104] more specifically, they started by fastening on the desirability of the state monopolies; and in the course of their discussions they touched on the aims, duties and methods of government; general policies of state; the means of administration; the state of contemporary society; and the value of past precedent.

In the early years of Huo Kuang's regency there is discernible some measure of retrenchment, or even a disengagement from responsibilities. The Hsiung-nu incursion of 87 BC was not followed by the despatch of a large scale punitive expedition;[105] in 82 the commanderies that had been established in Hainan Island were withdrawn, and the four that had been founded in

[104] *HS* 7:5a, *HFHD*, II, 160.   [105] *HS* 7:1b, *HFHD*, II, 152.

Korea were re-organised as two. There are also signs of the attention paid to the welfare of the population. Prior to the command for a debate on popular suffering in 81, a commission of enquiry had been sent out to the provinces to collect data on this matter in 86;[106] and in the next year relief measures had been taken to help those who were in material want. These were all steps that could be associated with the traditional virtues of Confucian government. However, it should be borne in mind that the men responsible for administration under Chao ti, i.e. Huo Kuang and Sang Hung-yang, were the same officials who had sponsored realist measures of government under Wu ti; and it is clear from the account that we have of the debate of 81 that the Government spokesmen, who included Sang Hung-yang, supported realist or Modernist principles, while the critics of contemporary government were men of a Reformist persuasion who had been nurtured in the scholastic tradition and harked back to the golden days of Yao and Shun.

The *Yen-t'ieh lun*, or *Discourses on Salt and Iron*, was probably compiled a decade or two after the debate took place. The disputants discuss the question of retrenchment as against that of expansion; of *laisser-faire* as against an attempt to control and exploit China's productive resources. Should the trading connections with central Asia be promoted or suspended? The critics of the government ask whether it is just and expedient to tax the population in order to expand Han territories; and the Modernist members of the government counter by asking whether Han can afford to relax the defensive measures needed to keep the Hsiung-nu at bay. The account of the debate is loaded on the side of the moralist critics of the day, who are always shown to be winning on points over their opponents; and the spokesmen for the government are on several occasions reduced to abject silence. But a significant contrast is to be noted in this respect between the force of argument as represented in the extant account of the debate and the measures

[106] *HS* 7:3a, *HFHD*, II, 155.

actually taken afterwards. The practical issue involved was the continuance or abolition of state monopolies. Of these, the control of the iron and salt industries was the more important and controversial, and that of the production of alcoholic spirits, which had only been introduced in 98, was of lesser significance. However, despite the arguments that were reportedly put forward, the only monopoly to be abolished in 81 BC was that of spirits. This was the compromise suggested by the Chancellor and the Imperial Counsellor, T'ien Ch'ien-ch'iu and Sang Hung-yang.[107]

It may be noted that the *Yen-t'ieh lun* alludes occasionally to the political events of Wu ti's reign that have been described above. The name Chiang Ch'ung appears in two passages,[108] when the Reformist critic of the government is protesting against the sharp practices, materialist attitude and rigorous administration practised by Wu ti's advisers; and Chiang Ch'ung was one of the named culprits. Elsewhere in the debate, the critic singles out Kung-sun Ho and Liu Ch'u-li as men who were responsible for the deterioration of moral standards in the Government of Wu ti's reign.[109]

In the dramatic incident of 80 BC Huo Kuang emerged with unimpaired authority and with no rival to challenge his position.[110] Motives of varying natures lay behind the participation of the different individuals in the plot to remove Chao ti and Huo Kuang in that year. Shang-kuan Chieh and his son Shang-kuan An, who had been appointed General of Cavalry (*chü-ch'i chiang-chün*) in 83,[111] were probably inspired by political jealousy. In the time of Wu ti, Shang-kuan Chieh had actually

---

[107] *HS* 6:34b, *HFHD*, II, 107; *HS* 7:5a, *HFHD*, II, 161; *YTL*, 41 (276), which adds that the agencies for iron situated within the passes were also abolished; *HS* 24B:20b, Swann, 320. For a fuller account of the debate, see Chapter 3.

[108] *YTL*, 14 (99), 28 (194).   [109] *YTL*, 30 (233).

[110] *HS* 7:6b, *HFHD*, II, 164; *HS* 63: 10b; *HS* 68:3a.

[111] *HS* 19B:27b.

held an office that was senior to that of Huo Kuang, and he now resented the reversal of their relative situations. Likewise, Shang-kuan An's arrogant behaviour after the nomination of his daughter as Empress (83) may have excited Huo Kuang's anger. The Princess O-i, who was Chao ti's elder sister, had tried with the help of Shang-kuan Chieh and Shang-kuan An to have her lover Ting Wai-jen promoted, but Huo Kuang had sternly refused the suggestion. Tan king of Yen believed that he had a prior claim to the throne, as he had already demonstrated in 87–6. There is, however, no immediate or fully satisfactory explanation for Sang Hung-yang's involvement. He was not related to the imperial house or to any of the consorts, as were all the others who were concerned. There is nothing in the *Han-shu* to indicate that he was competing for dictator's powers, other than a suggestion that he wished office to be conferred on his relatives, on the strength of his own successful management of the state monopolies.[112] Nor is there any record of his support being deliberately sought or bought by the others; and from what we know of Sang Hung-yang it would seem that he was a man of a sufficiently independent mind and strong character to avoid involvement in affairs of this nature without due reason. It is just possible that his implication was due to disgruntlement at the public enquiry of the previous year into policies which he, more than any other statesman, had sponsored and at the compromise which he had been forced to accept (see p. 72).

The conspirators waited for a day when Huo Kuang was away from court. They then had a document submitted to the throne in which he was accused of strengthening his own support by means of various appointments to office and of using his authority arbitrarily. Tan King of Yen took the opportunity to write to the Emperor, citing past precedent and referring to the measures taken at the outset of the Han dynasty to prevent families other than the Liu house from interfering in matters of

[112] *HS* 68:3a.

state.[113] He wrote that trusted ministers were ruining the dynasty in an atmosphere that was conditioned by calumny and lawlessness. Chao ti was now fourteen years old and angrily rejected the charges, promising legal processes for anyone who dared to renew the accusations. His authority was sufficient to stop Shang-kuan Chieh and Shang-kuan An from taking direct action, but the other conspirators continued in their course. Tan King of Yen started to recruit the help of the strong men of the provinces. Despite advice to the contrary and the warnings of a host of portents[114] he was confident that he could carry the day by virtue of his right, as Wu ti's son, to rule as Emperor. But his hopes were shattered by the discovery of his plans, just at the time when a similar attempt was being foiled at Ch'ang-an. Here the Princess O-i had prepared to have Huo Kuang murdered at a banquet, but prior information had reached the Chancellor, and in the event Shang-kuan Chieh, Shang-kuan An and Sang Hung-yang were executed. The Princess O-i and King Tan committed suicide.

Huo Kuang was able to retain his unique position for a further period of thirteen years, which saw Chao ti's attainment of majority in 77[115] and the problems of imperial succession in 74 BC. As an act of clemency, Hsüan ti created Tan's heir King of Kuang-yang in 73 and the line of succession continued without interruption until the time of Wang Mang.[116]

The dynastic events that followed the death of Chao ti are no less remarkable than those of the previous years and may serve to show that the old rivalries between the consorts of Wu ti were not yet dead.[117] Briefly, Liu Ho, a descendant of the Li family, succeeded Chao ti, but after a reign of a mere twenty-seven days he was deposed and replaced by Liu Ping-i, the only member of the Wei family to survive the scandals of 91–90. Liu Ping-i reigned as Hsüan ti for twenty-five years.

[113] *HS* 63:10b.   [114] *HS* 63:12b.   [115] *HS* 7:8a, *HFHD*, II, 169.
[116] *HS* 14:20a.
[117] *HS* 8:1a, *HFHD*, II, 199; *HS* 63:18a; *HS* 68:4b.

Chao ti died on 5 June 74 at the age of twenty, and it was represented at court that Liu Hsü the only surviving son of Wu ti had a good claim to succeed as Emperor. Hsü was a man of some seniority, having been created king of Kuang-ling as long ago as 117. According to the *Han-shu* his behaviour had been unprincipled, and the idea of his accession disquieted Huo Kuang. It may perhaps be surmised that Huo Kuang's unease arose from the thought of having an elderly man enthroned as Emperor who would be able to withstand manipulation. Whatever his motives Huo Kuang succeeded in having the idea scotched, and he sent a commission of officials to summon Liu Ho, king of Ch'ang-i and grandson of the Lady Li. Ho was asked to make all speed to reach Ch'ang-an where he was to attend to the late Emperor's obsequies.

Liu Ho set off from Ch'ang-i[118] immediately, with indecent haste and without a thought to spare for his horses who died under the strain. However—and here again we can only follow the *Han-shu*, whose account may well be coloured by subsequent developments—Liu Ho spent the journey in reckless indulgence and with a show of ostentation, and he refused to make any of the protestations of grief that the occasion demanded until he reached the gates of the palace. Further reference to his behaviour will be made shortly.

We do not hear for certain of Liu Ho's presence in Ch'ang-an until 18 July, i.e. about forty-two days after the receipt of the summons. On that day he formally acceded to the throne, taking custody of the imperial seals and seal-ribbons; and the title of Empress Dowager was conferred on Chao ti's widow, grand-daughter of Huo Kuang, and of the tender age of fifteen. The long interval between Ho's departure at break-neck speed from Ch'ang-i and his accession may lend some support to the allegation that he spent the journey in a prolonged bout of material indulgence; alternatively, he may have reached the capital city earlier and have spent the interval in performing

[118] For the situation of Ch'ang-i, see *RHA*, vol. I, p. 141, note 80.

the ceremonies and vigils prior to accession. At the time Liu Ho was aged eighteen or nineteen.[119] Chao ti's funeral was completed on 24 July.[120]

According to the *Han-shu*[121] the immoral behaviour of the new Emperor outraged and grieved Huo Kuang, who consulted T'ien Yen-nien. T'ien was *ta-ssu-nung* or Superintendent of Agriculture[122] and a man with whom Huo enjoyed friendly relations. He advised that a conference should be called to discuss the situation, and when Huo Kuang duly reported his fears for the safety of the realm, all the attendant officials maintained an embarrassed silence. The situation was saved by T'ien Yen-nien in a powerful speech urging immediate action and threatening violence, and a report was presented to the Empress Dowager, giving grounds for the fear that Liu Ho was not fit to receive charge of the Empire. By a dexterous manoeuvre, Liu Ho was brought into the presence of the Empress Dowager without any of his personal attendants, many of whom were arrested and sent down for judicial processes. The occasion—14 August, twenty-seven days after his accession—was marked by formality and dignity. Armed guards were drawn up and the senior officials of state took their places according to precedence.

Liu Ho was now obliged to listen to the text of a memorial which had been composed in the names of thirty-six senior members of the Government, including civil officials and generals. The document began by stressing that the Son of Heaven's powers and authority rest on qualities and judgment, and deplored the evident lack of these assets in the person of Chao ti's successor. Liu Ho had had no proper feelings of grief and had failed to accept the conventional proprieties. Even before Chao ti's funeral he had misused the imperial seals; he

[119] See Dubs, in *HFHD*, II, 181; *HS* 63:20b.

[120] *HS* 7:10a, *HFHD*, II, 174.   [121] *HS* 68:5a.

[122] *HS* 19B:30a. Dubs renders *Ta-ssu-nung* as Grand Minister of Agriculture.

had introduced his own retainers from Ch'ang-i, making merry with them in the imperial palace. There had been music and entertainments, both while Chao ti's coffin was still lying in state and after the interment, and the Dowager Empress's carriage had been used in the course of the imperial amusements. Liu Ho had had sexual relations with women who had been members of Chao ti's entourage, and had threatened execution for anyone who dared to divulge such practices. In addition he had made free with the precious metals, swords, jades and silks of the palace stores so as to find presents for his fellow revellers; he had drunk to a state of stupefaction in the company of his attendants and slaves, and abused his position so as to send out messengers on personal missions—altogether on 1127 occasions in the twenty-seven days since his accession. So far from taking heed of remonstrances, he had initiated judicial processes against the few men who had dared to voice their criticism. In this way the principles of imperial rule had been forfeited and the dynasty and empire lay endangered. The memorial ended with a request to report this state of affairs at the shrine of Kao tsu, founder of the dynasty.

With the predictable approval of this memorial by the Empress Dowager, granddaughter of Huo Kuang, the latter was free to have Liu Ho deposed and his seals returned to the keeping of the palace. Surprisingly Liu Ho was not exiled to the west as had been suggested, but allowed to return to Ch'ang-i; and his personal property was shared between his four daughters. However, his kingdom was brought to an end and the area was henceforth administered as the commandery of Shan-yang under the direct control of the central government. Of those who had encouraged him in his ways or shared in his indulgences 200 were put to death at Huo Kuang's orders. There is an elaborate account in the *Han-shu*[123] to show that by 64 BC, i.e. after Huo Kuang's death and a number of changes, Hsüan ti allowed himself to be persuaded that he had nothing

[123] *HS* 63:18a.

to fear from Liu Ho, and a nobility was conferred on him in that year.[124]

Huo Kuang now put forward his suggestion for filling the vacancy left by Chao ti's death, and he proposed that Liu Ping-i should be selected for the honour. Ping-i was aged eighteen and a grandson of the Wei family's Heir Apparent who had committed suicide in 91; and once again a commission set out to acquaint a nominee for the throne of his destiny and to invite his presence at Ch'ang-an. Ping-i's accession was dated from 10 September 74.[125]

Until his death in 68 BC, Huo Kuang was in an unassailable position. As he doubtless expected, his offer to return the cares of government to the Emperor was declined,[126] and he was treated with the greatest generosity in the bestowal of honours on those who had planned Hsüan ti's accession.[127] The nobility granted to him in 85 had entitled him to the emoluments collected from 2350 households,[128] and this was now increased by 17200 to a total of nearly 20000. In addition he received handsome gifts of gold, cash, silks, slaves, horses and a residence. By comparison it may be noted that the next highest reward given at this time was a nobility of 10000 households, and at the outset of the dynasty the two founding statesmen Ts'ao Ts'an and Hsiao Ho had received nobilities of 10000 and 8000 households, respectively.[129] Commenting on the period of Chao ti's reign the author of the *Han-shu*[130] praised Huo Kuang's regency. Very significantly, he compared it with that of the Duke of Chou, and he drew attention to Huo's policy of retrenchment, to his attempt to repair the ravages caused by the extravagance of the previous reign, and to his abolition of some of the monopolies of state.

The two acts of accession and the single act of deposal that

---

[124] *HS* 15B:13a.   [125] *HS* 8:3b, *HFHD*, II, 205.
[126] *HS* 8:4a, *HFHD*, II, 207.   [127] *HS* 68:10b, 11a.
[128] *HS* 18:11a; *SC* 20:38 gives the figure of 3000 instead of 2350.
[129] *HS* 16:4b and 11a.   [130] *HS* 7:10b, *HFHD*, II, 175.

took place in 74 illustrate how the form and proprieties of Han institutions were observed scrupulously while changes of a very serious nature were being contrived. The documents drawn up in preparation for the events take care to cite precedent, and in the case of the enthronement of the emperors, the documents stress that qualities are of greater importance than seniority. The nomination of Chao ti's widow as Empress Dowager[131] created the necessary authority in whose name decrees could be issued and actions taken, even to the point of making and unmaking an emperor. The niceties of the imperial cult were preserved by having Liu Ho's misdeeds announced at Kao tsu's shrine, and Liu Ping-i's accession was marked by his formal visit of respect there.[132] The bill of indictment against Liu Ho included charges of infringing several points of duly prescribed behaviour, and one of the complaints of his activities prior to accession concerned his refusal to comply with the stipulations for mourning.[133] When the decision had been taken to invite Ping-i to accede as Emperor, he was first created noble of Yang-wu:[134] and according to Yen Shih-ku (581–645) this step was taken so as to avoid creating a commoner Son of Heaven. Finally, formalism may be seen in the activities of officials. In the memorial indicting Liu Ho, it was the Chancellor's name which appeared at the head of the list,[135] not that of Huo Kuang. Although the decision to depose Liu Ho was taken by

[131] *HS* 8:3a, *HFHD*, II, 204. For the assumption of the power of decree by an empress or empress dowager, see Lien-sheng Yang, 'Female Rulers in Imperial China' (*Harvard Journal of Asiatic Studies*, 23 (1960–61), pp. 47–61; reprinted in Bishop, *Studies of Governmental Institutions in Chinese History* (Harvard 1968) and in Lien-sheng Yang, *Excursions in Sinology* (Harvard 1969).

[132] Similar visits to the ancestral shrines were paid by emperors on their accession by, e.g. Hui ti, Chao ti, Yüan ti, Ch'eng ti, Ai ti and P'ing ti.

[133] *HS* 63:18b.   [134] *HS* 68:10b.

[135] *Sic HS* 68:6b. This account is probably more authentic than the summary given in *HS* 8:3a, *HFHD*, II, 204, which simply mentions Huo Kuang's name.

two men only (i.e. Huo Kuang and T'ien Yen-nien), the request to do so needed the full backing of all senior officials, and obviously the incorporation of as many names as possible in the act would tend to preclude reprisals at a later stage, should further dynastic difficulties occur. Lastly, the two commissions appointed to summon Liu Ho and Liu Ping-i to the highest honour in the Empire, each included the *tsung-cheng* or Superintendent of the Imperial Family.[136] This post was the only one of the nine senior offices of state which was regularly filled by a member of the Liu house. The incumbent was responsible for keeping the records of the family and maintaining the correct order of precedence among its members.

Commenting on the incident of 91 BC, the *Han-shu*[137] states that the calamity of *wu-ku* started with Chu An-shih, i.e. the criminal who had accused Kung-sun Ching-sheng of these and similar practices (see p. 39); that it reached completion under Chiang Ch'ung and that it then involved princesses, the Empress and the Heir Apparent, who all met their deaths as a result. The statement is sufficient as far as it goes, but it has been shown above that the case was intricately connected with dynastic rivalries and institutional developments that persisted until 74 at least. It remains now to examine the nature of *wu-ku* and the associated practices that are mentioned, i.e. cursing the Emperor and the burial of human images; and account should be taken of other events that are deliberately linked to these incidents in the histories, such as the search for persons involved or for evidence. Above all it is necessary to glance briefly at the prevailing religious beliefs of the time, at least in so far as these affected the palace.

Tung Chung-shu's formulation of a philosophy of state had been evolved in the decades preceding the scandals of 91–90.

[136] The *tsung-cheng* (Dubs—Superintendent of the Imperial House) also took part in the demotion of the Empress Wei in 91 (*HS* 97A: 11a).
[137] *HS* 66:2a.

As far as may be known the intellectual climate of Ch'ang-an at that time was being coloured by the belief in Heaven's intervention in human affairs and its manifestation of warnings, and a faith was growing in the properties of *Yin-yang* and the Five Elements and their powers over human destiny. As the appointed arbiter of mankind and governor of temporalities, the Emperor was accustomed to take part in a variety of ceremonies, which shed some light on the importance paid to various spiritual powers on behalf of the dynasty. Fairly regularly he worshipped at the shrines of the Five Powers and he inaugurated the worship of the Earth Queen and the Supreme Unity.[138] In 110 he had worshipped to the Yellow Emperor, and in the same year he had performed the *feng* ceremony to Heaven at Mount T'ai. Other cults in which Wu ti participated included those devoted to the spirits of the hills and rivers, and to the souls of the legendary Emperor Shun and the ancestral founder of the dynasty. Little expense had been spared in these ventures, which included the construction of the Spirits' Hall (*Ming-t'ang*) in 109. In addition Wu ti had made several journeys and spent considerable effort in searching for the immortal beings of P'eng-lai, and in several famous incidents he had shown his susceptibility to the influence of shamans or mediums such as Shao Weng and Luan Ta. It is against this background that we can consider the belief and practice of *wu–ku* during the Han period.

The term *ku* can be traced from the oracle bones until modern times, and it has acquired a large number of meanings or connotations. The Yin bone character clearly represents insects or vermin within a pot or cauldron.[139] In literature it is taken by commentators to carry a variety of particular meanings, including insects living in grain or into which grain is transformed;[140] maggots breeding in a pot; objects that can be

---

[138] See Chapter 5, pp. 167f.
[139] See Karlgren *Grammata Serica Recensa*, 52b.
[140] In this connection see *Lun-heng* 49, Huang Hui edition, pp. 714, 716.

injurious to man; poisonous vermin contained within the human stomach; to bewilder or cast spells; emanations of evil; and the spirits of sentenced criminals whose heads had been exposed on stakes. In general the term is used to imply magical processes and has been translated as 'Black Magic'.[141]

The history of the belief and practice of *ku* has been traced by Feng and Shryock, who summarise the contemporary (i.e. 1935) situation as follows:[142]

At present, *ku* is used primarily as a means of acquiring wealth; secondarily as a means of revenge. The method is to place poisonous snakes and insects together in a vessel until there is but one survivor, which is called the *ku*. The poison secured from this *ku* is administered to the victim, who becomes sick and dies. The ideas associated with *ku* vary, but the *ku* is generally regarded as a spirit, which secures the wealth of the victim for the sorcerer.

This conclusion is based on an examination of a series of passages extending from the *Tso chuan* to the nineteenth century. From the tenth century AD onwards there is clear evidence of the use of *ku* to kill people directly, or to bring pressure to bear upon them; e.g. a man may have received a 'dose' of *ku* and be told that unless he returns by a certain time it will kill him, whereas, if he does comply, a safe antidote can be administered. There are accounts of various techniques of applying *ku* and different ways in which the victims are affected. When the poison has been introduced into a person it may manifest itself as a living insect or reptile that is highly active within his entrails. Sometimes there are fatal results, or the insect is expelled from the victim's body and killed, possibly leaving traces as a physical deformity.[143]

[141] Dubs, *HFHD*, 114, etc., uses the term 'witchcraft and black magic' to render *wu-ku*. H. Y. Feng and J. K. Shryock use the term 'Black Magic', in 'The Black Magic in China known as Ku' (*Journal of the American Oriental Society*, vol. 55, (1935), pp. 1–30). See also de Groot, *The Religious System of China*, vol. v, pp. 826f.

[142] Feng and Shryock, 1.   [143] See cases cited by Feng and Shryock.

These practices are evidenced far more fully for recent centuries than they are for the Han period, and although they may very well be based on long-standing belief and custom, the meagre nature of the early references renders it difficult to determine how far the evidence may be applied retrospectively. There is a further difficulty in regard to practices of the Han period, as these are mostly described not as *ku* but as *wu-ku*, i.e. *ku* in which shamans participate or are concerned. It is not clear whether the specific mention of the shamans necessarily introduces a new element in the concept; for the present purposes no distinction is made in translating the two terms, which have been rendered above as *witchcraft*.

The Han concepts of *ku* presumably lay at an intermediate stage between a descriptive statement in the *Tso chuan* (i.e. fourth century BC) and incidents recounted in the *Sou-shen chi* (fourth century AD) and the *Sou-shen hou chi* (falsely attributed to T'ao Ch'ien, 365–427, but certainly before the Sui period). The passage in the *Tso chuan* refers to the year 540 BC, and has been rendered as follows by Couvreur:[144]

> *Le prince de Tsin demanda un médecin à Ts'in. Le prince de Ts'in ordonna au médecin Houo d'aller le voir. Le médecin (y alla et) dit au prince de Tsin: 'Il n'y a rien à faire pour cette maladie. C'est le cas de dire que, quand le malade approche des appartements des femmes, il est comme halluciné. L'hallucination, la perte de la raison ne sont pas causées par les mauvais esprits ni par la nourriture, (mais par la passion). . . .'*
>
> *Tchao Meng demanda: 'Qu'appelez vous kòu hallucination?' Le médecin repondit: 'On appelle kòu ce qui produit l'excès, l'affection déréglée, l'erreur, le trouble. La lettre kòu est composée des deux lettres mìng récipient et tch'òung ver ou reptile. L'insecte aîlé qui naît dans le grain longtemps emmagasiné s'appelle kòu. Dans le I king de Tcheou koung, la femme qui séduit l'homme, le vent qui renverse une colline sont apellés kòu. Toutes ces choses se ressemblent.'*

[144] S. Couvreur, *Tch'ouen Ts'iou et Tso Tchouan, La chronique de la principauté de Lòu*, vol. III, pp. 35f. For a different version of this passage, see J. R. Ware, *Alchemy, Medicine, Religion in the China of AD 320* (Massachusetts Institute of Technology, 1966), p. 5.

Two points may be noted which concern the meaning attributed to the term in the period between this passage and the evidence for the fourth century AD. In a comment to the *Chou-li*, Cheng Hsüan (127–200) takes *ku* as meaning poisonous objects which harm human beings,[145] and the *Shuo-wen* defines *ku* as 'insects within the stomach'.

The following passages illustrate the belief in the manufacture and efficacy of *ku* some two or three centuries after the time of Cheng Hsüan. The translations are those given in Feng and Shryock.[146]

(1) In the province of Yung-yang, there was a family by the name of Liao. For several generations they manufactured *ku*, becoming rich from it. Later one of the family married, but they kept the secret from the bride. On one occasion, everyone went out except the bride, who was left in charge of the house. Suddenly she noticed a large cauldron in the house, and on opening it, perceived a big snake inside. She poured boiling water into the cauldron and killed the snake. When the rest of the family returned she told them what she had done, to their great alarm. Not long after, the entire family died of the plague.

(2) Tan Yu was a poor and devout monk. There was a family in the district of Yen who manufactured *ku*. Those who ate their food, died from haemorrhage. Tan Yu once visited this family, and the host prepared food for him. Tan Yu recited an incantation, and saw a pair of centipedes a foot long suddenly crawl away from the dish. He then ate the food, and returned home without being harmed.

(3) T'ang Tzu, of the Hsiang district, went to Chu Ch'i's mother P'en's house to drink wine. On returning home he became ill, and vomited more than ten *ku* worms. Seeing that

---

[145] *Chou-li*, 10, SPTK 7a; see note to *shu-shih*.

[146] Feng and Shryock, 7–8, cite these passages from (a) *Sou-shen chi* 12, *Ts'ung-shu chi-ch'eng*, p. 86; (b) *Sou-shen hou chi* 2, *Ts'ung-shu chi-ch'eng*, p. 28; (c) *Sung-shu* 81:10a (*Po-na* ed.).

he was about to die, he directed his wife Chang that after death she should cut open his abdomen in order to get rid of the disease. Later Chang cut open his body, and saw his 'five viscera' completely destroyed.

The evidence for the Han period may now be considered. In 122 BC a consort of one of the Han kings was brought up on a charge of having killed her predecessor by means of *ku*,[147] but no details are furnished of the means allegedly employed. For the whole of the scandal of 91 there is no description of the practices said to have occurred, but something may be inferred, indirectly, from the account of the actions taken by Chiang Ch'ung after his appointment as commissioner to bring the cases of *wu-ku* up for trial.[148] The passage is by no means clear, and interpretations have varied from the time of Chang Yen (third to fourth century) to that of Wang Hsien-ch'ien (1842–1918) or de Groot, who renders it as follows:[149]

'Now Kiang Ch'ung had the ground dug up by his Hunnish *wu*, to seek for human images; those men seized breeders of *ku* and nocturnal sacrificers; they saw the spectres; they defiled the ground (with sacrificial spirits) so as to make suspicious places. They continuously arrested people, examining them, belaboured them with hot iron tongs, and roasted them to extort confessions. . . .'

The passage would seem to mean that Chiang Ch'ung arrested men on charges of practising *ku* or uttering prayers by night. He had previously taken the precaution of having manikins buried where they lived, and he now had those sites smeared or defiled with other matter, in the pretence that they were traces of spirits. He then had foreign shamans[150] examine the defilation left by such spirits, so that it would be generally realised that these were sites where *ku* had been buried; and he then

---

[147] *SC* 118:45; *HS* 44:16b.   [148] *HS* 45:13b.

[149] *The Religious System of China* (1892), vol. v, p. 830.

[150] *Tzu-chih t'ung-chien*, p. 728, includes two characters which are taken as a proper name, which, however, is not traced in *SC* or *HS*.

proceeded to have the sites dug up. Whenever people were arrested, proof was sought and a trial instituted, and admissions of guilt were forced by the application of hot irons.

The exploitation of a belief in *wu-ku* for dynastic purposes in 91 BC is only too self-evident from our sources. There were also other instances in which *wu-ku* was used as a pretext for political action. In 130 it had been the instrument for deposing an empress.[151] We next hear of a parallel case in the Eastern Han period; in AD 102 a charge of harbouring *wu-ku* was brought against the Empress Yin, and imprecation was again involved.[152] The earlier case of Kung-sun Ao may also show how *wu-ku* could be exploited in the name of justice.[153] He had been condemned to death because of the very great losses of the campaigns of 97 and 96, but by simulating death he had managed to escape and to retire to live incognito in the country. Some five or six years later, i.e. at the height of the scandal, his presence was revealed and he was re-arrested. He was then brought up on a charge that his wife had practised *wu-ku*, and by way of punishment the family was exterminated.

Some slight information is available regarding the attention paid to *wu-ku* in Han institutions. The office of *ssu-li hsiao-wei*

[151] See p. 51. In the records of extraordinary phenomena and their interpretation as acts of Heaven's warnings of dynastic misdeeds, *HS* 27A:13a, b deliberately links two explosions which were reported to have occurred in the state-controlled iron mines in 91 and 27 BC respectively. The first is associated with the dynastic events of 91–90, and the second with the somewhat comparable incident of 18–17, when Ch'eng ti's empress Hsü was deposed and her position filled by the imperial favourite Chao Fei-yen. It is to be noted that *HS* 27A (*loc. cit.*) specifies that the Empress Hsü was deposed after a charge of *wu-ku*. However, this detail is not included in *HS* 10:10a (*HFHD*, II 398) or *HS* 97B:6b, and there is no record of the Empress's punishment for such a crime. The inclusion of *wu-ku* in *HS* 27 could well have been made in order to accentuate the comparison between the two phenomena and their interpretation.

[152] *HHS* 10A:14a, 16a; *HHS* 16 (biog. 6): 6b. For a further case, in AD 105, see *HHS* 10A.17a.

[153] *HS* 55:18b.

was first established in Han institutions in 89;[154] its responsibilities included the arrest of those practising *wu-ku* as well as the investigation of cases of treason. From a comment to the *Chou-li* by Cheng Hsüan that has already been cited[155] we learn that according to the Han Statutes 'Those who dare to poison people with *ku* or teach others to do it will be publicly executed'; and those who were punished for the crime in 130 finally had their heads impaled and exhibited publicly.[156] In this connection, attention may be drawn to one explanation of the term *ku* that appears in the *Shuo-wen*, i.e. the spirits of convicted criminals whose heads had been exposed on stakes.

Some of the passages in the *Han-shu* definitely associate *wu-ku* with imprecation and the great searches that were carried out at imperial orders from time to time. In 130 a charge of both *wu-ku* and cursing was used as a means of deposing Wu ti's first empress.[156] There is nothing to show that the great search of 100[157] was necessarily concerned with these matters, and it may have been restricted to a search for criminals; but the institution of the great search of 99 follows immediately on a ban that was imposed on shamans who were in the habit of making sacrifices on the roads, and it seems likely that the search was not unconnected.[158] In 86 Han Hsing, son of that Han Yüeh who had been put to death by the Heir Apparent in 91, was brought up on a charge and executed. According to one statement[159] the charge was one of *wu-ku*; according to another passage[160] it was one of imprecation, and the discrepancy in the accounts may reflect the historian's association of the two types of practice together.

Cursing the Emperor, *chu-tsu shang*, was a heinous crime that was described in official Han terminology usually as *ta-ni*

---

154 *HS* 19A:22a. Dubs-Colonel of retainers.

155 See p. 85, Feng and Shryock, p. 6, *Chou-li* as cited in note 145; see Hulsewé, 33.   156 *HS* 6:7a; *HFHD*, II, 41; *HS* 97A:11a.

157 *HS* 6:33a; *HFHD*, II, 103–4.   158 *HS* 6:34a; *HFHD*, II, 105.

159 See p. 41; *HS* 33:9b.   160 *HS* 16:68a.

wu-tao and once as *ta-ni*. This was 'great refractoriness and impiety' or simply 'great refractoriness', and those accused of the crime were either punished by execution or forced to commit suicide.[161] The principle source of information for cases of this crime is to be found in the tables of the *Han-shu*, which record occasions when a charge of *chu-tsu shang* brought about the end of a highly placed official's career or the line of a nobility. It is remarkable that of the total number of twenty-one cases recorded here for the two centuries of Western Han, at least sixteen and probably eighteen were dated between 90 and 85.[162]

One of these cases involved the wife of Liu Ch'u-li the Chancellor, as has been described above (see p. 45), and in this particular instance we are told that the curses were uttered by means of a shaman.[163] A further interesting case of cursing the Emperor is recorded[164] for Hsü, one of Wu ti's sons (see p. 58), who had been created King of Kuang-ling in 117 BC.

[161] See Hulsewé, pp. 156f. and 168 for the use of the term to mean 'swearing by the name of the emperor when entering into agreements'.

[162] There are three cases dated between 6 and 1 BC. In two cases that are recorded in *HS* 17:16b and *HS* 17:18b, the text dates the crime at two years after the investiture of the nobility, *hou erh nien*, corresponding with 111 and 108. However, it is very likely that this should be interpreted as *hou-yüan erh nien*, i.e. 87 BC, as has been suggested by Wang Hsien-ch'ien and Su Yü for two other cases (*HS* 17:8b and *HS* 17:18a). In view of the discrepancy regarding the crime of Wei K'ang (see note 7, p. 40) I have not included this case in the figures, despite the implication in *HS* 63:1b that he was brought up on a charge of cursing and executed. *See* notes to *HS* 18:8a. The figures given here do not include the cases of Kung-sun Ho, Kung-sun Ching-sheng and the two princesses (*HS* 63:1b). There is also a further case, in c. 123 BC, in which the King of Chiang-tu and his queen had a female slave from the south invoke spirits in order to curse the emperor (*HS* 53:6a; Wilbur, *Slavery in China during the Former Han Dynasty*, p. 316).

[163] *HS* 66:4b. Li Shou was an official who arranged to have the shaman killed, presumably to prevent leakage of the intentions harboured by Liu Ch'u-li and Li Kuang-li. Li Shou was executed for the crime; *HS* 17:24b; see Hulsewé, 181.   [164] *HS* 63:15a.

Conscious of Chao ti's youth at the time of his accession, he had his own ambitions to succeed as Emperor, and invoked the services of a local female shaman, of a type that was well-known in the south. She claimed that she had successfully brought about the appearance of Wu ti's spirit; those who had attended the scene were convinced by her claim, and Wu ti was alleged to have insisted on Hsü's succession to the imperial throne. Chao ti's death after the performance of certain ceremonies added verisimilitude to the witch's statement. Pleased at her success, Hsü employed her again to utter curses when Ho King of Ch'ang-i was summoned to be Emperor, and his immediate deposal added yet more support to Hsü's belief in her powers. After Hsüan ti's accession, Hsü was involved in a charge of complicity in rebellion. He managed to evade trial and gave up the practice of having curses uttered, but he is said to have taken it up later when involved in other charges. Unfortunately, little is recorded of the activities practised during these incidents. To bring about Chao ti's death, the witch uttered prayers at the Mountain of the Shamans, wu shan;[165] after the event cattle were killed and prayers of thanksgiving were offered.

Finally, attention may be drawn to further hints of the belief in the powers of invocation at the end of Wu ti's reign, and the susceptibility of the imperial mind to witchcraft. Following Li Kuang-li's defeat of 90, an edict was proclaimed pronouncing the need for retrenchment (see p. 64). The text includes the following passage:[166]

'Enemy patrols taken by the noble of Chung-ho inform Us that when the Hsiung-nu hear of the approach of Han forces they have their sorcerers bury sheep or cattle by the roads that they are taking and by the water, in order to bring a curse upon Our armies; and when the *Shan-yü* sends a present of horses or fur-garments to the Son of Heaven, he regularly has his sorcerers lay a spell upon them. . . .'

[165] *HS* 63:15b; see notes in *Han-shu pu-chu*. [166] *HS* 96B:19a.

CHAPTER 3

The Grand Inquest – 81 BC

A very simply worded edict of 81 BC[1] has had far-reaching results on our understanding of the controversial issues of that time. Not for the first time, the Emperor ordered senior officials and men of wisdom to confer in an attempt to ascertain the hardships which the population was suffering.[2] Acting under these wide terms of reference, the parties to the ensuing discussions took their responsibilities seriously, and in the account of their deliberations which was compiled subsequently, they are shown as taking stock of the major intellectual and political issues of the day. The first subject on which they fastened, and the one which is specified in the *Han-shu*'s brief account of these proceedings,[3] concerned the state monopolies which had been introduced some forty years previously for salt and iron, and more recently for alcoholic spirits. For this reason, and owing to the title of the written report of the debate, the incident is usually described as the Discussions on Salt and Iron (*Yen-t'ieh lun*).

This document is of almost unique value in so far as it sets out in the form of a dialogue and with remarkable clarity many of the controversial issues of the day. These are discussed by the spokesmen of the two opposing parties, whose views are

[1] See *YTL* I (I) and *HS* 6.5a (*HFHD*, vol. II, p. 160). Part of the *Yen-t'ieh lun* has been translated by E. M. Gale, as *Discourses on Salt and Iron*, Leyden, 1931, and in vol. LXV of the *Journal of the North China Branch of the Royal Asiatic Society* (1934), pp. 73–110. Both of these works were reprinted by the Chung-wen Publishing Company, Taipei in 1967.

[2] See *HS* 6.3a (*HFHD*, vol. II, p. 155) for the appointment of a similar commission of enquiry in 86.

[3] *HS* 6.5a (*HFHD* vol. II, p. 160); *HS* 66.7a.

those of the Modernist and the Reformist frame of mind. The Modernist view is put forward by those who were speaking in defence of the government's policies; the Reformist view is expressed as a matter of pungent criticism of contemporary practice and its abuses.

The *Yen-t'ieh lun* may be divided into two major parts that are of uneven length; sections (*P'ien*) 1–41, which are followed by a short statement of the recommendation made by the participants; and sections 42–59, which are followed by a final section giving the comments of the observer who reported the debate. The statement which follows the first part, coupled with the manner in which the debate is shown to be conducted, reveals the nature of the compromise that was reached in 81 BC. In the first part of the debate (sections 1–41), the spokesmen for the government were frequently shown to have been worsted in argument, and whereas it was possible for two spokesmen only to represent the view of the Reformists, no less than fourteen changes were necessary among those who defended the Modernists' principles and the government's record. Nevertheless the recommendation that was put forward at the close of the forty-first section of the debate was a compromise in which the government were vindicated.

'The critics do not understand the issues facing the central government and mistakenly believe that the State's control of salt and iron is not expedient. We ask for the abolition of the state's monopoly for the production of spirits in the provinces and for the withdrawal of the agencies of state that were established for the production of iron within the metropolitan area'.

This submission was duly approved.

No names are furnished in sections 1–59 for the spokesmen who took part in the debate and who are described as the man of learning (*wen-hsüeh*), the man of wisdom (*hsien-lang*), the counsellor (*ta-fu*), the imperial agent (*yü-shih*) and the Chancellor's aid (*ch'eng-hsiang shih*). The *ta-fu* may probably be identi-

fied as Sang Hung-yang, who held the post of Imperial
Counsellor (*yü-shih ta-fu*) from 87 to 80 BC;[4] and he is mentioned by name, with a number of other men, in the general
comment to the debate that forms section 60.[5]

There is a surprisingly small amount of duplication in the
points that are raised during the first part of the debate. In the
summary which follows below, the arguments that appear in
sections 1–41 have been re-arranged under the five headings of
the aims of government, general policies, the means and
measures of government, the view of contemporary society
and the view of the past; and there then follows a summary of
the second part of the debate (sections 42–59). No discrimina-
tion is made here so as to correspond with the changes made
between the various interlocutors for each side. Speakers for
the Reformist view, i.e. the *wen-hsüeh* and the *hsien-lang*, are
sometimes referred to as the critics, and the other spokesmen,
who were defending Modernist policies, as the Government
(i.e. the *ta-fu, yü-shih* and *ch'eng-hsiang shih*).

THE FIRST PART OF THE DEBATE

The Aims of government

At a number of points in the debate the critics raised the question of what were the ultimate aims, duties and responsibilities
of imperial government. They insisted on the overruling importance of ideals, and the spokesmen for the Government
maintained that practical considerations should take priority.

[4] See *YTL* 14 (100), where the *yü-shih* refers to the *ta-fu* as one who,
as *chih-su tu-wei*, had controlled agriculture. Sang Hung-yang had actually
held the post of *Sou-su tu-wei* before his appointment as *yü-shih ta-fu* in
87, and both these posts or titles occur somewhat exceptionally during
Han. Gale renders *wen-hsüeh* as *literati* (Dubs: teacher of the classics);
hsien-lang as *worthies*; *ta-fu* as *lord grand secretary* (Dubs: grandee); *yü-shih*
as *secretary* (Dubs: imperial clerk); and *ch'eng-hsiang shih* as *cancellarius*.

[5] *YTL* 60 (374). He is also mentioned in the appreciation at the end of
HS 66 (*HS* 66.16b).

The critics stressed the value of fundamental principles and deplored the way in which these had given way to purely material considerations.[6] The Counsellor replied that the art of government must be addressed to the needs of the prevailing situation and not to the attainment of a perfectionist state of society or to the diehard retention of traditional ways.[7] To the critics' charge that the statesmen of Wu ti's reign and later had devoted themselves exclusively to seeking practical expedients,[8] the Government replied that they had been doing their best to satisfy the material needs of the population.[9] They would couple this aim with that of ensuring the safety of the people from invasion as being the most important duties of government. The critics, on the other hand, insisted on the need to conduct the administration without imposing excessive demands on the people by way of tax, service as labourers, or service in the armed forces; for such demands would only prevent them from fulfilling their proper function, that of working the land.

When the Chancellor's aide observed that administration must move with the times rather than stick to tradition for tradition's sake, the critic replied that the force of some principles such as those of cultured morality are immutable and applicable at all times.[10] But the Government believed that such values, if unsupported by material plenty, are no more than a hollow mockery. There was further discussion of the value of moral precepts as against that of practical controls, as a means of ensuring an equable distribution of material resources.[11] Both parties preferred to avoid the imbalances and disparities that had been witnessed recently and which had drawn Tung Chung-shu's protests a few decades earlier. While the Government claimed that their measures would reduce disparities to a minimum, the critics alleged that they would enhance the evils of the day.[12]

[6] *YTL* 16 (116); 18 (128).   [7] *YTL* 20 (144).   [8] *YTL* 10 (73).
[9] *YTL* 12 (89).   [10] *YTL* 23 (168).   [11] *YTL* 4 (29).
[12] *YTL* 14 (100).

In a statement that comes near to defining the task of government the critic declared[13] that this lay in assisting the blessed ruler (i.e. the *ming chu*), in promoting the growth of civilisation, in harmonising the forces of *Yin* and *Yang* and in reducing popular suffering. He asserted roundly that the present Government, with its harsh measures and its eye to profit, was quite unfit to uphold the principles of proper rule. At one point[14] the critic conceded that material prosperity is not to be disregarded, in so far as it may enable the attainment of a higher standard of culture and morals. But when he claimed[15] that a balanced state of natural conditions, free from disaster, is brought about thanks to the ruler's character and powers (*te*), he was answering the Government's statement that, whatever the qualities of a ruler, they cannot prevent the occurrence of natural calamities or interfere with the operation of the natural cycle.

General Policies

The parties to the debate discussed how these principles should be applied to formulating general policies that were designed to satisfy the demands for material prosperity on the one hand and moral principles on the other. They were concerned with the direction of the economy, the conduct of foreign relations, the use of punishments and the value of precept.

At the outset of the debate[16] the man of learning complained that the state monopolies had deflected attention from agriculture, which was the fundamental occupation of the Chinese, and had encouraged people to turn to the secondary occupations of commerce, manufacture and transport. The government brusquely demolished this point of view, saying that it was out of date and absurd to conceive of contemporary society solely in terms of agriculture, as it depended equally on the results of manufacture and trade. He added,[17] for good measure,

[13] *YTL* 20 (145). [14] *YTL* 35 (247). [15] *YTL* 36 (251).
[16] *YTL* 1 (1). [17] *YTL* 1 (3).

that the controls of government had been essential to ensure that resources other than those of agriculture were being adequately exploited; that goods were being distributed efficiently; and that transport was available to serve production. At a later stage in the debate[18] a spokesman for the Government cited examples of planned projects in the economy of China in the past; but the critic refused to accept these as examples of an administration that was worthy of ideal sovereign rule.[19] He added that those who had practised such policies in the past were not conspicuously successful at enriching their population, however strongly they had believed in the merits of planning. The critic reiterated that the effort must be restored from secondary to primary occupations, so that popular prosperity would ensue.

Foreign relations formed a further point of controversy between the two parties. The Government claimed[20] that a suitable display of luxury, dignity and pomp at court would attract the loyal support of the non-Chinese communities and their leaders. The critic saw no valid purpose in a deliberate attempt to win over such peoples who could, if they so desired, make over to the Emperor's court on their own initiative. The critics were in favour of leaving the unsettled nomad foreigners such as the Hsiung-nu to their own devices, and saw no need for active interference or involvement in their affairs. The Modernist spokesman for the Government, however, was more than doubtful about this. He was conscious of the potential threats that the Hsiung-nu could present and he felt that it would be an act of supreme folly to abandon precautionary measures. He pointed to the violence of the Hsiung-nu attacks in the past and adduced this as a reason for continuing defensive measures of a type that had been necessary even in the period of the *Spring and Autumn Annals*. The critic replied that only very large expeditions would suffice to weaken the Hsiung-nu; if they were attacked by small-scale forces, they would be

[18] *YTL* 14 (98).   [19] *YTL* 14 (99).   [20] *YTL* 37 (257); 38 (262).

ready to yield ground without suffering any loss. However, China would be involved in very heavy expenditure and hardship by mounting the large-scale expeditions that would be needed to achieve effective results.

Quite apart from the value of an offensive policy, the spokesman for the Government referred[21] to the need to protect the inhabitants of the frontier areas, and insisted that government could not afford to ignore this responsibility. He claimed[22] that this was the real motive that lay behind the extension of Chinese interests and communication lines of the previous decades. The critics, however, could not accept this contention as valid and thought that expansion had taken place in a degree that was wholly beyond those needs. It was very wrong to expend public energy in the cause of territorial expansion; and how right it had been to refuse to plant a colony at Lun-t'ai, an outrageously distant spot which could not possibly bring material benefit to the people of Han.[23]

The spokesman for the Government referred to profit as a motive for mounting foreign ventures, and believed that there was a two-fold advantage in sponsoring a programme of imports and exports.[24] He saw with satisfaction how surplus Chinese goods could be used to earn foreign products, and how the caravans would follow one another with their beasts of burden heading their way to the passes nose-to-tail. Not only would China's strength and resources be increased by these exchanges but those of the foreigner would be appreciably diminished. The critics[25] objected to these theories on several grounds. They believed that the value of the imports was being grossly overrated and that there existed better ways of bringing about popular happiness and prosperity. Moreover the whole scheme depended on commerce, and this in turn rested on a

[21] *YTL* 1 (1).   [22] *YTL* 16 (114).

[23] *YTL* 6 (44); 16 (114–5). For the proposal to establish colonies at Lun-t'ai, see Chapter 7, p. 225.

[24] *YTL* 2 (12).   [25] *YTL* 2 (12–3).

basic fallacy. For although the Government maintained that commercial exchanges were an essential means of enriching the population, real increases of wealth could only be achieved by the sweat of one's brow; and in any event it was not justifiable to disperse China's wealth to the frontiers at the expense of popular hardship[26] such as corvée service and military service. When the spokesman for the Government suggested that imports and foreign expansion played a part in raising the low standard of living of the Chinese peasant, the critic observed that, on the contrary, campaigning had deprived the farmer of the animals that he used; and while necessities were in short supply owing to military exigencies, the sole material gain consisted of useless luxury goods with which the people of China could happily dispense.[27]

The contrast between the two points of view of the idealist and the realist is brought out forcefully in the discussion of the evils that can arise in the conduct of the administration; for there are many opportunities for officials to profit from their position and to practise oppression for their own material interests. As a preventative measure, the Government believed in instilling a healthy respect for the punishments of state and in using such methods as a means of disciplining the people.[28] The critic thought that the abolition of corrupt practices was to be achieved by *chiao*, i.e. the inculcation of moral principles, and if this were to be done effectively, the punishments of state need be used very sparingly, in the same way as a charioteer makes use of his whip. To the protest of the Government spokesman that scant use of the punishments of state would encourage idleness and extravagance, the critic upheld the view that the correct teaching would bring culture to the people; that it would reduce strife to a minimum; and that it would produce a higher moral standard and higher standard of living.[29]

---

[26] *YTL* 14 (100).   [27] *YTL* 15 (105).
[28] *YTL* 34 (245).   [29] *YTL* 35 (247).

The Means and measures of government

The debate included a long discussion regarding the qualities to be sought in appointing men to office. The spokesman for the Government thought it foolish to appoint those whose sole resource in times of difficulty lay in harking back to the precedents of the past without reference to change or to contemporary conditions.[30] To this observation the critic loftily replied that it was right to recruit men for service with the highest principles in mind, rather than simply to satisfy the demands of expediency; and he ignored the charge that the system of appointing men to office on the merits of their civil education did not produce good governors.[31] The spokesman for the Government, however, would not be denied. He pointed[32] to the abject failure of the moralists or idealists such as Confucius when they were brought face to face with the practical problems of government, and insisted that qualities other than scholastic ability are needed by successful statesmen. To his criticism of Confucius and Mencius on these grounds he added his praise for Shang Yang's successful achievements.[33] These points of view are repeated later in the debate, and when the Government's spokesman drew attention to the inability of Confucius' pupils to save their master from ruin, the critic attributed such results to their master's own actions.[34] To the cheap jibe that no value may be discerned in the lessons of a fancy education, the critic noted the lack of an educational background on the part of the contemporary officials and compared the situation with one in which one puts to sea without oars.[35] The Government's spokesman refused to accept the value of literary training: the critic would not yield his point and insisted on its value in promoting the integrity of government.

There was a further important point of variance between the two parties over the Government's sponsorship of economic

[30] *YTL* 10 (70).   [31] *YTL* 10 (71).   [32] *YTL* 11 (82).
[33] *YTL* 7 (5of.).   [34] *YTL* 21 (152).   [35] *YTL* 21 (153).

enterprises. This issue involved the imposition of controls or other measures so as to co-ordinate production and to preclude waste, and it brought the question of profiteering under review. The Government's spokesman argued the case for government controls on both positive and negative grounds: positively, so as to promote the general exchange of goods and thus improve the material standard of living; and, negatively, so as to prevent private individuals from acquiring excessively great advantages or opportunities. In addition he asserted that one reason for supporting the Government's monopolies lay in the additional revenue that could be raised thereby and used to supplement the funds available for defence.[36] In this way profits would be used for the benefit of the public, and the principle involved here was comparable with the measures and successful administration of Shang Yang.[37] The critic was unable to accept this. He thought that the principle of profiteering was in any event to be discouraged;[38] for the profits which appeared to be derived from the state monopolies ultimately came from the people, who thereby suffered loss.[39] For this reason the state monopolies could not be said to bring any benefit to the people. In defence of the controls imposed by government, the spokesman pointed out that profiteering would occur in any event; and without active measures by the state the profits would fall exclusively into private hands; and in this way large fortunes would be amassed by the lucky few at the expense of the general public.[40]

The critics were by no means happy at the increasingly large part that money played in the economy. They believed that it would be better to raise taxation as much as possible in local produce, without involving actual monetary exchanges; for such transactions open the way for officials and merchants to oppress the farming community and for the growth of the very great injustices that would arise out of price disparities.[41] In

[36] *YTL* 1 (1). [37] *YTL* 5, 6 (38, 42). [38] *YTL* 1 (3).
[39] *YTL* 7 (50). [40] *YTL* 5 (37). [41] *YTL* 1 (4).

reply the Government's spokesman noted the benefits that were brought by a system of coinage; money was the means of exchange and might be used to relieve distress or equalise prices rather than to encourage profiteering[42]; and it was only reasonable to impose a ban on the private minting of coin, so as to prevent the accumulation of private fortunes.[43] The critic took the opportunity to point out how the change-over from the older systems of coinage to the comparatively new centralised system had served only to confuse and bewilder the public and to enable merchants to exploit opportunities as they best could.[44]

The actual question of the state's monopoly of the mines, which was technically the main point over which discussions had been ordered, is mentioned early in the debate[45] as well as later. The critic thought that the state monopolies deprived the population of the full benefit of iron tools, and the Government's spokesman in his turn expatiated on the evils attendant on private ownership. For that would lead to the growth of powerful families, the exercise of private monopolies and the development of corrupt practices. A monopoly run by the state, however, provided the peasant with his tools and thus brought about a greater degree of material prosperity.[46] The critic contrasted this idealised state of affairs with actual contemporary practice. The iron agencies were bent on reaching their quota of production rather than on serving the needs of the public; the result was that agricultural tools were of poor quality and the farming community had to work desperately hard, only to achieve a poor yield.

In defence of state monopolies, the Government's spokesman pointed to their use of state labour, both conscript and convict, as a regular arrangement backed by a full supply of materials and equipment. Private enterprise, on the other hand, worked irregularly with poor technical methods, and its

[42] *YTL* 2 (11).　[43] *YTL* 4 (30).　[44] *YTL* 40 (30).
[45] *YTL* 5, 6 (37f., 42f.).　[46] *YTL* 36 (251f.).

products were of an uneven finish. Under the state's monopoly the work was co-ordinated, prices were stabilised and both public and private interests benefitted. Skills were applied to the work, the finish and quality was even, and the manufactures were made for easy use.

The critic pointed out that under private enterprise, salt and cereals had been priced consistently, and manufactures had been made to serve their requisite needs. When the state controlled manufacture, the goods were marked by many imperfections; there was no supervision of public expenditure and no guarantee that state labour was being employed to full capacity. Under private ownership, only the best manufactures had been retained for use. Tools had been transported to the farms at times when they were most needed and were displayed for sale publicly. There was a reduction in the use of the labour corps, with the result that the Government could put its convicts and amnestied convicts to work on the upkeep and repair of roads and bridges, and this had worked to the advantage of the public. But under the contemporary system of co-ordination, although there was a single price set for the goods, many of the tools were of poor quality and the public had no choice between fine or shoddy goods. Very often the officials in charge were absent from their posts so that the goods were difficult to acquire. Salt and iron were highly priced, to the detriment of the public, and the poorer people sometimes had to work the soil with wooden implements or with their bare hands. In addition the Government's labour force did not reach the quota of work set; there was no limit on the calls that were made on the people's service to help them out, and grave hardship ensued from the demands that were imposed for hard labour. In the past it had been possible to achieve a suitable balance between the different working elements of the population, with each man, be he potter or smith, craftsman or merchant, specialising in his own occupation. Each one was supplied with the products that the other had made and could apply them to his work; and the Government suffered no concern on this score. For this reason the Sovereign had been able to bend his efforts to the promotion of agriculture and had had no need to concern himself with work that was of a secondary nature. Extravagant luxuries had been eliminated; the population had become imbued with the rules of moral conduct and had been shown an example of singleness of mind; so the people had devoted themselves to the primary occupations without becoming involved in those that were of lesser importance.

Contemporary society
Mid-way through the first part of the debate the Government's spokesmen was reduced to silence.[47] Acting more as chairman than as a speaker for his masters, the Chancellor's aide urged both parties to look at matters from the point of view of contemporary conditions, for these were clearly very different from those of the reigns of Wen ti and Ching ti and of the early years of Wu ti. The critic seized the opportunity to decry the changes that had taken place since *c.* 130 BC; and he observed that since then public life had been marked by oppressive government; monopolies of power; economic imbalance; uncontrolled licentiousness; harsh exactions by the authorities; and the impoverishment of the people.[48]

Throughout the dialogue the critics threw out remarks to support this general thesis, and their charges were never answered effectively. They blamed the situation on the misrule of the previous decade or so.[49] Early in the debate[50] the Government's spokesman had pointed to the flourishing prosperity of China's most famous cities as evidence of the success of their policies; and the critics countered[51] by describing the poverty of many of the agricultural areas. The Government's plea that such inequalities could be rectified by the organised

[47] *YTL* 28 (192f.).   [48] *YTL* 28 (193).   [49] *YTL* 28 (191).
[50] *YTL* 3 (19).   [51] *YTL* 3 (20).

control of transport and exchange was answered by the asser-
tion that poverty is brought about by excessive luxury; and at
the invitation of the Chancellor's aide, the critic returned to
expound the theme at very great length. In the longest of the
sixty sections of the book[52] he drew several contrasts; first,
between the different stages of human development that
stretched from an age of material simplicity to one of civilised
sophistication; secondly, between the different classes of the
society of Ch'ang-an, ranging from the most affluent and
self-indulgent to the humblest and most indigent;[53] and thirdly,
between the scant attention that was paid to the essentials and
the concern that was lavished on the inessential trappings of a
life of luxury. At the same time the critic noted the discrepancy
in the contemporary way of life between an ostentatious show
of moral duties and a lack of sincerity and integrity, while, at
the same time, considerable faith was reposed in various cults
of the supernatural.

The critic's protests were also directed against the harsh
degree of government that was being practised.[54] Offices could
be bought for cash, and as a result they were falling into the
hands of men who were far from fit to be their incumbents.
Provincial units were now very extensive and their officials
exercised very wide powers over very large areas, irrespective
of whether they were fit for government or had the interests of
their flock at heart. Again, the system of tax was notoriously
harsh,[55] and with it the demands for service; but while these
severities were being felt so acutely by the peasantry, there had
arisen large families who could boast sufficient strength to withstand the authorities and to refuse to meet the demands of
officials. As a result of these harsh conditions the peasantry often
took to flight, leaving their fields unworked and running to
waste. The Government's spokesman tried to answer this
charge by claiming that the peasantry had been pampered by

[52] *YTL* 29 (201–9).   [53] See *Everyday Life*, pp. 137f.
[54] *YTL* 32 (240).   [55] *YTL* 15 (106).

bounties and measures of relief, and had become accustomed to a state of indolence;[56] once they had abandoned their lands these remained unproductive, with a consequent reduction of the state's revenue. In point of fact, with the age of liability for service now fixed at twenty-three to fifty-six, the demands were less than they had been.[57] The critic could not accept this point, and described the effect of the exactions on family life.

A few specific points were raised in connection with the corrupt nature of the times. Government offices were alleged to be overstaffed, without producing any benefit;[58] they supported a large number of dependents and employed large numbers of slaves,[59] to no purpose, who could nonetheless amass considerable fortunes. Moreover, politics were such that the Government was competing with the merchants for profits that were exacted from the people; and, finally, there was the system of leasehold tenure of officially owned land.[60] In effect this served to enrich the large families. Meanwhile the metropolitan area was over-populated, attracting people from all quarters, while at the same time being far from self-sufficient. It was scandalous that because of these conditions the land was not being exploited as productively as possible.

The Past

In a number of references to the past the critic appealed to the golden age of government over which the Duke of Chou had presided;[61] and it is worth noting a sharp interchange which took place in connection with Shang Yang and the regime of Ch'in.[62] The critic observed that, however highly Shang Yang's schemes had been praised by the Government's spokesmen, their success had been limited and short-lived.[63] But such

---

[56] *YTL* 15 (106).
[57] *YTL* 15 (107). The allusion is to the earlier period when obligations for service began at the age of twenty.
[58] *YTL* 13 (95).   [59] *YTL* 29 (208).   [60] *YTL* 13 (96).
[61] *YTL* 35 (247), 36 (251).   [62] *YTL* 7 (50f.).   [63] *YTL* 7 (52).

failures, said the Counsellor, were not inherent in Shang Yang's policies but due to the mistakes made by his followers. When the critic claimed that the Ch'in empire had rested on ignoble principles,[64] it was retorted that it was precisely Shang Yang's principles which had paved the way for Ch'in's success and the expansion of empire. The critic replied that it was Ch'in's exclusive attention to material profit that had led to its downfall; Ch'in's policies had been short-sighted and Shang Yang's measures had been highly oppressive.

At the end of the first part of the dialogue[65] the critics cited the shining examples of the past and denied that the traditions of the kings of old were irrelevant to contemporary problems. They drew a contrast between the harmonious days of old, when *Yin* and *Yang* rested in balance, and the contemporary conditions. For at present the people were beset by severe demands for long service; and the failure to direct the administration for the sake of those who were governed was leading to a state of unbalance, indiscipline and violence. The government spokesman[66] protested that the critic's views were merely theoretical and had no practical application; the critic replied that it was precisely theory that was needed. He painted a picture of the just and equitable dispensation of Chou as this had existed long ago before degeneration and corruption had set in; and before the ruling classes had enjoyed a life of luxury, oblivious of the sufferings of the masses. The critic ended with an impassioned indictment of the absence of a social conscience and vividly described the contrast between the comforts of the fortunate and the distress of the unfortunate.[67]

It was this speech which reduced the Government's representatives to silence for the eleventh occasion during the debate and the compromise suggestion that is described above[68] was submitted and approved.

---

[64] *YTL* 7 (53).   [65] *YTL* 39 (268f.).   [66] *YTL* 40 (272).
[67] *YTL* 41 (274).   [68] See p. 92.

THE SECOND PART OF THE DEBATE

In the second part of the debate the speakers touched on much the same subjects as those mentioned in the first forty-one sections and re-iterated the same arguments; and while the critics' case was conducted by a single speaker (the *wen-hsüeh*, or man of learning) the counsellor (*ta-fu*) was unable to sustain the defence of the Government without relief and replacement by a colleague. In the final sections of the debate the Counsellor resumed his place as the chief spokesman.

For some time the speakers concentrated on questions of foreign policy, with special reference to the Hsiung-nu. The Counsellor's case was that China's security could only be maintained by means of an offensive policy, as had been shown in the past under Ch'in and at other times; and this policy failed only if there was insufficient determination to carry it through to its logical conclusion.[69] Appeasement (i.e. *ho-ch'in*) would never achieve a long-term settlement;[70] and nothing could be more unrealistic or ludicrous than the belief that this could be brought about by trusting to the good faith of the Hsiung-nu.[71]

The man of learning believed in curtailing expansionist activity to a bare minimum.[72] The effort involved in the expeditions was far in excess of the gains that could be won; and in view of the type of terrain wherein the Hsiung-nu operated, very large scale expeditions would be necessary and the expense of launching them would be prohibitive. Past experience had shown that military expansion did not lead to security, and the attempts to penetrate in strength to the Far West had weakened the Chinese rather than their enemy.[73] It was

[69] *YTL* 42 (281); 44 (290f.); 45 (294).
[70] *YTL* 43 (285). For appeasement (*ho-ch'in*) see Ying-shih Yü, *Trade and Expansion in Han China* (Berkeley and Los Angeles, 1967), pp. 36f.
[71] *YTL* 47 (301f.).   [72] *YTL* 46 (298).
[73] *YTL* 44 (291); 45 (295).

essential to relieve the people of China of the arduous labour involved in campaigning, which had already led to some disaffection.[74] Long-lasting victories might be won only by the exercise of character, and for this reason Chou had left a more permanent heritage to posterity than Ch'in.[75] It would be best to arrange a peaceful settlement.

For some time the debate continued on the relative need and values of material strength and integrity of motive. There then followed a highly interesting exchange[76] concerning the theories of *Yin* and *Yang* and the Five Elements, and the part played by Heaven in cosmic destiny. The counsellor referred to the dissatisfaction voiced by Tsou Yen at the failure of the latter-day scholastics (*ju-chia*) and Mohists to comprehend the extent of the cosmos; he went on to argue that Tsou Yen's cosmological theories bore universal application, and that particular concepts should be reviewed in the light of that major concept. The critic replied that such concepts of unseen and intangible powers had served only to confuse governments, and he gave warning of the danger of becoming involved in unknown and incomprehensible realms, in the same way as Confucius had urged his followers to refrain from becoming involved with the spirits. As a positive contribution, however, he added a further dimension to the discussion by introducing Tung Chung-shu's doctrine of creation and the rhythmical succession of the seasons.[77] This doctrine is bound up not only with the forces of *Yin* and *Yang*, but also with the part played by Heaven in bestowing rewards and punishments in accordance with good or evil behaviour; and the critic showed how Tung Chung-shu's opinion could be supported from texts such as the *Book of Changes* and the *Spring and Autumn Annals*. The Counsellor, however, was quite unable to accept the part played by Heaven in the cosmic or human drama. For him everything was explained on the theory that the Five Elements replace one

74 *YTL* 43 (285); 46 (297).   75 *YTL* 43 (287).
76 *YTL* 53, 54 (331f., 334f.).   77 *YTL* 54 (335).

another by means of conquest,[78] and he in his turn, could call on the *Book of Changes* and the *Book of Documents* for support.

The allusions made by the critic to bounties and punishments are reminiscent of the views expressed by Tung Chung-shu.[79] The Government's spokesman defended the use of punishments as being a necessary instrument of government; the critic deprecated their use in so far as they were unsuitable and ran counter to the principles of Heaven (*T'ien tao*). The critic regarded the operation of the laws as unjust;[80] for they were applied in an inequable way in different parts of the imperial domains and the punishments of state were far too complex and detailed for people to understand or for officials to interpret. As it stood, the system of laws and punishments operated to the detriment of justice and against the interests of humanity. To the Government's claim that laws are as necessary to the administration as a bridle is to a rider, the critic replied that these may be excellent as tools, provided that they are manipulated by riders of suitable quality; but they cannot of themselves inculcate moral lessons. Moreover, they were being exploited by officials most unfairly and to the injury of the public; for while innocent men were becoming involved in the processes of the law, there was no certainty that services to the state would be rewarded appropriately.[81]

For the critic, morality and cultural influence was of far greater importance than the prescriptions of the law, as morality had a pervasive and universal effect; while to the defendants of the Government, the law was indispensable as a means of governing a population. The Government's spokesman alluded to measures advocated by Shen Pu-hai and Shang Yang in successfully strengthening the states of the Warring States period.[82] For such measures were directed at the repair of

---

[78] *YTL* 54 (336); for the succession of the Five Elements, either by conquest or by production, see Chapter 1, p. 29 and Chapter 9, p. 302.

[79] *YTL* 54 (335f.). For Tung Chung-shu, see *HS* 56.5a, *et seq.*

[80] *YTL* 55 (342).   [81] *YTL* 56 (350f.).   [82] *YTL* 56 (349).

obvious deficiencies and did not depend on the existence of ideal figures such as the Duke of Chou, whom the critics held up as a paragon. The riposte of the critic, as usual, was to point to the failure of Shang Yang in the long run, and to emphasise the need for radical measures to improve a situation that was vitiated by crime and violence. Nothing less would save a state of affairs in which the major principles of morality had been abandoned.

The discussions about the laws and their severities brought into question the principle of collective responsibility within a family or small group for the crimes committed by any single member.[83] The critic complained that owing to this principle, the punishments were being applied indiscriminately, useful as they were as isolated measures designed to maintain social order. As guilty and guiltless alike were liable to become involved in the processes of the law, it had come about that there was no generally accepted revulsion at being treated as a criminal; and it was only natural that members of a family should try to protect each other from the severities of the law. The Government's spokesman defended the idea of group responsibility as being reasonable, and believed that in a sophisticated society a simple system such as that of the famous Three Clauses that were attributed to Kao tsu would be impractical.[84] The critic drew a distinction between two types of governmental ordinance; those which were designed to guide the people and those which were designed to punish criminals.[85] Finally the argument resolved itself into the counsellor's view of humanity as needing repression, and the man of learning's belief that human nature needs guidance along the path to better standards.[86]

There are a number of occasions in the *Yen-t'ieh lun* where

[83] *YTL* 57 (353f.).
[84] *YTL* 58 (361). For the Three Clauses of Kao tsu, see Hulsewé, pp. 333 and 368, note 143.
[85] *YTL* 58 (363).   [86] *YTL* 59 (368).

the critic is reported far more fully than his opponent; and although the Government's spokesmen were often left speechless, such a fate never overtook the critic. It is not impossible that the account of the debate was compiled as an exercise in political propaganda on behalf of those statesmen who were leaning towards reform and away from organisation, and it could well be that such a document would have acquired a growing appeal during the age of transition of Hsüan ti's reign. The attitudes adopted by the two parties to the debate correspond very closely to those expressed by the two groups of statesmen who are characterised in these pages as Modernists and Reformists.

The critics of the *Yen-t'ieh lun* stood midway between the time of Tung Chung-shu and the religious reformation of 31 BC; and they led forward from Tung Chung-shu's doctrines regarding the role of Heaven to the time when the worship of Heaven would become a state cult. Like his predecessors in Han imperial governments, the Counsellor and his colleagues thought of Ch'in as an exponent of imperial government whose fall had been due to errors and weakness, but which was not to be discredited on moral grounds. The men of wisdom and learning were ready to cite the example of Chou and its famous Duke,[87] in the same way as Wang Mang would do a few decades later. The critics saw nothing to justify measures of expansion that were undertaken simply to increase the strength of Han, and their misgivings were to be revealed in subsequent decisions of state. However, the Counsellor's support for an outward looking policy was completely in line with the decisions taken by Wu ti's advisers. The critics' complaint about extravagance was re-echoed by the reformist statesmen of Yüan ti's reign and was followed by measures of retrenchment that were taken at that time.[88] But although the cogent arguments adduced against the state monopolies and against the imposition of other

[87] *YTL* 35 (247); 36 (251); 55 (345).
[88] See Chapter 5, pp. 159f.

controls on the economy were to lead to some measure of change, those changes did not derive from a formal and final renunciation of the principles that were involved. The monopolies fell into disuse by default rather than by deliberate decision, at a time when China could not boast of the existence of a single effective imperial regime.

CHAPTER 4

The Fall of the House of Huo – 68-66 BC

On several occasions in the history of Western Han, members of a certain family rose to occupy the highest places in the realm, owing to their close relationship to the throne, and if for any reason that relationship was threatened, prejudiced or severed, the fortunes of the family suffered abruptly and dramatically. On such occasions the demise of a family's influence could involve sudden and merciless extermination; for such ruthlessness was essential if a rival family could hope to establish itself securely and without threat of retaliation. So it fell out with the families of Lü, Wei, Li and Huo, and later with several other families whose leaders had for a short time occupied the most powerful positions of state. When the Huo family fell in 66 BC none of its male members who had been appointed to high office survived, and the succession of the nobilities which had been conferred upon them fell into abeyance. Only a few female members of the family lived on, bereft of the position which they had once enjoyed and of the powers they had been used to wield behind the scenes. These included Huo Kuang's grand-daughter, the Dowager Empress of Chao ti, who was then still in her twenty-third year; and Huo Kuang's daughter Ch'eng-chün, Empress of Hsüan ti from 70 to 66, when she was deposed from her noble station and relegated to the seclusion of a detached palace.

With this virtual demise of the Huo family, the fortunes of the Hsü family rose correspondingly, in a series of events which cost considerable bloodshed. The first blow had actually been struck in 71, when Hsüan ti's first empress, who was of the Hsü family, had been murdered in particularly brutal circumstances, at the orders of Huo Kuang's wife. However, the principal incidents, and those which closed the fortunes of the Huo family, followed the death of Huo Kuang in 68, for it was only then that the Emperor learnt of the murder of his former Empress. He reacted by demoting a number of members of the Huo family from their positions of honour; by nominating the infant son of the late Empress Hsü as his Heir Apparent; and by appointing as his chief advisers men whose affiliations lay with the Hsü family. Realising the desperate nature of their plight the Huo family determined to put all to the test by plotting the murder of the Heir Apparent; and they intended to remove the Emperor and to replace him by one of their own members, Huo Yü. However, as has occurred so frequently in China's history, news of the plot was revealed prematurely and the Huo family were punished by virtual extermination. Members of the Hsü family and those who were concerned with revealing the plot were rewarded with honours and high office; and under their dispensation there may be discerned a change of political climate and the emergence of attitudes which were markedly different from those of previous reigns, and which were destined to become far more pronounced in the succeeding decades.

The intrigues of 68 to 66 BC form part of an incident in which political and dynastic destinies were subject to strain, change and upheaval, and in which the fate of a number of prominent individuals was intimately concerned. The story stresses once again that the development of Han politics can only be understood in the context of the rivalries and scandals within the palace. In addition, the events of 66 BC mark an important stage in the transition from one set of attitudes to another. Policies of state that had been introduced from *c*. 130 and practised with growing determination until *c*. 90 were now deprived of some of their most powerful supporters; and they were soon to yield place to different standards and values which were to be fully adopted from the reign of Yüan ti (49 to 33) onwards.

Attention has been drawn elsewhere[1] to the circumstances in which Huo Kuang rose to stand possessed of ultimate powers of government in the Han Empire. He was a nephew of the Empress Wei (Wu ti's consort) and a half-brother of the famous General Huo Ch'ü-ping. The latter brought him to Ch'ang-an when he was about ten, perhaps shortly after 120 BC, and Huo Kuang soon saw service as Commandant of the Imperial Carriages and Counsellor of the Palace.[2] In a valedictory edict, Wu ti named him as leader of a regency during the reign of the next Emperor, and in this capacity Huo Kuang easily secured a dominant position among his two colleagues. He was considerably more experienced than they were in the affairs of court and government; he could look back on some thirty years' service to the state, rendered at a time when Modernist policies were being adopted so as to consolidate the control of the Empire and enhance its prestige in central Asia. But it is noticeable that during these years he had held no major office of state, preferring to exert his influence in other capacities.

Huo Kuang had taken care to marry his daughters in such a way that his superior position would be maintained. One was married to Chin Mi-ti, a second member of the triumvirate who constituted the Regency. Shang-kuan An, who was the son of the third member (Shang-kuan Chieh) was married to another, and it was their daughter who was in time to become Chao ti's empress. Other daughters of Huo Kuang were married to the statesmen or generals Fan Ming-yu, Jen Sheng and Teng

[1] See Chapter 2, pp. 66f.
[2] *HS* 68.1b. *Feng-chü tu-wei* and *Kuang-lu ta-fu* are rendered by Dubs as Chief Commandant of the Emperor's Equipages and Imperial Household Grandee.

Table 3. Huo Kuang and his family

(ALL DATES BC)

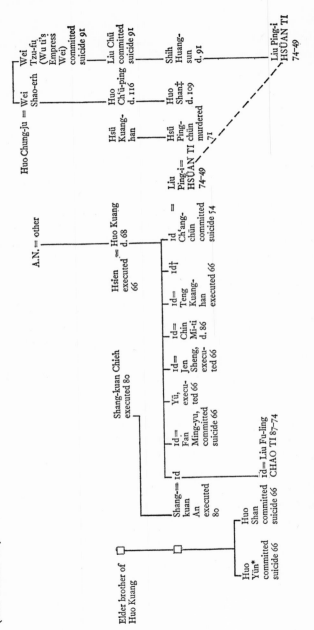

* In *HS* 97A.24b, Huo Yün and Huo Shan are referred to as grandsons of Huo Ch'ü-ping, but this statement conflicts with the entries in *HS* 18.9a, b. See *HS* 8.10b, and notes.

† At one time Huo Kuang offered a daughter in marriage to Chüan Pu-i (see Chapter 2, p. 71); it is not clear which of his daughters was suggested.

‡ See *HS* 18.9a and *HS* 25A.38a.

Kuang-han;[3] and at one time Huo Kuang had promised the hand of a daughter to the one official who had been brave enough to expose an imposture practised on the court in 82 BC.[4] As will be seen later, the highest honour to which any woman of the Han Empire could aspire, that of being consort and legitimate empress of the Emperor, was in time due to fall to yet another of Huo Kuang's daughters.

The manner in which Wu ti had called Huo Kuang to his high responsibilities is of some interest.[5] As early as *c.* 91 BC the Emperor had had a painting made showing the Duke of Chou, in the course of rendering assistance to the young King Ch'eng and he had had the painting sent to Huo Kuang as a present. The implication was clear; when the appropriate time should come, Huo Kuang should be prepared to take on a similar role to that of the famous Duke, i.e. that of acting as regent should this be necessary and of being ready to yield place when the need for such services was past. As he lay on his death-bed in 87, Wu ti referred pointedly to his earlier action, but it is unlikely that either then or on the occasion when he had had the painting ordered the Emperor had it in mind to hold up the examples, ideals or institutions of Chou for praise. For as yet those ideals were not accepted as conforming with the spirit of the times, and it was only the example of the regency that was relevant.

Nevertheless the comparison was of some importance during subsequent developments of Han history. Some hundred years

[3] Fan Ming-yu served as a military officer in campaigns against the Wu-huan and the Hsiung-nu and was appointed General of the Trans-Liao Command in 78 BC. Later he was appointed Superintendent of the Palace (67) and played a part in the political events of Chao ti and Hsüan ti's reigns; he was ennobled for his services in 77, but committed suicide in 66 (*HS* 7.9a, *HFHD*, vol. II, p. 171; *HS* 17.28a; *HS* 19B.29a, 32a, b). Nothing is known of Jen Sheng other than his punishment for complicity in the plot of the Huo family and his appointment as governor of An-ting Commandery (*see* note 61 below). For Teng Kuang-han, see note 61 below.

[4] *HS* 71.3a; see Chapter 2, p. 71.   [5] *HS* 68.1b.

later, Wang Mang was seeking to pass himself off as one who followed the example of the Duke of Chou, and he was also seeking to compare himself with the great Huo Kuang. If Wang Mang could succeed in showing that Huo Kuang had also been regarded as a second Duke of Chou, his own case would be supported substantially. Later still, when the appreciation of Chao ti's reign was being compiled for the *Han-shu*, the comparison was reiterated and Huo Kuang's measures of government deliberately praised.[6]

Wu ti's final action before his death on 29 March 87 BC was to nominate Huo Kuang as *Ta-ssu-ma* or Marshal of State. He also held the title of General, as did the other two members of the triumvirate, and at the same time the team was strengthened by the appointment of Sang Hung-yang to be Imperial Counsellor. As a man, Huo Kuang is said to have acted with the greatest circumspection. He took care to avoid committing any error during his service at Wu ti's court where he was generally liked and trusted. He is described as being self-possessed and placid, and as paying great attention to detail. Somewhat exceptionally the records include information about Huo Kuang's personal appearance; he was of short stature, pale-faced, with twirling eyebrows and a fine beard and side-whiskers. The regularity of his habits was such that he would halt at exactly the same spot in his perambulations within the palace grounds, and the courtiers quickly learnt to recognise the man who never deviated an inch from his accustomed stance.[7]

But it is perhaps not surprising that this composed and calculating man of affairs fell out with his colleagues over

[6] See Chapter 2, p. 79, and *HS* 7.10b (*HFHD*, vol. II, pp. 174-5). For the circumstances of Chao ti's nomination as heir apparent and his accession, see Chapter 2, p. 55. For the suggestion that Wang Mang's achievements and honours were comparable with those of Huo Kuang, see *HS* 99A.5a, b (*HFHD*, vol. III, p. 141); for Wang Mang's pose as a second Duke of Chou see Chapter 9.

[7] *HS* 68.1b, 2a.

matters of patronage. He steadfastly refused to allow offices or honours to be given to the protegés of Shang-kuan Chieh and Shang-kuan An or to the relatives of Sang Hung-yang. For his part Shang-kuan Chieh was only too well aware that in earlier times he had held a position that was senior to that of Huo Kuang, and Sang Hung-yang felt justly proud at the success of his schemes to enrich the state and exploit its resources. Their resentment at Huo Kuang's stern refusals can easily be understood.[8]

Owing partly to dynastic plots, Huo Kuang was able to maintain and assert his superiority over his colleagues throughout the reign of Chao ti (87 to 74 BC) and thereafter until his death in 68. Chin Mi-ti, who might have constituted a powerful rival to his ambitions, had died as early as 86,[9] and the abortive plot (80) to enthrone Tan, king of Yen, as Emperor resulted in the execution of Shang-kuan Chieh and Sang Hung-yang.[10] Before the plot broke, the conspirators had had a report sent to the Emperor accusing Huo Kuang of assuming unwarranted liberties in his behaviour and of appointing some of his own favourites to high positions of state.[11] Chao ti, the historian tells us, had rejected the charges out of hand and the perspicacity with which, at the age of fourteen, he had seen through the conspirators' insinuations had astonished the court.

Even after attaining his majority, Chao ti still delegated charge of the Empire to Huo Kuang. In the series of dramatic events which followed Chao ti's death in 74—the accession of

[8] *HS* 68.3a; for Sang Hung-yang's hatred of Huo Kuang, see *HS* 24B.20a (Swann, p. 321) and *HS* 66.7a.

[9] *HS* 17.26a; *HS* 19B.26b; *HS* 68.20a, b.

[10] See Chapter 2, pp. 73f.

[11] *HS* 68.3b. These included the appointment of Su Wu (see note 13) to the post of *Tien-shu-kuo* (superintendent of the Dependent States: Dubs—Director of Dependent States) and his own aide Yang Ch'ang to be *Sou-su tu-wei* (Commandant for Grain Collection: Dubs—Chief Commandant who searches for Grain). Yang Ch'ang became Chancellor in 75.

Liu Ho, king of Ch'ang-i, his deposal after twenty-seven days, and the accession of Liu Ping-i—Huo Kuang played the dominant part.[12] The memorial in which Liu Ho's crimes were brought to notice was submitted under the names of Yang Ch'ang, formerly Huo Kuang's aide and now the Chancellor; Huo Kuang, Marshal of State and Supreme General; and a host of other dignitaries who were related to Huo Kuang or may have owed him a debt for his patronage.[13] Once the memorial had received the approval of the Empress Dowager (i.e. Chao ti's empress, and Huo Kuang's grand-daughter), it was Huo Kuang who insisted that Liu Ho should accept its validity. With his own hands he loosed the imperial seal from Liu Ho's person and had it presented to the Empress Dowager; and when he escorted Liu Ho out of the palace to the quarters assigned to him as king of Ch'ang-i, there took place a touching, and perhaps hypocritical scene. With tears in his eyes, Huo Kuang explained that his action in deposing Liu Ho had been necessary in the major interests of the empire; and, saved from the fate of banishment, Liu Ho was allowed to return to his kingdom of Ch'ang-i, with the promise of a sufficient allowance for his needs. However, Huo Kuang's behaviour was by no means as generous when it came to the case of some 200 persons who were believed to have led Liu Ho into the paths of in-

---

[12] See Chapter 2, pp. 75f.

[13] These included Chang An-shih (see p. 124), Fan Ming-yu (see note 3 above), Tu Yen-nien (see p. 121), Ping Chi (see p. 121), Wei Hsien and Su Wu. Wei Hsien (*HS* 73.1a) held the posts of Superintendent of State Visits (*Ta-hung-lu*: Dubs—The Grand Herald) from 76 to 72 and Chancellor from 71 to 67, from which he was honourably discharged on account of age (*HS* 19B.29b, 31a). For Su Wu, see *HS* 54.16a, and K. P. K. Whitaker, 'Some notes on the Authorship of the Lii Ling/Su Wuu letters' (*Bulletin of the School of Oriental and African Studies*, 1953, vols. xv/1 and xv/3, pp. 113–37 and 566–87). Su Wu is known for his negotiations with the Hsiung-nu and held the post of Superintendent of the Dependent States immediately before Ch'ang Hui held that post (*HS* 70.3b).

dulgence and wickedness. They were now brought out of prison and executed publicly.[14]

It was likewise Huo Kuang and his immediate associates who brought about the accession of Liu Ping-i—the future Hsüan ti—and Huo Kuang took a leading part in the ceremonies and formalities of the occasion.[15] Liu Ping-i had been the sole survivor of the Wei family to escape extermination in 91 to 90. He had been brought up as a commoner outside the dangerous atmosphere and intrigues of the palace. He was still in his eighteenth year at the time of his accession and he was ignorant of the procedure at court and of affairs of state. It was only to be expected that he would follow the lead given by his patrons who had brought him to his high position; and when Huo Kuang went through the formality of offering to return the powers of government to the throne, the offer was declined.

Attention should now be drawn to three other men who featured in this story and subsequently held high offices of state—Ping Chi, Tu Yen-nien and Chang An-shih. Ping Chi, who was an expert in legal administration, had served as one of the officers of the judiciary in his native kingdom of Lu; later he had been promoted to be one of the inspectors who were subordinate to the Superintendent for Trials in the central government.[16] When the witchcraft scandals broke out in Ch'ang-an (91 BC), he was called upon to take charge of one of the prisons, and it was in the course of these processes, which were extended over some years, that Ping Chi arranged for Liu Ping-i's survival. Being a descendant of the Wei Empress and of the Wei Heir Apparent, the boy could not avoid implication in the intrigues and plots of those years. But Ping Chi recognised that he was far too young to be involved personally and succeeded in saving him from the destruction which was visited upon all those other members of the imperial family in whom

---

[14] *HS* 68.10a.   [15] *HS* 68.10b.

[16] *HS* 74.6b. Dubs renders *T'ing-wei* as Commandant of Justice.

the supreme power of state could conceivably be invested.

Later Liu Ping-i was to owe another debt to Ping Chi. Serving as Huo Kuang's aide at the time of Chao ti's death, Ping Chi had already earned Huo Kuang's appreciation and high opinion. He was one of the men who were sent to welcome Liu Ho to the imperial throne, but when it was apparent that the latter's moral strength and standards were not adequate to meet his high responsibilities, Ping Chi strongly urged Huo Kuang to have Liu Ping-i enthroned as Emperor. He wrote[17] that he had had occasion to observe the young man during his infancy; he knew that he was fully conversant with the canonical writings and that he was a person of no mean ability; his behaviour was placid and his actions were suited to circumstance. Ping Chi therefore asked Huo Kuang to ascertain by divination whether Liu Ping-i would be a suitable incumbent of the imperial throne, and when in fact he acceded, Ping Chi received the honour of a minor nobility.[18]

Tu Yen-nien[19] was another statesman who recommended Liu Ping-i to Huo Kuang as a suitable successor to Chao ti. It was he who had given advance information which led to the disclosure of the plot of 80 BC, and he had been rewarded by the gift of a nobility. At the time he was serving on Huo Kuang's staff; the latter had him promoted Superintendent of Transport[20] and he held that senior office of state until his dismissal in 65.[21] Tu Yen-nien is said[22] to have taken due note of the aftermath which had followed the extravagance and military adventures of Wu ti's reign and to have asked Huo Kuang to introduce some measures of economy. There was also a further

---

[17] *HS* 74.7b.

[18] *Kuan-nei-hou*: Dubs—marquis of the imperial domain. This was a nobility without the rights of hereditary succession or of levying taxation on a specified number of households. (See *Aristocratic Ranks*, pp. 152f.).

[19] *HS* 60.3a, *et seq.*

[20] *T'ai-p'u*: Dubs—the Grand Coachman.

[21] *HS* 19B.28b, 33a.   [22] *HS* 60.4b.

sign that Tu Yen-nien had Reformist sympathies. It was allegedly owing to his initiative that the review on national policies, including the value of the State's monopolies of the industries, had been arranged in 81 BC.

It so happened that one of Tu Yen-nien's younger sons, Tu T'o,[23] had been on intimate terms with Liu Ping-i while the latter was still living away from the capital. It was possibly owing to this friendship that Tu Yen-nien found opportunity to assess Liu Ping-i's qualities, and his impressions were such that he urged Huo Kuang to have him succeed as Emperor. As a result of this advice, the size of Tu's nobility was increased, so that it comprised the emoluments that were drawn from a total of 4300 households.[24]

At the time of Chao ti's accession (87),[25] Huo Kuang had already formed a highly favourable impression of Chang An-shih's integrity. When the King of Yen staged his abortive revolt in 80, Huo Kuang realised that there was a dearth of senior statesmen on whose loyalties he could depend, and he had Chang An-shih appointed Superintendent of the Palace.[26] He was first ennobled in 75, and in the following year he was closely associated with Huo Kuang in the events which led to the accession and deposal of Liu Ho and the accession of Liu Ping-i. Subsequently an edict singled out Chang An-shih for praise in view of his high qualities, meritorious service and honesty. For his successful efforts in bringing peace and stability to the realm, his nobility was increased by 10600 to a total of 13640 households, and the size of this honour together with its degree of precedence was second only to that of Huo Kuang.[27]

[23] *HS* 60.5a.

[24] The figure of 4300 is given in *HS* 60.5a. *HS* 17.26a gives two figures which total 5360; see the notes to *HS* 60.5a, where Wang Hsien-ch'ien takes 4360 as the correct total.

[25] *HS* 59.7a.

[26] *Kuang-lu-hsün*: Dubs—Superintendent of the Imperial Household.

[27] *HS* 18.12a; *HS* 59.8a.

Chang An-shih had previously taken a part in arranging for Liu Ping-i's marriage. His elder brother, Chang Ho, had had ambitions to marry his granddaughter to Liu Ping-i, but Chang An-shih had angrily scotched the idea on the grounds that this would entail too great an advance for the Chang family. As a result of Chang An-shih's intervention, Chang Ho arranged for the boy to be married to Hsü P'ing-chün, daughter of Hsü Kuang-han. The latter had served as a courtier to the king of Ch'ang-i, and owing to a mistake or accident he had had the misfortune to suffer the punishment of castration. The incident reveals the starkly cruel nature of the times, for he was subjected to such treatment as a matter of mercy. Hsü Kuang-han had once been attending Wu ti on an expedition to the shrines and summer retreat of Kan-ch'üan, and on this occasion he had saddled his horse with a fellow courtier's saddle. For this all too understandable error he was brought up on a charge of carelessness and robbery, and it was decided that the crime merited the death penalty. It was only due to the intervention of an imperial edict that such punishment was commuted to that of castration. Shortly before Chao ti's death (5 June 74 BC), his daughter Hsü P'ing-chün bore a son who was later to become the Emperor Yüan ti.[28]

These then were some of the men who were closely associated with Huo Kuang and who contrived with him to bring about the accession of Liu Ping-i, great-grandson of Wu ti's empress Wei, and in his eighteenth year at the time when he was called to the supreme honour of the Empire. Huo Kuang remained in control of the government, and his position was re-affirmed publicly by the increase of his nobility to the quite exceptional size of nearly 20 000 households[29] and by lavish gifts. These are recorded as comprising over 7000 catties of gold, 60 million cash, 30 000 rolls of silk, 170 slaves, 2000 horses and one residence. At the same time some of his close

[28] *HS* 18.14b; *HS* 71.3b; *HS* 97A.21b.
[29] *HS* 68.11a; see Chapter 2, p. 79.

relatives retained the positions of responsibility and the powers that they had enjoyed during the previous reign. His son Huo Yü and his great-nephew Huo Yün were leaders of the courtiers of the palace,[30] and his great-nephew Huo Shan held the post of Commandant of the Imperial Carriages.[31] In these capacities the three men all held direct command over certain troops, and Huo Kuang's two sons-in-law, Fan Ming-yu and Teng Kuang-han commanded the guard units in the Wei-yang and Ch'ang-lo palaces. A number of other relatives held positions in the inner and outer courts which enabled them to act as Huo Kuang's personal supporters.

Huo Kuang fell seriously ill in 68, and it was clear that he could not live long. The Emperor visited him in person, gravely affected by the situation; and as a result of their discussions and of consultation with the Chancellor, Huo Kuang's son Huo Yü was appointed to be General of the Right. Later, the Emperor and Empress attended Huo Kuang's funeral in person, and the lavish style of his obsequies reached a standard that had never before been equalled except for His Imperial Majesty in person. The Emperor's gifts included not only gold, money, silks, jades and pearls, but also a jade suit in which Huo Kuang's body was to be dressed for the life in the hereafter (see the frontispiece). The suit was made up of some two to three thousand pieces of jade, delicately sewn together with fine thread.[32] The tomb was laid out and constructed in a manner that had hitherto been deemed appropriate for members of the imperial family. The coffin was duly escorted to its final resting place, and a settlement of 300 families was established to

[30] *Chung-lang chiang.* Dubs renders *chung-lang* as Gentlemen of the Household.

[31] Dubs—Chief Commandant of the Emperor's Equipages.

[32] *cf.* the examples of jade-suits found recently at Man-ch'eng (*Kaoku* 1972, 2, pp. 39f.; *Wen wu*, 1972, 1, Plate II; *Historical Relics Unearthed in New China*, Peking 1972, Plates 95–6).

maintain the site and the necessary observances. In a special edict the Emperor referred to the services which Huo Kuang had rendered for over thirty years during Wu ti's reign and ten years in Chao ti's reign. When faced with a major crisis, he had remained steadfast to his principles and had taken the lead over the most senior officials of state. His policies were such as to promote peace for all time and thereby to bring rest to the realm. All the peoples of the world had thus enjoyed a time of tranquillity, and the Emperor wished to express his heartfelt gratitude and appreciation for Huo Kuang's magnificent achievements. He therefore granted exemption from tax and state services to Huo Kuang's descendants in perpetuity, so that from one generation to the next they would have no obligations to meet; for Huo Kuang's services had been no less valuable than those of Hsiao Ho.[33]

On his death-bed Huo Kuang had asked that his great-nephew Huo Shan should receive a nobility, so that he would be properly equipped to maintain the rites in honour of Huo Kuang's half-brother Huo Ch'ü-ping.[34] This request was granted along with the other funerary honours; and, what was to be of greater significance, while Huo Shan retained his title as Commandant of the Imperial Carriages,[35] he was also assigned general responsibility for the work of the secretariat. By virtue of an edict issued in the following year, Huo Yün, another great nephew, was also honoured with a nobility.[36]

There are two matters of interest in these events which merit consideration. Attention has already been drawn (p. 117) to the comparison which was subsequently made between Huo Kuang and the Duke of Chou, and it has been noted that in his

[33] *HS* 68.12b, *et seq.* For Hsiao Ho's achievements at the time of the foundation of the Han dynasty, see *HS* 39 and *HFHD*, vol. I, pp. 24-5.

[34] See Chapter 2, p. 51.

[35] Dubs—Chief Commandant of the Emperor's Equipages.

[36] *HS* 68.12b; Dubs renders *Shang-shu* (Secretariat) as Office of the Masters of Writing.

commemorative edict the Emperor compared Huo Kuang with Hsiao Ho. The achievements of Hsiao Ho were of a very different nature from those of the Duke of Chou. For Hsiao Ho's work had been directed to the establishment of the Han Empire on the model that had been provided in the institutions of Ch'in; it had not been directed to the demonstration of Confucian virtues that were associated with the house of Chou.

Secondly, the *Han-shu* records an incident in which Huo Kuang is shown to cast doubt on the extent of his son's ability.[37] Chang An-shih's eldest son, Chang Ch'ien-ch'iu, had served with Huo Kuang's son Huo Yü in the capacity of leaders of the courtiers of the palace.[38] They had led the forces under their command to take part in the campaign which was being fought against the Wu-huan under the direction of Fan Ming-yu, General of the Trans-Liao Command[39] (78 BC). On returning from the war, the two officers had called to pay their respects to Huo Kuang. When the latter questioned Chang Ch'ien-ch'iu about the tactics of the campaign and its topography, he had given a verbal answer about the fighting, drawing plans of the terrain in the form of a map, and there were no details wherein he found himself at a loss. Huo Kuang then turned to Huo Yü, who was unable to describe a single incident, and remarked that there were written reports about all such matters. It was subsequent to this exchange that Huo Kuang began to think highly of Chang Ch'ien-ch'iu's intelligence, while believing that Huo Yü lacked ability. 'The family of Huo will die out in this generation,' he sighed, 'but the family of Chang will prosper.'

The *Han-shu* adds the comment[40] that of all those families

---

[37] *HS* 59.13a.　　[38] See note 30 above.

[39] In 78 BC; see *HS* 7.8a (*HFHD*, vol. II, p. 168).

[40] *HS* 59.13b. 'Later, Huo Yü was punished and the Huo family was eliminated, but members of the Chang family succeeded one after the other. From the reigns of Hsüan ti and Yüan ti they served as attendants at the palace [*Shih-chung*: Dubs—palace attendant], regular attendants [*Chung*

who served the state with distinction, only those of Chin and Chang enjoyed the same degree of friendship, favouritism and honours that was lavished on those families who had provided an imperial consort. It will be seen below how speedily Huo Kuang's fears were to be realised and with what validity the statement of the *Han-shu* may be accepted.

Despite the apparent strength and favouritism which the family of Huo could boast at the time of Huo Kuang's death in 68, and despite the advantages to be expected in a family whose members included both the Dowager Empress and the Empress, there ensued a dynastic and political crisis which was to end two years later in the family's elimination. The political issues concerned the struggle for the control of the government, and the question of whether this would be vested in the Emperor himself, in the Chancellor and the duly appointed officials of state, or in the Leader of the Inner Court (or secretariat).[41] The dynastic issues concerned the imperial succession and the rival ambitions of two families for the glory, powers and influence pertaining to the mother of the declared heir apparent to the imperial throne.

To understand the situation it is necessary to revert slightly in time. It has already been noted that Liu Ping-i had been married to Hsü P'ing-chün, and some months before his accession she bore him a son.[42] Shortly after his accession, which took place on a day corresponding with 10 September 74 BC,

---

ch'ang shih: Dubs—Regular Inner Palace Attendant], in other offices and as supernumerary cavalrymen [*san chi*: Dubs—cavalier attendant], and more than ten of them acted as colonels. Among those families whose members served with distinction, only the Chin and Chang enjoyed the same degree of friendship, favouritism and honours as did the families whose members included imperial consorts.'

[41] For the emergence of the Secretariat and the Inner Court, see *HFHD*, vol. II, pp. 10f., 144f., Wang, pp. 166f., and p. 313 below.

[42] *HS* 8.3b (*HFHD*, vol. II, 205); *HS* 97A.22a, *et seq.*

Hsü P'ing-chün was given the title of *Chieh-yü*. At that time this was the title of the highest grade of concubine in the imperial establishment, but it still remained in a completely different category from the title of *Hou* or Empress; and the nomination of a particular consort as *Hou* was necessary in order to secure the succession legitimately. At the discussions which were held at court regarding this all important question, the senior statesmen were all in favour of nominating Huo Kuang's daughter as Empress, but before this view had been fully expressed, the Emperor made it abundantly clear that he wished to nominate his consort Hsü P'ing-chün; this was accordingly accomplished on 31 December 74. After the event, Huo Kuang pointed out that the father of the new Empress had suffered the punishment of castration and was not fitted to be related to one who held the position of sovereign in the realm; but within a year the father had been given the title of *Ch'ang-ch'eng chün*,[43] and this mark of respect served to reaffirm the confidence and determination of the Emperor.

At this juncture Huo Kuang's wife Huo Hsien took a hand in the drama.[44] She realised only too clearly that unless some drastic action were taken the Huo family would shortly be ousted by the Empress Hsü and her supporters; and there were already signs of political activity which served to confirm her fears. Without confiding in her husband or in any other members of the family, Huo Hsien planned for her daughter Ch'eng-chün to take the place of the Empress Hsü. For the latter was pregnant once again, and should she bear Hsüan ti another son, the Huo family could give up all hope of the future. By promising that an appointment of his own choice should await her husband, Huo Hsien was able to win the co-operation of the nurse who was attending the Empress, then suffering somewhat from her condition. Huo Hsien's plan was carried out in a singularly unpleasant and unsavoury fashion. When at last the Empress had been delivered, the nurse contrived to have poison

[43] *HS* 18.14b; *HS* 97A.22a.   [44] *HS* 68.14a; *HS* 97A.22b.

inserted in the medicine prepared for the patient and which had, in accordance with custom, already been tasted. The Empress drank the potion; very soon she complained of a headache, and asked if the medicine had been poisoned. Her attendants assured her that this was not so, but her agony became acute, and she died on 1 March 71 BC.[45] A year later, on 17 April 70, Huo Hsien's daughter was nominated Empress, and the occasion was celebrated in the usual way by the gift of gold, coin and silk to all officials and by an amnesty that was declared throughout the Empire.[46]

It would surely have seemed, in 70 and 69 BC, that the Huo family could not be better placed; their leading member controlled the government; one of his daughters was the Empress; other members of the family held key positions and could command the use of troops if necessary. Nevertheless, the situation was about to be changed radically and catastrophically so far as the Huo family was concerned. If the *Han-shu* gives us a true account, and if the author did not merely insert details that were deemed suitable for justifying subsequent events, there were some members of the family who took occasion to behave with indecent arrogance, immediately after Huo Kuang's death in 68. With an ostentatious show of extravagance, Huo Hsien enlarged and embellished the mausoleum that had already been prepared for her later reception, and she indulged in illicit relations with Feng Tzu-tu, formerly Huo Kuang's slave-master and confidant. Huo Yü and Huo Shan had their mansions beautified, and used to ride on horseback at will, halting only at the doors of the imperial buildings. Huo Yün frequently excused himself from attending court, on personal grounds or on a plea of sickness. He kept a large company of retainers, enlarged his pleasure grounds and used to go hunting; and he would send his slaves to present themselves at court in his place. There was none who dared to

[45] *HS* 8.6a (*HFHD*, vol. II, 212).
[46] *HS* 8.6b (*HFHD*, vol. II, 213).

remonstrate over such matters, and Huo Hsien, together with her own slaves, was wont to enter the buildings of the Ch'ang-hsin Palace by day or night without restriction.[47]

Huo Kuang died in 68. For the first time the Emperor, now in his twenty-fourth year, took a personal interest in matters of state,[48] and far-reaching changes set in which affected the procedures of government and the opportunities which had been open to the Huo family for exploiting their position. Important changes also occurred in the tenure of the senior offices of state. While the exact sequence of events cannot be determined for certain, they resulted in the reduction of the powers of the Secretariat and the corresponding growth of the strength of the Chancellor's post. At the same time the powers that had been associated with the title *Ta-ssu-ma* or Marshal of state were transferred from the Huo family to Chang An-shih.

Hitherto the procedures for handling documents of state had lent considerable force to the Leader of the Secretariat. All reports to the government were regularly submitted in duplicate, and the copy which was marked 'second' was opened by the leader himself. If he felt that the contents did not call for further action, he was able to conceal the document and prevent its presentation elsewhere.[49]

It was on the request of Wei Hsiang that this procedure was changed, so as to put an end to the practice of concealment; and the change was greeted by the Huo family with anger and dismay.[50] Wei Hsiang had once been involved with one of Sang Hung-yang's clients. He had served as a prefect of Mao-ling, in the metropolitan area, before being promoted governor

---

[47] *HS* 68.12b, *et seq.*

[48] *HS* 68.13b.

[49] *HS* 74.2b.

[50] *HS* 68.14a; *HS* 74.8a attributes Hsüan ti's personal attention to government and the change of procedure to the period after the punishment of the Huo family.

of Ho-nan Commandery; and, as happened to many servants of
the Han Imperial government, he had at one time been brought
up on a charge before the Superintendent of Trials,[51] and had
been imprisoned. Thanks to an amnesty (77) he was released,
and he was subsequently appointed to a number of posts. His
friend Ping Chi warned him that he should bide his time and
take care to behave with circumspection. In due course he
reached full 'ministerial' rank by appointment as Superintendent of Agriculture (72) and then Imperial Counsellor (71).[52]

As mentioned earlier (p. 125), following Huo Kuang's death
Huo Yü was appointed General of the Right, and Huo Shan
was given authority to act as Leader of the Secretariat. Wei
Hsiang took the opportunity to protest against the monopoly
of power which was being invested in the Huo family. He did
so by means of a written address to the throne which was
presented through the intermediacy of Hsü Kuang-han, father
of the recently poisoned empress. He wrote as follows:[53]

'In its protests against the statesmen of the day, the *Spring and
Autumn Annals* expresses regret that in the state of Sung men of the
same family were appointed counsellors for three successive
generations, and that full powers of government were monopolised
by the Chi-sun family in Lu; for these were both states which fell
into danger and ruin.

'Ever since the Hou-yüan period [i.e. since 88 BC] the gift of
office has been taken away from the imperial house and the power of
government has been exercised by the chief minister. And now that
[Huo] Kuang is dead, his son has in his turn been appointed Supreme
General;[54] his nephew grasps in his hand the instruments for govern-

---

[51] *T'ing-wei*: Dubs—Commandant of Justice.

[52] *Ta-ssu-nung*: Dubs—Grand Minister of Agriculture. *Yü-shihta -fu*:
Dubs—Clerk Grandee or Grandee Secretary.

[53] *HS* 74.2a. For the identification of Hsü Po and Hsü Kuang-han, see
HS 71.3b notes.

[54] *Sic.* Huo Yü had in fact been appointed General of the Right (see
p. 125).

ing the state, and his close relatives occupy substantially important positions in the armed forces. [Huo] Kuang's widow [Huo] Hsien and his daughters possess authority to come and go as they please in the Ch'ang-hsin palace. They issue their orders when they like, as often as not by night, and their extravagances and indulgences are beyond control. It is only right that their personal powers should be curtailed and that the schemes which they are harbouring should be brought to nothing, so as to provide generations to come with a strong basis of security and to preserve intact for the future the achievements of those who have rendered service to the state.'

Immediately after Huo Kuang's death, and while he was Imperial Counsellor, Wei Hsiang took further steps which weakened the authority of the Huo family. In a carefully phrased memorial he pointed out that Huo Kuang's death had left a vacuum, and that the ensuing struggle for power could be dangerous. He urged that Chang An-shih, whose part in the events of 74 has been described above (p. 123), should be nominated as Marshal of State. After some hesitation and reluctance Chang An-shih agreed to accept these new responsibilities. Since 74 he had held the appointment of Superintendent of the Palace,[55] and he was now to become Marshal of State, coupled with the title of General of Chariots and Cavalry;[56] and he was at the same time ordered to assume leadership of the Secretariat. Three months later his title of General of Chariots and Cavalry was replaced by that of Guards' General;[57] and in place of the garrison troops which he had formerly commanded, he now controlled the guard units at the two imperial palaces,[58] the forces attached to the gates of the city and those of the northern barracks.

[55] *Kuang-lu-hsün*: Dubs—Superintendent of the Imperial Household.

[56] *Chü-ch'i chiang-chün*. Wang (p. 185) renders this as General of the Chariot and Mount.

[57] *Wei chiang-chün*: Dubs—General of the Guards.

[58] *HS* 59.8b. These were the Wei-yang and Ch'ang-hsin palaces, whose guards were previously controlled by Fan Ming-yu and Teng Kuang-han.

This appointment was originally made in the fourth month of 67.[59] In the sixth month Wei Hsiang was promoted from Imperial Counsellor to Chancellor, and in the seventh month Chang An-shih's military responsibilities were strengthened in the way that has been described. At the same time Huo Yü's position was correspondingly weakened. He already held the title of General of the Right, and he was now given the further honorary title of Marshal of State. However, this title did not carry the power that might have been expected. It was held simultaneously by Chang An-shih with the result that it had lost the unique prestige that it had conferred on Huo Kuang. Simultaneously, the garrison forces under the command of Huo Yü as General of the Right were disbanded, with the result that while his glory was enhanced by the bestowal of honours that lacked substance, the following on which he could rely was in practice taken from him.

Effective as these changes were in altering the balance of power in politics, they were contrived without the need for any manipulation of Han institutions. The office of Chancellor had never been abolished, although its influence may have lapsed; that influence was now restored in so far as one of the most able men of the day (Wei Hsiang) was appointed to hold the office. The title of *Ta-ssu-ma* had never been more than an honorary title which was conferred as a mark of recognition for services rendered. It was not until 8 BC that it was formerly established as an office of state, with an appropriate seal and complement of subordinates; in the meantime there was no reason why it could not be given simultaneously to two senior officials. While the Leader of the Secretariat had come to wield considerable powers, these had never been described by statute; they had simply arisen as a result of practice; so, when practice and procedure were changed, there was no need to make any formal declaration regarding the responsibilities of the Secretariat. In this way the form of Han government remained un-

[59] *HS* 19B.22a, b.

changed, while the power to exercise government moved from one circle to another.

At the time when Huo Yü was deprived of real power a number of other prominent persons experienced a change of fortune, and it is likely that these changes were brought about by a further circumstance, the Emperor's discovery of the truth about his late Empress' death. These facts became known to him some time between the third and the seventh months of 67. At the time of her murder (71) the medical staff of the palace had been put under arrest, and Huo Hsien was only too afraid that the whole story would be revealed. She had therefore confided eventually in Huo Kuang, who was utterly dismayed at what he was told, and remained undecided whether to bring the matter into the open or to protect his wife by silence.[60] In the end he took no action, and it was only after Huo Kuang's death that the Emperor learnt the truth. He reacted (seventh month of 67) by depriving Huo Yü of substantive power in the way that has been described and by demoting several of the sons-in-law or other relatives of Huo Kuang to junior posts. In some cases they were relegated to virtual exile, by appointment to distant provinces.[61] By contrast the conferment of nobilities on Hsü Kuang-han and Shih Kao showed how the Hsü and Shih families had risen in imperial favour; and some of their members were also given command of forces which had

[60] *HS* 68.14a; *HS* 74.2b; *HS* 96A.23a, *et seq.*

[61] *HS* 68.14a, *et seq.* The men included Fan Ming-yu, Superintendent of the Guards at the Wei-yang palace and general of the trans-Liao command, who became Superintendent of the Palace (*Kuang-lu-hsün*); Jen Sheng, who had been leader of the courtiers of the palace and became governor of An-ting Commandery; and Teng Kuang-han, who had been Superintendent of the Guards at the Ch'ang-lo palace and became Superintendent of the Lesser Treasury of the Ch'ang-hsin Palace. In addition, Chang Shuo (Counsellor of the Palace, *Kuang-lu ta-fu*: Dubs— Imperial Household Grandee) became governor of Shu commandery; and Wang Han (Leader of the Courtiers of the Palace) became governor of Wu-wei Commandery.

previously been subordinated to members of the Huo family or their associates. These steps, in fact, followed a slightly earlier event which marked the promotion of the Hsü family. In the fourth month of 67 the eight-year-old son of the Empress had been nominated Heir Apparent.[62] At the same time Ping Chi, who, it will be recalled, had been responsible for Hsüan ti's survival, was appointed senior tutor to the Heir Apparent.[63]

With these developments the Huo family realised the gravity of their situation and determined that they must risk all by staging a revolt. Huo Shan, who had acted as Leader of the Secretariat until Chang An-shih had been ordered to assume this responsibility, summarised the state of affairs to his close relatives, Huo Hsien, Huo Yü and Huo Yün. He observed[64] that the Chancellor, Wei Hsiang, enjoyed the confidence of the Emperor. He had deliberately altered the methods of government that had been practised during Huo Kuang's time, and by the dexterous gift of bounties to the poor, he was trying to expose Huo Kuang's deficiencies. He said that the Emperor loved to talk with the professional civil servant scholars; these were men who lacked resources and manners and who indulged in abandoned talk; and they were the very persons whom Huo Kuang had hated. Huo Shan continued that a number of accusations had been levelled at the Huo family; it was said that in Huo Kuang's days the sovereign had grown weak and one of his subjects strong, to the point of seizing a monopoly of power. It was also being alleged that, now that Huo Kuang's relatives were in office, they were behaving with pride and arrogance, and this was the cause ascribed to the many portents which had been reported and which were interpreted as forecasting danger to the realm. Huo Shan added that he had done his best to pre-

[62] *HS* 8.8b (*HFHD*, vol. II, pp. 220–1); *HS* 9.1a (*HFHD*, vol. II, p. 299); *HS* 18.14b, 15b.
[63] *HS* 74.8a.
[64] *HS* 68.15a, *et seq.*

vent these calumnies from being brought forward but his efforts had been unsuccessful.

When Huo Hsien suggested that the Chancellor, Wei Hsiang, could be incriminated for the remarks that he had made about the Huo family, Huo Shan replied that this would be impossible, in view of the Chancellor's integrity. Unfortunately, he said, members of the Huo family had been far less careful in their behaviour, and he had been told of a popular rumour, which of course could not be true, that the Huo family had murdered the Empress Hsü. Huo Hsien now feared the worst, and she felt unable to withold the truth of the last allegation from her relations. Understanding, at last, why so many members of the Huo family had been dismissed, Huo Shan, Huo Yü and Huo Yün reviled Huo Hsien for keeping them in ignorance; and they knew that their only chance of survival lay in staging a plot.

A suggestion was now made that an edict should be published in the name of the Empress Dowager, grand-daughter of Huo Hsien, which would authorise putting the Chancellor and Hsü Kuang-han to death; but news of this stratagem leaked out, possibly owing to loose talk on the part of the grooms and stablehands who were working in the residence of the Huo family; [65] and in due course an edict ordered Huo Yün and Huo Shan to leave their posts and repair to their private quarters. For good measure the edict expressed the imperial censure of Huo Kuang's daughters for their discourteous behaviour towards the Empress Dowager, their niece, and it rebuked Feng Tzu-tu, Huo Hsien's lover, for his many infringements of the laws.

A second and much more serious attempt was made by the conspirators some time before the seventh month of 66 BC.[66] Huo Shan suggested that a charge could be brought against

[65] *HS* 68.16a; see the note by Ho Cho.

[66] *HS* 8.10a, *et seq.* (*HFHD*, vol. II, pp. 225f.); *HS* 68.16b; *HS* 74.2b.

Wei Hsiang for ordering a reduction in the sacrificial arrangements for the imperial shrines, without due authority to do so, but there is no record that such a charge was actually preferred. Instead it was planned that Wei Hsiang, Hsü Kuang-han and their subordinates should be invited to a banquet; and once there they would be executed by Fan Ming-yu and Teng Kuang-han, on the authority of an edict which would purport to come from the Empress Dowager. At the same time the Emperor was to be deposed, Huo Yü was to be established in his place, and the Heir Apparent was to be poisoned.[67]

While these plans were afoot, orders had been given to appoint Huo Yün to the distant post of governor of Hsüan-t'u. This was one of the commanderies in Korea, where he would be virtually exiled and powerless to harm the court. At the same time Huo Shan was brought up on a charge of making copies of secret documents; Huo Hsien made a plea to save him from extreme punishment by delivering her residence and 1 000 head of horse to the state, but this was not allowed. It was now that news of the plot was disclosed, and the Huo family met its deserts. Huo Yün, Huo Shan and Fan Ming-yu committed suicide; Huo Hsien, Huo Yü and Teng Kuang-han were arrested; Huo Yü was executed at the waist; and Huo Hsien, together with Huo Kuang's daughters and relations, was put to death in public. The only members of the family to survive were Huo Hsien's daughter, who was the Empress, and her granddaughter, who was Chao ti's late Empress. Her daughter was deposed from her position (17 September 66) and sent off to live in the Chao t'ai, within the grounds of the Shang-lin Palace. Twelve years later, when she was removed elsewhere, she took the opportunity to take her own life. Huo Hsien's grand-daughter, who was still in her twenty-third year at the time of the plot, survived until 37 BC. It may be noted that a

[67] The intention of poisoning the heir apparent is revealed in *HS* 8.10b (*HFHD*, vol. II, p. 226), but not in *HS* 68.16b. The fullest details are otherwise given in *HS* 97A.24a.

further unsuccessful plot was staged in 62, under the leadership of Huo Cheng-shih, of Ho-tung commandery; but there is no evidence to show whether or not he was related to the family of Huo Kuang.[68]

Large numbers of families[69] were implicated in the plot, and the punishment of the chief offenders was followed by the publication of an imperial edict, whose text is carried twice in the *Han-shu*.[70] This was in the seventh month of 66. The conspirators were accused of plotting treason,[71] and of having practised deceit on the populace; but thanks to the holy spirits of the imperial ancestors their plans had been disclosed and the conspirators had all been duly punished. The edict granted an amnesty to all those who had been tricked by the Huo family into compliance and whose degree of complicity had not yet been reported; and nobilities were conferred on a number of men who had been concerned in revealing the plot. These included Yang Yün, that grandson of Ssu-ma Ch'ien who had been concerned with the publication of the *Shih-chi*, and Shih Kao, who was destined to receive the title of Marshal of State in 49. The conferment of these nobilities was dated in the eighth month of 66.[72]

Wei Hsiang had constituted one of the prime objectives against whom the efforts of the Huo family had been directed. His survival in the office of Chancellor until his death in 59 BC, coupled with what is known of his character and his preferences, suggests that the events of 66 may have marked an important stage in the development of Han politics, i.e. in the

---

[68] *HS* 8.10b (*HFHD*, vol. II, p. 226); *HS* 8.15b (*HFHD*, vol. II, p. 238); *HS* 17.30a; *HS* 97A.19a, 24a.

[69] *HS* 68.17a reads 'numbered by the thousand'. The *Tzu-chih-t'ung-chien* (SPTK ed., 25.7b) reads 'by the ten'.

[70] *HS* 8.10a, *et seq.* (*HFHD*, vol. II, p. 225) and *HS* 68.17a.

[71] *Ta-ni*. More properly 'great refractoriness' (see Hulsewé, pp. 156f.).

[72] *HS* 17.29a, b; *HS* 18.15b.

transition from the Modernist policies of expansion, control of the population and exploitation of resources, to the Reformist policies of retrenchment and *laissez-faire*. A number of administrative decisions which were taken in these years support this view.

The Modernist policies had been introduced in increasing intensity from about 130. With military setbacks and the large expenditure involved in the campaigns the policies began to lose momentum, and by *c*. 90 they were becoming mitigated in favour of retrenchment. However until 66 the Modernist attitude still remained dominant, despite certain clear signs of retrenchment such as the reluctance to embark on a military campaign in 87; the withdrawal of certain commanderies in 82; the consideration of popular welfare in the debate of 81; or the reduction in the activities and staff of the Office of Music *c*. 70.[73]

It was presumably decisions such as these which inspired the comment written about a century later in the *Han-shu*, to the effect that Huo Kuang's attempts to repair the extravagances of Wu ti's reign deserved proper appreciation.[74] However, it is clear from contemporary criticism that the Modernist attitude still coloured Hsüan ti's government. Such criticism was voiced by Wang Chi in his capacity as Academician and Political Counsellor,[75] and it concerns the period immediately after 66, when the Hsü and Shih families were in favour and Hsüan ti was taking a personal part in the Government. According to the *Han-shu*[76] the Emperor was emulating Wu ti's example of extravagance, with the result that his buildings, carriages and robes were more splendid than those of Chao ti. Wang Chi made a plea for a more simple type of government. He protested that it was habitual for officials to depend on legal prescription rather than on ethical precept; and he begged

[73] See Chapter 2, p. 71f. and Chapter 6, p. 200.
[74] *HS* 7.10b (*HFHD*, vol. II, p. 175).
[75] *Po-shih chien-ta-fu*: Dubs—erudit, grandee remonstrant.
[76] *HS* 72.5b.

Hsüan ti to look for examples of good administration in the precedents set by the good kings of Chou. Hsüan ti thought that Wang Chi's ideas went too far.[77]

But despite the failure of these strictures to persuade, signs were not lacking that a new intellectual attitude was emerging which was destined to affect the government of the Han Empire, and some steps were already being taken which harked back to the past. One of the acts of Wu ti's Modernist ministers had been to bring to an end nearly all the nobilities which had been founded at the beginning of the dynasty and which were still held by the original noble's heir in 112.[78] This action had probably been intended to decrease the influence of a traditional aristocracy and to make way for the rise of new men, whose views were in keeping with the progressive attitude of the times. Sixty years later, and four years after the fall of the Huo family, Hsüan ti's government made a gesture which pointed in precisely the opposite direction. A search was instituted for the surviving members of the families of those nobilities which, having been founded at the outset of the dynasty, had been brought to an end in 112; the descendants of over a hundred were found and partly reinstated in their traditional honours, by a grant of exemption from statutory obligations together with a present of gold.[79] This measure can only be interpreted as being an overt demonstration that the government of 62 relied on principles that differed from those of its predecessor of 112.

Further signs that Hsüan ti's reign witnessed the transition

[77] *HS* 72.7b, particular in connection with Wang Chi's protest against imperial extravagance and the irregular methods of appointing officials. See Chapter 6, note 61.

[78] See *HFHD* vol. II, pp. 126f.

[79] There is some doubt whether this action took place in 65 or 62, and whether the number of nobilities concerned was 123 or 136. See *HS* 6.22a (*HFHD*, vol. II, p. 80); *HS* 8.12a and 15b (*HFHD*, vol. II, pp. 230, 238); *HFHD*, vol. II, pp. 126f.; Hulsewé, p. 218; *Aristocratic Ranks*, p. 143.

from one set of attitudes to another are revealed in an examination of the fifty-seven edicts that were proclaimed between 178 and 2 BC and which refer specifically to the occurrence of phenomena and their bearing on human affairs. It may first be noted that before Hsüan ti's reign there had been relatively few such edicts (only thirteen in the ninety-five years between 178 and 83) as compared with the greater number issued from 72 BC onwards (forty-four in the seventy years from 72 to 2). Of perhaps greater significance is the change in attitude that becomes apparent. For, up to 72 most of these edicts referred to phenomena that could be interpreted as good omens, and the strange events which called for explanation were linked with the religious beliefs and cults that had been inaugurated in the Ch'in empire or earlier and taken over by Han on its foundation. However, from 48 BC the portents to which these edicts referred were regarded as omens of catastrophe; and the edicts explained these events as signs of the displeasure of Heaven or of an imbalance that had occurred between the influences of *Yin* and *Yang*.

It is shown below that the worship of Heaven was promoted by Han imperial governments with growing emphasis, and in place of earlier cults, probably from 31 BC;[80] and Heaven was associated not with Ch'in but with Chou. The change of emphasis which is noticeable in the edicts that are under consideration corresponds both with changes in religious practice and with the major shift from a Modernist to a Reformist attitude. For in many cases political measures of a Reformist nature, which were designed to reduce the extent of taxation or to restrict the extravagance of the palace, accompanied the edicts which were issued from 48 onwards and which explained the strange phenomena in terms of the cult of Heaven. In addition it may be shown that in this respect as in others the reign of Hsüan ti formed a period of transition. Of a total of seventeen edicts referring to these matters which were proclaimed between

[80] See Chapter 5.

72 and 51 BC, ten drew attention to events which were regarded as being of a happy nature; and in this way their treatment of the strange events conformed with earlier practice. However, seven of the edicts drew attention to events that were of a disastrous type. While ascribing the cause of these events to the wrath of Heaven, the edicts sometimes ordered palliative measures of a Reformist nature, such as reductions in imperial expenditure (71), in the price of salt (66) and in the imposts of government (64).

The fall of the Huo family involved attention to the supernatural in several ways which merit consideration in view of the contemporary interest in phenomena and spiritual powers. Some of the principal actors in the drama are said to have experienced premonitions of their fate; and another, who observed the outcome of these incidents, was even prepared to predict the downfall of the Huo family. In addition, the events which occurred at this time feature in subsequent lists of phenomena and are cited retrospectively as verifications of Heaven's habit of issuing warnings to man by means of portents.

When, after Huo Kuang's death, the leading members of the family realised the perils in which they stood encompassed, Huo Hsien dreamt[81] that the waters of a well which was situated in her household had overflowed and inundated the courtyard, so that the family had been forced to take refuge in the trees. She also dreamt that Huo Kuang had appeared to her and warned her of the impending arrests. In addition there had been a plague of rats in the house. People had kept running into them, and the rats had drawn pictures on the ground with their tails. Then there had been a number of occasions when owls had hooted in their evil way in the trees which overlooked the main rooms; and the gates of the residence had suddenly and spontaneously collapsed. The same thing had occurred in Huo Yün's house. Even more strange, it was generally said in the neighbourhood that

[81] *HS* 68.16b.

someone had been seen on the roof, tearing up the tiles and casting them down to the ground below, but on investigation no one was to be found there. Huo Yü too had had his dreams; he had heard the clatter of carriage wheels and horses' hooves and a great shout had arisen of 'Arrest Huo Yü.'

The prediction that the Huo family would be ruined was voiced by a man named Hsü Fu on moral grounds;[82] their extravagances constituted an insult to the Emperor and their behaviour was unethical. In addition he believed that their monopoly of power had caused widespread harm and that a reaction would be bound to set in. He reported his views to the throne in no less than three written statements, asking that the powers of the Huo family should be curtailed in their own interests and so as to prevent their ultimate ruin. When the drama had been played out, Hsüan ti somewhat grudgingly rewarded Hsü Fu for the warnings that he had chosen to leave unheeded at the time.

Shortly after Huo Kuang's death, Chang Ch'ang, who rose to hold the office of Metropolitan Superintendent of the Right from 61 BC,[83] presented a submission to the throne.[84] He cited examples from China's pre-imperial past to prove the dangers of the contemporary situation. He added that at the height of the powers that he had enjoyed during his twenty year long dictatorship Huo Kuang had upset the cosmic balance between Heaven and Earth and had disrupted the rhythms of *Yin* and *Yang*. He referred to a number of phenomena, such as the strange tilt of the moon; solar eclipses; the descent of darkness by day or the glory of brilliant lights by night; earthquakes and land fissures; outbreaks of fire in the earth; irregular motions of the heavenly bodies; and other omens of catastrophe. All

[82] *HS* 68.17b.

[83] *Ching chao yin*: Dubs—Governor of the Capital. Chang Ch'ang held this post for eight years from 61, when he was demoted to be *Tso-p'ing-i* (Metropolitan Superintendent of the Left: Dubs—Eastern Supporter); *HS* 19B.34a.

[84] *HS* 76.13a.

these strange events should be attributed to the excessively dominant position of *Yin*, i.e. to the strength of the females attached to the imperial personage and the monopoly of power which their relations were wielding.

The chapters of the *Han-shu* which are specifically concerned with phenomena and portents and their relation to actual events mention the drama of 68 to 66 at least three times, and in some cases they allude to incidents that have already been described. In these passages the *Han-shu* is seeking to prove that the prior notification or warning of Heaven's wrath was verified by the subsequent occurrence of catastrophe in human affairs. The record reports[85] irregular motions of the stars and the appearance of comets in the first, sixth and seventh months of 69 BC; and it associates these reports with the rebellion of 66. Elsewhere[86] there is a reference to phenomenal rain and hail that fell in east China in the fifth month of 66 to a depth of two and a half feet with hailstones as large as hens' eggs; twenty people died in these unseasonal events, and all the fowls of the air perished. Such matters are associated with the plot of the Huo family that broke out almost immediately afterwards.[87] Finally attention should be drawn to the statement of the spontaneous collapse of the gates at the residence of Huo Yü.[88] Here the *Han-shu* attempts to verify the force of this warning by referring to Huo Yü's lack of discipline and respect, his failure to take heed of the admonitions he had received, and the final catastrophe in which the family was liquidated. It needed the sharp pen of Wang Ch'ung to cast doubt on the association between the collapse of those gates and the ruin of the Huo family.[89]

---

[85] *HS* 26.55a.   [86] *HS* 27B2.15b.

[87] The text of the *Han-shu* reads tenth month, but as frequently occurs the figure ten is an error for seven.   [88] *HS* 27B1.16a.

[89] *Lun-heng* 15 (43), Huang Hui ed., p. 659; Forke's translation, vol. 1, p. 116.

As is usual in Chinese history it is difficult, if not impossible, to determine the character and motives of the men who were intimately concerned with government or responsible for major changes of policy. However, the meagre information regarding the attitudes of those who took a leading part in public life after the crisis of 68 to 66 affords a few further hints of the transition from one set of ideals to another.

As has already been noted (p. 123), Tu Yen-nien had tendered certain advice to Huo Kuang in 81 BC, and in so far as he was anxious to relieve suffering which he ascribed to the government's interference with popular activities, he can be said to have been Reformist at heart. After the attempted revolt of 66, Hsüan ti regarded Tu Yen-nien as being a 'Huo party man',[90] and he intended to have him removed from public life. However, although Tu Yen-nien was actually brought up on a charge and dismissed, he was re-appointed a few months later to be governor of Pei-ti commandery; and he later (55) rose to hold the post of Imperial Counsellor, the second highest position in the structure of government.[91]

Shih Kao was one of those who had been ennobled for the part they played in exposing the plan to revolt. Right at the end of Hsüan ti's reign, he was created Marshal of State, with responsibility for leading the Secretariat,[92] and he remained in this position from 49 until 43. Two incidents show his character as Reformist; he was one of those who promoted the cause of the *Ku-liang* commentary on the *Spring and Autumn Annals* as against that of the *Kung-yang* commentary,[93] and it was he who sponsored K'uang Heng for appointment to office. K'uang

[90] *HS* 60.5b.   [91] *HS* 19B.35b.

[92] *HS* 18.15b; *HS* 19B.36b; *HS* 82.5a.

[93] *HS* 88.23b. The full significance of this choice and the importance of the debate of 51 BC is examined in Tjan Tjoe Som, *Po Hu T'ung, The Comprehensive Discussions in the White Tiger Hall* (Leiden, 1949). In a later study I am hoping to consider the incident in the context of political and religious developments.

Heng's part in the reform of the religion of state is described elsewhere.[94]

It is not so clear wherein the sympathies of Ping Chi lay, and it is likely that he owed his prominence in public life to Hsüan ti; for he had taken steps to save Hsüan ti's life and to recommend him for succession to the throne. Ping Chi served as Imperial Counsellor from 67 BC until his promotion to be Chancellor in 59; and he held that position until his death in 55. The only sign of his support for the reformist cause is seen in his recommendation of Hsiao Wang-chih and several other men of the 'scholastic' type[95]—men of the sort with whom Hsüan ti had been glad to converse, to the indignation of Huo Shan (see p. 136). In his time Hsiao Wang-chih emerged as one of the strongest exponents of Reformist policies, but it cannot be known how far his views had become clear at the time when Ping Chi sponsored him for service.

Like Shih Kao, Yang Yün, grandson of Ssu-ma Ch'ien, had been ennobled for laying information which led to the exposure of the plot of the Huo family in 66. In 61 he was appointed to the 'ministerial post' of Superintendent of the Palace,[96] but some five years later he was deprived of his nobility and relieved of his post on the grounds that he had been criticising the conduct of government; and he was duly executed.[97] It seems possible, or even likely, that his protest, which was allegedly conveyed in a somewhat reckless and tactless manner, was directed against those points wherein Han government could be compared with that of Ch'in. In this way Yang Yün is another statesman whose sympathies appear to have been more with the Reformist than with the Modernist attitude.[98]

---

[94] See Chapter 5.   [95] *HS* 78.1b.

[96] *Kuang-lu-hsün*: Dubs—Superintendent of the Imperial Household.

[97] The date of his execution is given variously as 56 or 55; see *HFHD*, vol. II, p. 249, note 19.6.

[98] *HS* 8.19b; *HS* 9.1b (*HFHD*, vol. II, pp. 249, 300); *HS* 17.29b; *HS* 19B.24a.

But it is in the actions and statements of Wei Hsiang, Chancellor from 67 BC until his death in 59, that there appear the clearest signs of the Reformist attitude for this time. Wei Hsiang had been known for his scholastic ability. He was recommended for service and he held a few posts in the provinces, being promoted Superintendent of Agriculture in 72. In the following year he became Imperial Counsellor, and it was in that capacity that he appointed Hsiao Wang-chih to his staff. He held that post until his elevation to Chancellor in 67.[99]

During the years 65 to 62 BC Wei Hsiang came out with strong Reformist views regarding foreign policy. He believed in the value of retrenchment and of avoiding any upset in the balance of *Yin* and *Yang*; and although the punitive campaign against the rebel Ch'iang tribes was fought while he was Chancellor, he successfully persuaded Hsüan ti to refrain from embarking on an expedition in central Asia. His nostalgia for the past, real or idealised, was very noticeable, and he cited no less than twenty-three Han edicts of earlier days as precedents for the measures which he favoured. He stated openly that he believed that past and present relied on different institutions of state, and that the duty of the present time lay in honouring and practising the precedents of the past. In this respect he was somewhat eclectic and undiscriminating; for his reverence for the past led him to cite the statements of a number of men, whose opinions were very varied and whose views were not necessarily relevant to his own. Thus, while he could call on Tung Chung-shu as an earlier exponent of the principles which are described here as Reformist, he did not hesitate to quote from the statements of Chia I and Ch'ao Ts'o, who had been some of the early exponents of the principles of Modernist government. However, in the course of these citations he took care to specify particular courses of action as being ideal examples of imperial administration in the past, and the examples which he chose were very much like the steps

[99] *HS* 19B.30b; *HS* 74.1a; *HS* 78.2a.

advocated by Reformist statesmen such as Hsiao Wang-chih.

Thus Wei Hsiang held up for praise the way in which earlier emperors had opened the state granaries to help the indigent and needy; or the occasions when they had sent commissioners to tour the empire so as to ascertain the degree of popular hardship. Similarly he recalled instances in which emperors had cut down imperial expenditure and reduced the load of taxation. Finally the *Han-shu* carries[100] the text of a long speech in which he stresses the importance of *Yin* and *Yang*, the influences of the Five Elements, and the need for man to conform with the cosmic patterns that informed Heaven and Earth; and he closed his eloquent address with an appeal to the Emperor to select four men who were well-versed experts in the ways of *Yin* and *Yang*. Each one was to specialise in one of the four seasons, and when his particular season came round he was to advise wherein the duties of government lay, so that the forces of *Yin* and *Yang* could be maintained in their proper balance. Much of Wei Hsiang's lesson can probably be traced to Tung Chung-shu; many of the policies which he advocated recur in the speeches attributed to the Reformist statesmen who succeeded him during the reigns of Yüan ti and Ch'eng ti.

The transitional nature of the reign of Hsüan ti is partly reflected in the somewhat conflicting evidence and hints that we have regarding the character and predilections of the Emperor. It seems that he saw virtue in both the Modernist and the Reformist causes, and his relations with the Huo family changed drastically from dependence, to toleration and finally to hatred.

Hsüan ti had a realistic appreciation of the nature and demands of imperial government and he understood the reasons that lay behind the Modernist policies of expansion and control. At the same time, either through personal choice or by force of circumstance, he was much in sympathy with those statesmen

[100] *HS* 74.4b.

of a scholastic frame of mind who expressed Reformist views or upheld those ideals of a past age to which the Reformists looked for guidance.

The circumstances of Hsüan ti's accession were such that he owed his position very largerly to Huo Kuang's leadership, and as a young man who was new to the ways of the court he depended on him for guidance and the retention of his position. It is perhaps not surprising that from this dependence there developed resentment and rancour; and it is more than understandable that Hsüan ti was not prepared to allow Huo Kuang's relatives the same liberties that that statesmen had been able to enjoy. We know nothing of Hsüan ti's personal or emotional attachment to his Empress, Hsü P'ing-chün, but again it is understandable that her murder by Huo Hsien can only have filled the Emperor with bitter fury.

An an elder statesman whose word would not be gainsaid and as the young Emperor's father-in-law, Huo Kuang was unlikely to brook interference, even from an Emperor. How far Huo Kuang made Hsüan ti aware of his position will never be known, but there are signs that Hsüan ti preferred the company and friendship of others. Reference has been made above to Huo Shan's criticism of the company which the Emperor chose (see p. 136) and to Huo Kuang's acid comment on the Empress Hsü's father (see p. 129). Elsewhere we read that while the Emperor respected and feared Huo Kuang it was Chang An-shih whom he took to his heart and with whom he shared greater affinities.[101] Not surprisingly Wei Hsiang earned the hatred of the Huo family, if only for his successful reduction of the powers of the secretariat; but they were also afraid of him and when Wei Hsiang had been appointed Chancellor his conduct of affairs accorded very closely with the ideas of his Emperor.[102]

The unprecedented honours paid to Huo Kuang at his death and the Emperor's personal attendance at his funeral need

[101] *HS* 59.10b.   [102] *HS* 74.2b, 3a.

hardly be taken as evidence of Hsüan ti's personal love for the Huo family; and should his attentions be regarded as excessive for a son-in-law to pay to a father-in-law who had served the state for some fifty years, there is a further incident which reveals a somewhat different aspect of the Emperor's personal feelings. This concerns the behaviour of Chao Kuang-han, who had been appointed Metropolitan Superintendent of the Right in 71 and held the same post at the time of Huo Kuang's death.[103] Previously he had been willing enough to serve Huo Kuang, but now, 'understanding the mind of the Emperor' he called out the officials in Ch'ang-an over whom he had charge, and taking personal command he made his way with them to the residence of Huo Kuang's son Huo Yü. They burst through the gates and sought out Huo Yü's private store of liquor. They then hammered the wine-jars to pieces, cut down the barriers of the gates with axes and made off. When the Empress, Huo Yü's sister, heard of this raid she confronted the Emperor and burst into tears; anxious to placate her, he summoned Chao Kuang-han for questioning. In the event the latter was imprisoned and finally executed at the waist (65).

From the time when Hsüan ti first took a personal part in government he put his best talents into the work of administration, disciplining his officials and discriminating carefully between appearance and reality. His realistic approach to government and its instruments is mentioned in the *Han-shu's* appreciation of his reign, which notes the care with which he insisted that the rewards and punishments of state must be reliable and trustworthy.[104] The same point emerged in an account of a conversation which he once had with his son, the future Emperor Yüan ti, and which stands out in some contrast to Huo Shan's complaint that the Emperor was indulging too much in the company of scholastics.

[103] *Ching chao yin*: Dubs—Metropolitan Superintendent of the Right; *HS* 19B.31a; *HS* 76.4a.

[104] *HS* 8.25a (*HFHD*, vol. II, p. 265); *HS* 74.2b, *et seq.*

The conversation took place[105] at a banquet, at an unspecified time. The Heir Apparent taxed his father with excessive reliance on punishments and suggested that he would do better to employ officials who had had a scholastic training. Hsüan ti's expression was seen to change, and his reply shows that on this occasion, at least, he favoured Modernist rather than Reformist principles. He affirmed that the institutions of the Han dynasty derived from those of the non-Confucian sovereigns of the pre-imperial age, i.e. the *pa*, and he asked angrily how he could depend alone on ethical precept and the administrative example of the kings of Chou. 'The understanding of these ordinary scholastics', he continued, 'does not penetrate the realities of the times. They love to praise the past and to denigrate the present, and they confuse people's ideas of appearance and reality, so that they do not appreciate what practices should be retained. How could such men be entrusted with the responsibilities of state ?'

According to the *Han-shu* the incident closed with Hsüan ti's sighs and the fears that he expressed for the future of the dynasty when the Heir Apparent should come to succeed. These details may be due to no more than the hind-sight of the compiler of the history, who was about to describe the further changes that took place in Yüan ti's reign, whereby Modernist policies were effectively replaced by those of the Reformist.

This chapter may fittingly conclude with a comment on the rise and fall of the Huo family that is ascribed to Ssu-ma Kuang.[106] That shrewd critic applauds the loyal services which Huo Kuang rendered in upholding the Han dynasty and then asks how it came about that he was unable to protect his family. The reasons are attributed partly to Huo Kuang himself and partly to Hsüan ti; for statesmen or officials who succeed in

[105] *HS* 9.1b (*HFHD*, vol. II, p. 300).

[106] *Tzu-chih-t'ung-chien*, SPTK ed., 25.9a (Peking Punctuated ed., p. 821).

grasping the control of government, which is properly an instrument that the sovereign should wield, nearly always hold on to it as long as possible. Thanks to his long monopoly of power and his establishment of private coteries, Huo Kuang excited the anger of his sovereign and the indignation of his inferiors. He was fortunate to have escaped intact before these feelings broke out in the open; and had his descendants with their arrogant and extravagant ways succeeded in doing so they would have been all the more lucky. However, Hsüan ti deserved some of the blame: he could have requited Huo Kuang's services by rewarding his descendants with limited powers and responsibilities, but instead he conferred upon them some of the highest powers of civil and military government, with the result that they became hated and feared. For these reasons it must be admitted that Hsüan ti had had a part in fostering the downfall of the Huo family; and guilty as Huo Hsien, Huo Yü, Huo Yün and Huo Shan had been, their crimes did not merit the utter ruin of the family, for which Hsüan ti's lack of human kindness was partly the cause.

CHAPTER 5

K'uang Heng and the Reform of Religious Practices – 31 BC

Panic broke out in Ch'ang-an city in the late summer of 30 BC.[1] Earlier in the year incessant rain had fallen for over thirty days in the three metropolitan districts, bringing floods in its wake. Rainfall had also been reported in nineteen other provinces, and the waters were said to be rushing down the valleys in torrents. More than 4,000 persons had lost their lives and over 83,000 buildings had been destroyed, including government offices and dwellings. The alarm spread in the capital city, defying all reason, and in the stampede people were trampling each other down in the streets. The old and infirm were crying out,[2] and the city, which housed some 80,000 inhabitants, was in a state of utter turmoil. From within the palace the Emperor summoned a conference of ministers, and Wang Feng, Marshal of State[3] and uncle of the Emperor, gave his advice. He suggested that the Empress Dowager and the Emperor, together with the other female inhabitants of the palace, should take to boats, and that officials and civilians should be told to climb the city walls so as to avoid the floods that must surely be coming.

With one exception all the officials present agreed with

---

[1] The principal references for this incident are *HS* 10.4a (*HFHD*, II, 380); *HS* 27A.22a; *HS* 27C.1.21a; and *HS* 82.1b. The second of these passages is incomplete.

[2] I have included text which is omitted in Wang Hsien-ch'ien's edition but which is included in the *Po-na* edition (82.1b).

[3] *i.e. Ta-ssu-ma*: Dubs—Commander-in-chief.

Wang Feng. The exception was Wang Shang, a northerner, recently demoted to be General of the Left. He was no relation of Wang Feng, nor of Wang Feng's sister the Empress Dowager, nor of their nephew Wang Mang, who was soon to figure in dynastic history. Wang Shang pointed out that there was no cause for panic. When floods had struck the notoriously wicked states of the past they had not submerged the city walls; Ch'ang-an at present enjoyed a peaceful administration; there had been no outbreaks of armed conflicts and the upper and lower orders of society lived together in amity. There could be no reason for floods to strike, and it was absurd to order people to clamber up the walls, thereby exciting them to even greater alarms. Wang Shang's calm words convinced the Emperor that no evasive action was necessary, and in a short space of time peace and stability were restored in the city.

The incident is perhaps slight and should not be regarded as being typical of the behaviour of Ch'ang-an's inhabitants. But, somewhat exceptionally, the histories provide a vivid and realistic account of what was happening in the city at a particular moment of time, and it is possibly of some interest to pause and take note of the attendant circumstances of the day and their implications, which concerned political change and dynastic complication, the attention paid to omens and the observance of religious rites.

Ch'eng ti was in his nineteenth year when he acceded to the throne in 33 BC. He was the son of Yüan ti (reigned 49–33) and his Empress Wang Cheng-chün, and in his youth he had shown promise of a generous and prudent disposition.[4] However, as he grew up his habits of self-indulgence dashed the hopes that his father had reposed in his character. Yüan ti thought quite seriously of replacing him as Heir Apparent by a son borne by his favourite concubine, Miss Fu, and he was only dissuaded from doing so with difficulty, as will be seen below. At a date

[4] *HS* 10.1b (*HFHD*, II, 374); *HS* 98.3a.

Table 4. Hsüan ti and the imperial succession

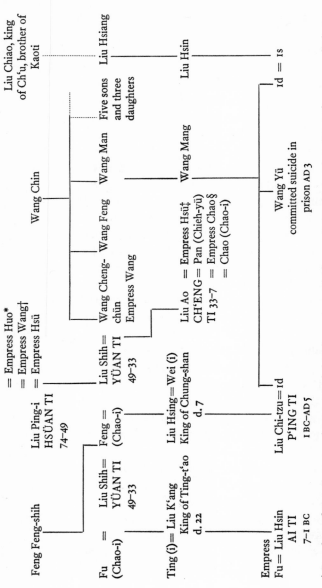

* Daughter of Huo Kuang.   † Later entitled Ch'iung-cheng T'ai hou to distinguish her from Yüan ti's empress; died 16BC.
‡ Daughter of Hsü Chia.   § Called Chao Fei-yen.

which is not known, the future Ch'eng ti had been married to a daughter of Hsü Chia, who was a cousin of Yüan ti's mother. It is stated that the match had been arranged by Yüan ti as a means of recompensing the Hsü family for the wrongs that they had suffered in the past; for Yüan ti's mother, the Empress of Hsüan ti (reigned 74–49), had been poisoned in 71 BC by a member of the Huo family in an attempt to promote their own cause.[5] At the time of his accession Ch'eng ti had not yet begotten an heir, and one of the underlying causes of dynastic disquiet during his reign was the continued failure of his consorts to bear a son, whether his favours were granted to the Empress Hsü, the concubine Pan, to Chao Fei-yen (raised to the status of Empress in 16) or to her sister the concubine Chao. Only as late as 12 and 11 BC were two sons born, and according to the *Han-shu* Ch'eng ti had these two infants put to death in order to assuage the jealousies of his favourite.[6]

Throughout Ch'eng ti's reign the Wang family formed the dominant element at court and in government offices. The Empress Dowager, who continued to take an active part in dynastic decisions until the reign of P'ing ti (from 1 BC to AD 5), exercised a strong influence over the young Emperor Ch'eng ti. One of the first acts of the reign was to appoint her brother Wang Feng to the title of Marshal of State and to invest him with powers of leadership over the secretariat (*i.e. Shang-shu*).[7] The combination of this title and those powers served to provide the Wang family with the status and security whereby their political fortunes could be founded. The days had long passed since the post of Chancellor (*ch'eng-hsiang*)[8] carried with it the highest authority and responsibilities of the realm below those of the Emperor, and the use that Wang Feng made of his position to eliminate the chances of rivalry may be

[5] *HS* 97B.1a; see Chapter 4, pp. 129f.
[6] For a summary of these events see Dubs in *HFHD*, II, 369f.
[7] Dubs—Office of the Masters of Writing.
[8] Dubs—Lieutenant Chancellor.

illustrated by a number of incidents.[9] Wang Feng held this distinctive position until 22 and was followed by no less than four members of the Wang family until the change of political balance of 7 BC.[10]

The advice tendered by Wang Feng on the occasion of the panic of 30 BC has already been mentioned. Nothing, however, is recorded of the attitude of the Chancellor of the day, K'uang Heng, and a possible reason for his silence will be suggested below. Indeed, when it finally appeared that the rumours which had given rise to such alarm were groundless, the steadfast attitude and sound advice of Wang Shang was suitably appreciated; and after a few months he was appointed to the vacant post of Chancellor from which K'uang Heng had been dismissed.[11] But K'uang Heng had been concerned with political measures during the previous two decades, and he was involved in some of the live issues of the early years of Ch'eng ti's reign. His previous career and his recorded pronouncements shed some light on the climate of opinion of the day.

Early in his life K'uang Heng had won a reputation as a scholar;[12] he had been graded in the first class in the somewhat rudimentary tests of the time; but as his answers had not corresponded with the ordinances of state he had only been appointed to a minor position in the central government.[13] Hsiao Wang-chih, a statesman of note, had done his best to bring K'uang Heng's talent to official notice; but Heng's main call to fame lay in his learning, which left Hsüan ti, the practical

[9] See Dubs in *HFHD*, II, 358f.

[10] Wang Yin, who held the position from 22 to 15; Wang Shang (15–11); Wang Ken (11–7); and Wang Mang for a short time in 7 BC.

[11] *HS* 19B.41a, b and *HS* 82.1b. K'uang Heng was dismissed on a day corresponding with 14 January 29 BC; Wang Shang's appointment was dated from 10 April.

[12] *HS* 81.1a, *et seq.*

[13] At the beginning of Ch'eng ti's reign, types of appointment sometimes depended on the grade reached in the official tests; see *HS* 81.15a, 22a.

minded Emperor of the day, somewhat unimpressed. It was only after the accession of Yüan ti, in 49 BC, that K'uang Heng came into prominence. He owed his rise partly to the recommendation of Shih Kao, a somewhat unsuccessful official who was trying to raise a following at court, and the occasion of an eclipse and earthquake[14] gave K'uang Heng an opportunity to impress Yüan ti with his qualities. In presenting his views on the contemporary scene, he pointed out that the frequent amnesties of the previous few years,[15] so far from allowing people to reform their conduct as was hoped, had failed dismally to reduce the extent of their lawlessness. He drew attention to the oppressive government practised by officials and the prevalence of crime, and he declared himself shocked by the extravagant way of life at Ch'ang-an which, as the Emperor's capital, should rather have been the scene of plain living and high thinking and a dedication to cultural pursuits. He made a plea for the removal of grasping officials and for a return to the ethical ideals of government. Pleased with the terms of his submission, Yüan ti had K'uang Heng promoted Counsellor of the Palace[16] and junior tutor of the Heir Apparent.[17]

Some of the measures that were taken during Yüan ti's reign indicate the acceptance of K'uang Heng's Reformist views. The reaction that he was voicing against an excessive degree of state interference[18] had already been expressed by Hsiao Wang-chih, and the same views were put forward more forcefully by Kung Yü. The measures included the withdrawal of the

[14] Presumably the eclipse reported for 28 March 42; *HS* 9.8b (*HFHD*, II, 321, 354) and the earthquake of 14 December 41; *HS* 9.9a (*HFHD*, II, 323).

[15] *i.e.*, 48, 47 and 46.

[16] *Kuang-lu ta-fu*: Dubs—imperial household grandee.

[17] *T'ai-tzu shao fu.*

[18] At this time the main protagonist for the Modernist view that had been accepted as a basis for state policy during Wu ti's reign was Keng Shou-ch'ang; see Swann, pp. 192f.

Han commanderies *(chün)* that had been established on Hainan Island (46 BC); the abolition of the state monopolies of salt and iron (44);[19] the abolition of the state's agencies for the control of staple goods; economies in the luxuries and entertainments of the imperial palaces (47 and 44 BC); and the distribution of material relief to the destitute.[20]

Attention has been drawn above to Yüan ti's desire to replace his heir apparent, a son of the Empress Wang, by another son, who had been born by a favourite concubine.[21] In raising objections to such an idea,[22] K'uang Heng appealed to the history of the Chou period and to the authority of the *Book of Songs* and other texts regarding the principles of true kingship. He wrote that order was attained in the world when dynastic arrangements were correctly regulated. It was essential to respect the claim of the legitimate consort and heir and to keep commoner descendants at a lower level; and it was also necessary for a ruler to sacrifice his private partialities in the interests of public morality.

Yüan ti was evidently impressed by K'uang Heng's ability and the further examples of his advice on political matters, which was based on references to classical texts and frequently mentioned the cause of law and morality. In 38 K'uang Heng reached 'ministerial rank' by appointment as Superintendent of the Palace;[23] in the next year he was promoted Imperial Counsellor;[24] and in 36 he became Chancellor, receiving the honour of a nobility at the same time.[25]

K'uang Heng was not the only official to whom the future Emperor Ch'eng ti owed his survival as Heir Apparent. Accord-

[19] These were actually restored in 41; *HS* 9.9a (*HFHD*, II, 324).

[20] *HS* 24A.20a; Swann, pp. 196f.

[21] i.e. the concubine Fu, entitled Chao-i; her son had been given the title of king of Ting-t'ao.

[22] *HS* 81.6a.

[23] *Kuang lu hsün*: Dubs—superintendent of the imperial household.

[24] *Yü-shih ta-fu*: Dubs—imperial clerk grandee.

[25] *HS* 19B.39a, b; *HS* 81.7b.

ing to another passage in the *Han-shu*,[26] so far from being able to assess the abilities of officials at this time (i.e. 38–34), Yüan ti was too ill to take any part in government. Indulging his love of music to the full, the emperor also engaged in frivolities, such as dropping bronze pellets on to drums from a height, and hoping to score a bull's-eye. The concubine Fu's son was the only other expert in this pastime who could rival his majesty's skill, and this quality excited Yüan ti's admiration of his 'talent'. Such a view provoked the scorn of Shih Tan a favourite courtier of Yüan ti who was distantly related to the imperial family. Shih Tan did not hesitate to rebuke the Emperor. 'What is usually meant by talent', he said, 'is intelligence and love of learning, familiarity with the precedent of the past and an understanding of the new, contemporary world; and the Heir Apparent is the one who is blessed with these gifts. But if you value people for their performance at stringed instruments or drums, why, then Ch'en Hui and Li Wei[27] rank more highly in the scale than K'uang Heng and should be appointed to the post of Chancellor.'

During Yüan ti's last illness (33 BC) Shih Tan again had to intervene on behalf of the Heir Apparent. Both he and his mother the Empress had been all but excluded from the Emperor's bedside, where Miss Fu and her son were in attendance. Shih Tan insisted on the right of the Heir Apparent to succeed, as the legitimate descendant of the Emperor. He said that the heir commanded the loyal support of the people; officials would refuse, to the point of death, to accept an edict ordering a change in the succession; and he himself would seek permission to die first in such a cause. By these means Yüan ti was made to realise that he was beaten, and before he died he asked Shih Tan to assist and guide the Heir Apparent in his new task.[28]

[26] *HS* 82.5a, b.   [27] Two well-known contemporary musicians.
[28] For Shih Tan and the heir apparent, see also *HS* 10.2a (*HFHD*, II, 374) and *HS* 98.3b.

At Ch'eng ti's accession (33 BC) K'uang Heng submitted a long memorial to the Throne,[29] which, if the record of the *Han-shu* is trustworthy, must surely have struck the new Emperor as being both self-satisfied and irritating. K'uang Heng devoted his efforts to warning Ch'eng ti of the dangers of a *mésalliance* and to pointing out the value of classical learning and dignified behaviour. He reminded his Emperor that he had no leisure now for amusements or indulgences, and that he should bend his will to implementing the ideals of imperial rule. He cited from the *Book of Songs* to recall the good example of King Ch'eng, of Chou, and touched on the importance of proper matrimony as being the start of procreation and the origin of happiness. Only when these matters were conducted correctly would the material world reach fulfilment and the destiny of heaven be completed. He cited Confucius' treatment of the *Songs* to show the need for rulers and their consorts so to conduct themselves that they conformed with the purposes of Heaven and Earth, and thus respectfully receive the direction of the blessed spiritual powers; only when private indulgences were discountenanced would a ruler meet the demands of the most highly respected values and act as lord of his ancestral house and shrine. K'uang Heng begged Ch'eng ti to study the examples whereby thrones had been won and lost, how government had prospered and decayed; he should beware of music and sex, surround himself with men of stern integrity, keeping away those who simply boasted sharp wits. Complete familiarity with the lessons of the six classical texts would mean that the principles of Heaven and Man would be harmonised; and that the plants and creatures of the animal world would be safely nurtured; and in particular the *Analects of Confucius* and the *Book of Filial Piety* contained the epitome of the words and actions of a holy man and must be understood thoroughly. In the final part of his submission, K'uang Heng made due reference to the personal behaviour that was required of a monarch,

[29] *HS* 81.7b.

in the interests of securing his people's awe and love and their imitation of his example.

Despite the support that K'uang Heng had given to the Wang family and his successful efforts to ensure the accession of one of their sons, his career during Ch'eng ti's reign was neither long nor easy. Possibly there is a hint of arrogance or smugness in his character which may have made him unlikable; possibly this was due to his puritanism; but his immediate difficulties lay with the person of Shih Hsien.[30] This eunuch had been one of Yüan ti's favourites. Appointed to the key position of Leader of the Secretariat he had imposed his will on the court, and officials from the Chancellor downwards had stood in fear of his authority. Shortly after Ch'eng ti's accession, K'uang Heng and a few colleagues gathered their strength together and submitted an itemised list of Shih Hsien's misdeeds, extending their charges to cover his faction. But K'uang Heng met bitter opposition, and found himself facing a counter charge that, knowing of Shih Hsien's misdemeanours previously and being himself in a position of authority, he had failed to bring them to notice, preferring to build up his own connections. Like K'uang Heng, Shih Hsien had done his best to support the cause of Ch'eng ti in the question of the succession, but K'uang Heng's charges had enough validity to bring about the dismissal of Shih Hsien's closest supporters. Shih Hsien himself was ordered to return to his native commandery of Chi-nan, but died of starvation and grief on the way.

Nevertheless the discomfiture of Shih Hsien did not serve to allay the anxieties that K'uang Heng felt for his own safety. On several occasions he offered his resignation, only to be refused; and even when his son K'uang Ch'ang had murdered a man in a fit of drunkenness and another son had tried to free him from arrest, Ch'eng ti still refused to allow their father to offer his resignation by way of expiation. Finally (29) he was dismissed from his position as Chancellor and reduced to commoner status

[30] *HS* 81.9a; *HS* 93.4b.

on the ground that he had misappropriated some territory.[31]

When, in 30 BC, the inhabitants of Ch'ang-an believed that their lives were in immediate danger and that their city would soon lie in ruins about them, there may have been some men and women who reflected on the ultimate causes of the disaster they were about to witness. And, if one may speculate for a moment, some officials may well have wondered whether the rush of mighty waters was the just recompense brought about by certain occult powers or by the souls of deceased ancestors. For some would doubtless be convinced that those powers had been slighted and angered by reforms that had been but recently introduced in the religious observances of state.

The reforms were probably of a more radical nature than has sometimes been supposed,[32] and affected the site of worship, the objective of the state cult and the manner of its service. Newly built sites of worship at which the emperor took part were substituted in place of those where his predecessors had sought to make contact with sacred powers for decades, or, in one case, for centuries. In addition there are signs of a distinct change of emphasis in the concept and object of the worship which the Emperor led; simultaneously a large number of shrines dedicated to a variety of cults were suppressed, and a simpler form of ritual was introduced for practice at the newly established places of worship. While it must remain a matter of idle speculation whether or not these changes were blamed for the floods of 30 BC, it is certain that their validity was brought into question during the next thirty years, usually when the future of the dynasty was in question. On no less than four

[31] The circumstances of this case provided valuable details regarding nobilities, their tenure of land and their definition in territorial terms.

[32] e.g. the reforms are described in *HFHD*, II, 361 simply as the 'removal of the great imperial sacrifices to the capital'. For the place of the reforms among other changes, see Fujikawa, *op. cit.*, particulary pp. 204f., 214f.

occasions between 30 BC and AD 5 the reforms were counter-manded or reintroduced, in conformity with contemporary per-suasion or expediency.

During Yüan ti's reign (49–33) the conduct of state affairs had been influenced by the presence of men such as Kung Yü, Wei Hsüan-ch'eng and K'uang Heng. Early in their careers they had been set to study some of the 'classical' texts; their frame of mind was traditionalist and they were opposed to the excesses of contemporary religious practice; and it may not be altogether misleading to describe them as protestant or puritan. Thus they were ready to break with the immediate past, to dismantle current observances and to introduce change, in the interests of maintaining what they believed to be the essential elements of service to the sacred beings; they sought support for their reforms in the practices attributed to the remote past.

The move to reform religious practice was but a single part of the major cause which came into prominence during the last fifty years of Western Han and which is associated with the *Ku-wen* school. Opponents, of the *Chin-wen* school, called on textual authority to support and regularise the contemporary practice of government; this was based on the strength of imperial authority and had evolved from the methods (*shu* and *fa*) of the Ch'in régime. The *Ku-wen* school wished to purge such contemporary practice of what they regarded as abuses, and to replace these by the immutable rules of *li*; such a code had been ascribed to the Duke of Chou.

Two examples may be cited to illustrate how the attitude of the two schools to matters of religious practice was in close parallel with their attitudes to the operation of government. Statesmen of the *Chin-wen* school such as Chu Po wished to retain the devolution of authority through a supreme official (i.e. the *ch'eng-hsiang*, chancellor) and his subordinates; the *ku-wen* school, however, (e.g. Ho Wu) preferred a traditional division of the highest responsibilities among three senior states-men, whose status and seniority were on a par, and who were traced back to the glorious days of Chou. Secondly, while the *Chin-wen* school hoped to uphold the authority of government by the current system of regional inspectors (*tz'u-shih*) the *Ku-wen* Reformists proposed to substitute for them a system of *chou* and *mu*; and these officials were similarly ascribed to the remote past.[33]

It was under the guidance of the *Ku-wen* men that reforms were introduced in the conduct of services to the imperial ancestors. In addition, in place of the worship hitherto carried out by the Emperor to the Five Powers at Yung, the Grand Unity at Kan-ch'üan and the Earth Queen at Fen-yin, the state cult was now to be concentrated in the worship of Heaven and Earth, at sites built to the south and north of Ch'ang-an city. The reforms were represented as restoring old and proper practices from which departures had been made; they were to uphold the position of the emperor and save him from unnecessary indignity and hardship; and they were to bring economies to the state and reduce the exacting contributions of the populace to the maintenance of the ceremonies. It also seems that greater attention would be paid in the new concepts than hitherto to the forces of *Yin* and *Yang*. As yet these had hardly appeared in the context of the cults of state, although they had been cited frequently enough in Han documents such as imperial edicts. By now the concept of *Yin* and *Yang* was sufficiently deep rooted to form part of the Chinese tradition. It has also been suggested, by Fujikawa, that the reforms of 32 BC mark a reaction against the influence that the magicians (*fang-shih*) had exercised in the past, particularly over Wu ti.

Before the reforms were introduced it had been the practice of Han emperors to take part in the seasonal worship of the Five Powers, and, as will be seen, this cult was conducted at Yung and had been inherited from previous dynasties. In addition Wu ti had instituted new state cults in 114–113 BC which were conducted at Kan-ch'üan and Fen-yin, respectively.

[33] For these changes, see Chapter 8.

Since the eighth century BC the dukes of Ch'in and their successors had worshipped various powers at designated sacred sites (*chih*). The powers were principally the *ti*, who included *Shang ti* the Supreme Power; the *ti* of fire (*Yen ti*); and the *ti* that were associated with the colours white, green and yellow. Of all the sites where these powers were worshipped, those of Yung came to assume the greatest importance. Yung was situated in an area that was much later to be designated as the Han metropolitan division of the *Yu-fu-feng*. This area spanned the northern and southern banks of the upper reaches of the Wei river, and included the site of the Ch'in imperial capital of Hsien-yang.[34] Yung lay to the west of the later city of Ch'ang-an; but close as it was to the Han capital, it was not particularly secure, being penetrated by patrols of the Hsiung-nu in 166.[35]

By the time of the unification (221 BC) the importance of Yung as a religious centre had grown beyond all recognition. In addition to the four sacred sites (*chih*) dedicated to the worship of four of the *ti*, there were over a hundred shrines which served powers such as the sun, moon and constellations, or the lords of the winds and the rain. Regular services were held, sometimes with blood sacrifices, and the Ch'in Emperor sometimes attended in person. The significance of Yung was enhanced by its proximity to the Emperor's seat of government and due account was taken of this situation.[36]

As part of the process of substituting his own authority for that of Ch'in, in 205 Liu Pang adopted responsibility for worshipping the four *ti* that were associated with the colours white, green, yellow and red;[37] in addition he instituted the worship of a fifth *ti*, the power of black. However, the first of the Han Emperors did not apparently attend these services in person. The first occasion when this was done occurred in 165, when Wen ti visited Yung and performed the *chiao*, or seasonal

[34] *HS* 28A.1.34a.   [35] *HS* 94A.13a.   [36] *HS* 24A.15a.
[37] *HS* 25A.17b. There do not appear to be specific references to the worship of the *ti* of Red in the pre-imperial age.

worship of the boundaries, in honour of the five *ti*.[38] Wen ti also had the worship of the five *ti* performed at new shrines which were built at Wei-yang, and attended there personally (164).[39] Ching ti carried out the rites at Yung in 144, and from 134 onwards it was intended that the Emperor should visit Yung regularly, once every three years.[40] However, according to the record, imperial visits were far from regular; they are noted for the years 123, 122, 114, 113, 110, 108, 92, 56, 44, 40 and 38.[41]

The worship to the Earth Queen (*Hou t'u*) was inaugurated in December 114. It apparently followed from Wu ti's personal suggestion and the recommendations that senior officials made at his behest to consider the matter. They proposed that five altars should be prepared, on a circular mound that lay encompassed by a lake.[42] Light brown calves together with the grand offering of one bull, one sheep and one pig were to be sacrificed at each of the altars; and once the ceremony was ended the victims were to be buried underground. Yellow was to be the dominant colour in the robes of the celebrants. Wu ti had heard that a bright effulgence had been seen descending by the Fen river, and this occurrence determined him to establish the altars on the mound at Fen-yin, in Ho-tung commandery. Wu ti's personal obeisances were of the same type as those that he offered to the Supreme Power; he and his successors returned to perform these rites at Fen-yin in 107, 105, 104, 103, 100, 61, 55, 45, 39 and 37.[43]

---

[38] *HS* 4.16a, *HFHD*, I, 258; *HS* 25A.20a.

[39] *HS* 25A.20a.   [40] *HS* 25A.21b.

[41] *HS* 6.13a; 14a; 18b; 20a; 26b; 28a and 36b (*HFHD*, II, 57, 60, 74, 76, 89, 93 and 113); *HS* 8.19a (*HFHD*, II, 248); *HS* 9.5b, 9b, and 10b (*HFHD*, II, 313, 325, and 329).

[42] *HS* 25A.26b; see also *MH* III, 475. For the concept of this divinity as female, being paired with the male divinity of Heaven, see Chavannes, 'Le T'ai Chan', *Bibliothèque d'études, Annales du Musée Guimet* (Paris, 1910, pp. 521–5), where the distinct emergence of this concept is dated in Wu ti's reign.

[43] *HS* 6.28b, 30b, 31a, 32a, 33a (*HFHD*, II, 93, 97, 98, 100, 103); *HS*

In the meantime there had been instituted a further regular act of worship on the part of the Han Emperors.[44] This was the service to *T'ai i* the Grand Unity, which was carried out for the first time, by Wu ti in person, at the winter solstice of 113. The site for this ceremony was at Kan-ch'üan, in Yün-yang prefecture, within the metropolitan division of the Tso-p'ing-i. Kan-ch'üan lay to the east of Ch'ang-an, and Wu ti had a summer palace situated there. Worship of the sun and the moon was included in the ceremonies, and the Standard Histories preserve the texts of two formal documents that date from this solemn occasion.[45] At the inaugural ceremony the Emperor was robed in yellow. Lights blazed forth in rows upon the altar and vessels were set by at the side for dressing and cooking the sacrificial victims. Officials presented the ceremonial discs of jade, and the oblation of the animals was duly performed. That night a brilliant light was observed, and when day broke a yellow cloud rose to the skies. As with the ceremonies at Yung, so at Kan-ch'üan it was envisaged that the Emperor would attend personally every second (?) year.[46] But again the observance was anything but regular, being conducted by Wu ti in 106, 100 and 88; by Hsüan ti in 61, 57, 53, 51 and 49; and by Yüan ti in 47, 45, 43, 39 and 37.[47]

A further change of religious practice under Wu ti may possibly be seen in the new emphasis placed on the worship of

---

8.15b, 19b (*HFHD*, II, 239, 250); *HS* 9.5b, 10b, 11a (*HFHD*, II, 313, 328, 330).

[44] *HS* 6.20b (*HFHD*, II, 76); *HS* 25A.33a; *MH*, III, 491.

[45] *HS* 6.20b (*HFHD*, II, 77); *HS* 25A.33a; *MH* III, 492.

[46] See *HS* 25A.33b and notes. The corresponding text of *SC* and some editions of *HS* read three rather than two years. Whatever the textual evidence, it appears from the record that at certain periods the visits were made every two rather than every three years. See also *HS* 25B.19b and notes.

[47] *HS* 6.30a, 33a, and 38b (*HFHD*, II, 96, 103, 118); *HS* 8.15b, 18b, 20b, 22a and 23b (*HFHD*, II, 239, 247, 254, 258 and 261); *HS* 9.3a, 5b, 7a, 10b, 11a (*HFHD*, II, 306, 313, 317, 328 and 330).

Huang ti, the power of Yellow, and its association with the procurement of immortality (see p. 184).

It will be noticed that a long break in continuity occurred between imperial visits to the three sites during the end of Wu ti's reign, the whole of Chao ti's reign and the first twelve years of Hsüan ti's reign.[48] The *Han-shu* observes the break and attributes it to the youth of Chao ti, who actually attained adulthood in 77, and the dictatorship of Huo Kuang during the early part of Hsüan ti's reign.[49]

As a result of K'uang Heng's influence, a major change was introduced in the seasonal worship of the bounds (*chiao*), shortly after Ch'eng ti's accession. Under the new arrangement these services were to be held no longer at Yung, Fen-yin or Kan ch'üan, but at Ch'ang-an. In addition, whereas previously the services had been directed to the Five Powers, the Earth Queen and the Grand Unity, they were now to be held in honour of Heaven (*T'ien*) and Earth (*Ti*). As will be seen from the text of the memorial attributed to him, K'uang Heng argued his case skilfully, invoking precedent from the past and reminding the palace of the real purpose that lay behind the observance of the rites at Kan-ch'üan. In addition he was shrewd enough to refrain from suggesting outright the substitution of Heaven and Earth in place of the other powers. But his memorial, and the subsequent documents, will only be understood fully if it is assumed that when the services were moved such a change would also be effected. And, as will be shown below, while veneration for Heaven and Earth was not altogether new in Han thought, active participation in sacrifices and worship by a Han emperor was an innovation. So K'uang Heng simply asked that the senior officials of the government should discuss

[48] The rites were not attended by an emperor between 92 and 56 at Yung, between 100 and 61 at Fen-yin, and between 88 and 61 at Kan-ch'üan.

[49] *HS* 25B.7a, b.

whether it was suitable to remove the services to Ch'ang-an; but it may be noted that the fifty men who supported K'uang Heng during the course of the discussion did not mention the Five Powers, the Earth Queen or the Grand Unity; they argued in terms of worshipping Heaven and Earth.

The initial memorial was presented under the names of K'uang Heng, the Chancellor, and Chang T'an the Imperial Counsellor:[50]

'In the affairs of emperors and kings, nothing is of greater moment than their acceptance of the order of Heaven, and in such a task nothing is more important than the seasonal services of worship. It is for this reason that the holy kings bent their minds and thoughts to the utmost to institute regulations for those services. They worshipped Heaven at the southern bounds of their domains, and the meaning of this lay in their attendance at the realm of *Yang*; they sacrificed with burial rites to Earth at the northern bounds, and the symbolism of this lay in their approach to the realm of *Yin*.

'Heaven's relations with its son are such that it attends the place where he has built his city to accept the offerings that are due. In the past when the Emperor Hsiao Wu resided in the palace of Kan-ch'üan, a site was dedicated in Yün-yang for the worship of the Grand Unity, and services were held south of the palace. Nowadays the imperial presence is regularly in Ch'ang-an; to carry out the worship of the boundaries to Heaven, the emperor turns north to go to the realm where *Yin* reigns supreme; and to perform the services to the Earth Queen, he turns east to the realm where *Yang's* influence is slight. In this way practice is at variance with the institutions of old.

'In addition, in his journey to Yün-yang his way passes through ravines and along a narrow passage that extends for a hundred *li*. To reach Fen-yin he crosses mighty rivers, with the danger that boat and oar may be buffeted by wind or wave, and his train consists of anything but the many carriages that befit a holy ruler. The commanderies and prefectures through which he passes put the roads in order and supply the necessary provisions, so that the officials and

[50] *HS* 25 B.11a.

the civil population suffer hardship, and the government offices are put to great trouble and inconvenience. Thus the people whom the Emperor protects are made to labour and he himself journeys through lands that are dangerous; these are difficult conditions in which to pay reverence to sacred and spiritual beings or to pray for prosperity; and they can hardly conform with the Emperor's role of receiving the order of Heaven and treating mankind as his children.

'In the past kings Wen and Wu of Chou performed the seasonal sacrifices of the bounds at Feng or Hao, and king Ch'eng did so at the town of Lo. From these examples it may be seen that Heaven accompanies the site of the King's residence to accept his offerings. It is right that the sacred site dedicated to the Grand Unity at Kan-ch'üan and the worship of the Earth Queen in Ho-tung should be removed and set up at Ch'ang-an, so as to fit with the practice of the emperors and kings of the past. We beg leave to discuss the matter with senior officials so that a decision may be reached.'

Ch'eng ti duly gave his consent. Eight officials, including Hsü Chia, the Emperor's father-in-law, believed that no change should be made in view of the long tradition behind contemporary usage. But fifty others, including Wang Shang,[51] Shih Tan[52] and Chai Fang-chin[53] supported K'uang Heng. They cited the authority of the *Li-chi*[54] 'Burning victims on brushwood at the Grand Circular Altar constitutes the worship of Heaven; the burial of sacrificial victims at the Great Rectangular Altar constitutes the worship of Earth.' They argued that the dedication of a site at the southern bounds of the city would be a means of determining the site where Heaven would respond; and the isolation of a sacrificial site at the Great

[51] i.e. General of the Left who advised the Emperor to hold fast during the panic of 30 B C. At this time (32) he still held the more senior post of General of the Right; *HS* 19B.41a and *HS* 82.1a.

[52] Rose to be Superintendent of the Lesser Treasury (Dubs—Privy Treasurer) from 14. See Chapter 8.

[53] Rose to be chancellor from 15 until his death in 7; see Chapter 8, p. 265.

[54] *Li-chi* 20, *Chi-fa*; Couvreur, *Li ki* 1913, Vol. II, p. 259.

Rectangular Altar, situated at the northern bounds, would meet the requisite site for *Yin*. They went on to observe:[55]

'The sites of the seasonal services of the bounds have in all cases been at the south and north of the holy kings' cities; as the *Book of Documents* says:[56] "On the third day, *ting-ssu*, he sacrificed victims on the suburban altar, namely two oxen". The Duke of Chou's sacrifice was a notification of his removal to a new town and his foundation of the rites for the seasonal service of the bounds.

'Kings endowed with spiritual blessings and holy rulers serve Heaven and Heaven is shown forth; they serve Earth and Earth becomes manifest; and when Heaven and Earth are clearly shown forth, the powers of the spirits are made apparent. Heaven and Earth take the one who is king to be the master, and so, when the holy kings instituted the correct procedure for the sacrifices to Heaven and Earth, they invariably arranged for this to be done at the bounds of the rulers' cities. Ch'ang-an is the residence of our holy master and lies under the observation of August Heaven. The sacrifices performed at Kan-ch'üan and in Ho-tung have not been accepted by the sacred spirits and it is right to remove them to places where *Yang* is in its regular position and where *Yin* is in full force. It is right to reject contemporary modes and to restore ancient practice; to follow the institutions of the holy kings and to determine the requisite situation of Heaven; and to follow what the procedure prescribes.'

This support encouraged K'uang Heng and Chang T'an to proceed further, and in a second submission[57] they fastened on the principle of following the views of the majority; and they did not omit to point out that the fifty men who supported them were well versed in their classical writings, while their eight opponents had no text or precedent on which to draw. K'uang Heng concluded his case by citing from the *Book of Songs*[58] and

---

[55] *HS* 25 B.12a.

[56] *Shu-ching, Shao kao*, 5; the translation of this citation is taken from Karlgren, *Book of Documents*, p. 48.   [57] *HS* 25 B.12b.

[58] *Shih-ching*, No. 288, *Ching chih* (Karlgren, *Book of Odes*, p. 249); and No. 241 *Huang i* (*Ibid.*, p. 193).

interpreting the text as favouring the establishment of the *chiao* to the south and north of Ch'ang-an. Ch'eng ti again accepted their advice.

K'uang Heng's next step was directed towards eliminating the elaborate rituals and the symbolism that had characterised the state cults hitherto.[59] He objected to features such as the brilliantly coloured altar[60] of the Grand Unity at Kan-ch'üan, whose eight corners pointed symbolically to the eight directions. He protested that he could find nothing in the past which justified the use of a highly embellished and carved altar, the interment of models of the imperial carriage with its chestnut colts, or the figurines of fine hunters. Similarly he took exception to the display of jades and the performance by the women's choir. He believed that the real significance of the burning of the woodpile[61] and the provision of sacrifices for the *ti* lay in the purification of the site, in the act of worship and in the value placed on the essential qualities of such worship.

K'uang Heng named the songs and dances that should properly be performed to await the presence of the spirits of Heaven and Earth. Calves should be used as the sacrificial victims, dried straw for matting, and earthenware or calabashes for vessels. In each case one should follow the natural order of Heaven and Earth, giving first place to sincerity and simplicity, and not daring to elaborate. K'uang Heng believed that

'the achievements and character of the spirits are of the highest order, and neither the most delicately refined objects nor a plethora of material goods are adequate to give thanks for their work; only by

[59] *HS* 25 B.13a.

[60] *Tzu-t'an.* The implications of this term are not certain. One commentator explains it as an altar constructed with the use of purple shells. See Hawkes, *Ch'u Tz'u, The Songs of the South* (Oxford, 1959), p. 39. The term is also used of altars that featured in some Taoist rites.

[61] I follow the reading of the *Po-na* edition (*HS* 25 B.12a; Wang Hsien-ch'ien edition *HS* 25 B.13b).

the utmost sincerity may they be brought nigh; and by respecting the stark essentials so may the blessed character of Heaven be illuminated. Gaily painted altars; meretricious décor; women's choirs; the imperial carriage; chestnut colts or fine hunters; the appurtenances of stone altars; none of these should be maintained.'

As the next part of his reforms[62] K'uang Heng pointed out that kings are free to establish their own forms of worship and are not obliged to continue the practices inherited from the past. This principle applied in particular to the services held hitherto at Yung, which had been instituted arbitrarily by the leaders of Ch'in; but they were not prescribed by the *li*. It would be quite improper to respect the practices that had been started indiscriminately by the *chu-hou* of the pre-Han period; and even the service at the northern site of Yung, i.e. the one initiated by Han Kao tsu to the Power of Black, should not be maintained. Ch'eng ti again accepted the advice of his Chancellor, and the shrine of Ch'en Pao[63] was included among those that were abolished. In the following year a Han emperor performed the *chiao* sacrifices at a site south of Ch'ang-an for the first time (17 February 31 BC).[64]

It will be shown below that previously, in the reign of Yüan ti, a large number of shrines dedicated to the service of the ancestral spirits of the Emperors had been suppressed. The final change which K'uang Heng and Chang T'an effected[65] was a similar suppression of a whole host of services, supported by the central government and performed in the provinces by various types of intermediary.[66] Of a total of 683 such sites, only 208 were regarded as conforming with the prescribed

---

[62] *HS* 25B.13b.

[63] *HS* 25A.4b. The worship of this deity was established by Duke Wen of Ch'in in the eighth century BC; see *MH*, III, 421; see also *HS* 25A.15a.

[64] *HS* 10.3a (*HFHD*, II, 378).

[65] *HS* 25B.14b.

[66] These are described as *hou shen, fang shih* and *shih-che*.

rites; the other 475 were abolished. Similarly of the 203 sites at Yung,[67] only fifteen, which were dedicated to the mountains, rivers and constellations, were saved from destruction. Elsewhere in the provinces there took place a wholesale abolition of sites of worship that had been established under the auspices of Kao tsu, Wen ti, Wu ti and Hsüan ti.[68]

K'uang Heng's reformation did not pass without question at the time, and when he was dismissed from his appointment as Chancellor (29) there were those who said that the changes should not have been made. What was worse, to the consternation of the Emperor, on the very day that worship was suspended to the Grand Unity at Kan-ch'üan, a violent storm destroyed the Bamboo Palace there and uprooted over a hundred well-matured stout trees that had been growing in the site dedicated to the sacrifices. Ch'eng ti consulted Liu Hsiang,[69] whose answer forms the clearest statement that survives in support of the practices which had just been abolished.[70]

'Members of a family would not willingly discontinue the services they inherit from their forebears, and it would be even less reasonable for a dynasty to give up the worship of its hallowed and precious beings at the sites of yore. Moreover at the foundation of these services at Kan-ch'üan, Fen-yin and the five dedicated sites of Yung, so far from being set up indiscriminately the shrines were only built after the spirits had made themselves felt. The rites were respected meticulously during the reigns of Wu ti and Hsüan ti and the glory of the spirits was particularly conspicuous; so the sites of worship set up by our ancestors may certainly not be removed lightly. In the

[67] There is some doubt whether this figure should be 203 or 303; see *HS* 25B.14b. notes *ad loc*. In view of the multiplicity of sites of worship at Yung, 303 is perhaps the more likely.

[68] For details of the places involved and the deities worshipped see *HS* 25B.14b.

[69] Liu Hsiang was a descendant in the fourth generation of Kao tsu's half-brother Chiao, king of Ch'u. For Liu Hsiang's career and his part in the intellectual movements of the day see *HS* 36.6a, *et seq*.

[70] *HS* 25B.15a.

case of the worship to Ch'en Pao,[71] 700 and more years have passed from the time of Wen kung of Ch'in until now. Since the foundation of the Han dynasty the spirit has paid a regular visit from one generation to the next. Its brilliant light of scarlet or yellow extends for forty or fifty feet and has come to rest by the shrine. Voices have reverberated and the fowls of the air have given tongue. Each time the spirit has appeared at Yung, the directorate of prayer[72] has offered a grand sacrifice and sent a watchman to ride post-haste to the palace, in the belief that the occurrence has been a most felicitous event. The spirit came to the shrine five times in the reign of Kao tsu, twenty-six times in that of Wen ti, seventy-five times in that of Wu ti, twenty-five times in that of Hsüan ti and twenty times since the first year of Ch'u-yüan [48 BC]. This is the traditional worship of the pulsating force of Yang.

'The rites devoted to the ancestral shrines of the Han dynasty may not be discussed without due authority;[73] for in each case they have been jointly founded by the sovereigns of the ancestral house together with their wise counsellors. There is no written authority covering the varying institutions of past and present; in the most highly respected and most important matters, heterodox usage can hardly be used as a criterion for explaining standard practice.

'A number of counsellors have succeeded one another since Kung Yü's advice was first accepted, and there are many features that have been subject to change and upheaval. The *I ta chuan*[74] says that the calamities which attend the abuse of the spirits will be visited until the third generation, and I fear that the dire effects will not stop short with Kung Yü.'

Ch'eng ti was impressed by Liu Hsiang's arguments and regretted having made the changes. In addition he still had no heir. In 14 BC he had the Empress Dowager issue an edict

---

[71] See note 63 above.

[72] *T'ai-chu*: Dubs renders *T'ai-chu ch'eng* as Assistant Grand Supplicator. See note 98 below.

[73] For the suppression of ancestral shrines at the advice of Kung Yü see p. 179.

[74] For this concept, see *Ta Tai li-chi* 80 *Pen ming* SPTK edition 13.6b.

ordering the restoration of worship[75] to the Grand Unity and the Lord of the Soil, at Kan-ch'üan and Fen-yin, respectively; and it is noteworthy that in the two subsequent changes it was again an edict of the Empress Dowager whereby practice was altered. After 14 Ch'eng ti made a habit of visiting the three sites regularly until his death, Yung in one year and the two sites of Fen-yin and Kan-ch'üan in the next.[76] The services were restored at Ch'ang-an after Ch'eng ti's death in 7;[77] and on that occasion the edict admitted frankly that the return to Yung had failed to procure an imperial heir.[78] Clearly the motive for these changes was one of expediency. In 4 BC the[79] state cults were moved once more to Kan-ch'üan and Fen-yin; but the Emperor (Ai ti) was not able to attend in person, and sent officials to act on his behalf. The final change that took place in Western Han, which brought the ceremonies back to Ch'ang-an again, resulted from a memorial which Wang Mang submitted in AD 5; his text summarises the history of religious change and stresses some of the points that have been considered above.[80]

At the same time Wang Mang proposed[81] certain changes in the ritual of the services, so that the symbolism would correspond more closely with the concepts of Heaven and Earth. His proposals concerned musical performances, sacrificial animals and the mode of venerating the sun and the moon. In a further memorial he suggested the establishment of ancillary shrines at the new sites of Ch'ang-an, to serve a whole variety

[75] *HS* 10.12a, b (*HFHD*, II, 404); and *HS* 25B.15b; the edict followed Ch'eng ti's performance of the rites at Yung. Fujikawa (pp. 219 and 235, note 7) dates the change in 16 B C.

[76] Imperial visits were paid to Yung in 14, 12, 10 and 8; and to Kan-ch'üan and Fen-yin in 13, 11, 9 and 7 (*HS* 10.12a–16a; *HFHD*, II, 404–17).

[77] *HS* 25B.18b.

[78] See also *HS* 25B.17b for the advice given to Wang Shang by Tu Yeh sometime between 14 and 11.

[79] *HS* 11.6b (*HFHD*, III, 33); and *HS* 25B.18b.

[80] *HS* 25B.19a.   [81] *HS* 25B.20a.

of deities and spirits; and by the end of his reign there was a total of 1700 sites of worship at which blood sacrifices were offered. By now the attempt to restrict the state cults solely to the worship of Heaven and Earth seems to have lost much of its original purity of purpose. However, from now on a final break had been made in the services instituted under Wu ti to *T'ai-i* and *Hou t'u* and those that had been maintained at Kan-ch'üan. During Eastern Han, the state cults were based on the reforms of 31 BC, and the *chiao* sacrifices were instituted to the south and north of Lo-yang in AD 26 and 57, respectively.[82]

It has been noted that under Yüan ti, and before the religious changes that were introduced at the suggestion of K'uang Heng, a few measures had been taken with the avowed intention of restoring ancient practice and altering recent policies. But perhaps the most striking example of the Reformist or puritan movement is seen in respect of services held to honour the imperial ancestors. Here again the reforms had been introduced in Yüan ti's reign and they had been sponsored by men whose names have already been mentioned, i.e. Kung Yü and K'uang Heng. Wei Hsüan-ch'eng was another official who was concerned with this aspect of the reforms. He had taken part in the famous discussions about the classical texts in 51 and held the posts of Superintendent of the Lesser Treasury[83] (from 48 to 43) and Imperial Counsellor (43). He rose to be Yüan ti's Chancellor in 42 and held that appointment until his death in 36.[84]

By Yüan ti's reign there had occurred an enormous proliferation of expense and effort in the cult of the imperial ancestors.[85] There were 167 shrines established for the purpose in sixty-eight provincial divisions of the Empire, and at the capital city

[82] *HHS* (tr.) 7.3a and 8.1a.
[83] *Shao-fu*: Dubs—Privy Treasurer.
[84] *HS* 19B.36b, 38a, b, 39b; and *HS* 73.8a.
[85] See Dubs in *HFHD*, II, 289f.

176 sites of worship were kept to the souls of the departed
ancestors. At each one, four daily offerings of food were made
in funerary chambers; twenty-five sacrifices were performed
annually in the main temples, including the oblation of animals;
and services were held in the side chapels at each of the four
seasons. In addition there were a further thirty sites where
reverence was paid in similar fashion to the souls of deceased
Empresses. According to the *Han-shu*[86] the total number of
meals offered annually was 24,455; the sites were guarded by
45,129 men; and the priests, cooks and musicians totalled
12,147, not counting the servicemen engaged in looking after
the sacrificial animals. Kung Yü protested[87] at the number of
these establishments and at the failure to follow ancient practice
at the provincial shrines. His strictures were but the start of a
series of submissions made by senior statesmen in response to
Yüan ti's orders for a full discussion of the subject, and in each
case they recommended drastic reductions. By *c.* 40 BC these
had been put into effect; services at almost 200 of the separate
shrines were abolished. Special treatment was reserved only
for the three most noteworthy of the Han Emperors, i.e. Kao
tsu, Wen ti and Wu ti, and services dedicated to the souls of
the Empresses were discontinued.

However, as in the case of the services to the Five Powers
and the Grand Unity the change was not accepted as permanent. When Wei Hsüan-ch'eng died in 36 BC, K'uang Heng
took his place as chief spokesman for the traditionalist point of
view. He needed considerable strength of mind to maintain his
attitude. Yüan ti lay ill; he had dreamt of spiritual beings who
had warned him of dire consequences that would follow the
abolition of so many shrines, and his fears were confirmed when
his younger brother had a dream of a similar content.[88] Yüan ti
now came to believe that he should restore the shrines; for
some time K'uang Heng was able to maintain his deep-seated
opposition to such a return to former ways, but he was not un-

[86] *HS* 73.10a.   [87] *HS* 73.10a.   [88] *HS* 73.14b.

naturally alarmed by the Emperor's continued illness. He offered prayers to the three select Emperors, asking that the consequences of abolishing so many shrines should be visited on his own person. Moreover, acting against his own principles, he felt obliged to make propitiatory statements to the shrines where services had been discontinued.[89] But there was still no improvement in the Emperor's condition, and after some time the shrines in the capital were restored, with their full quota of services as before (34). Nevertheless Yüan ti died within the year. K'uang Heng tartly pointed out that the restoration of the shrines had had little effect and had failed to procure a state of bliss, and once more he was able to have the services discontinued.[90]

In 28 BC the services were restored, at a time when the next Emperor, Ch'eng ti, was very conscious that he had no heir; but at the accession of Ai ti (7 BC) a move was made for their abolition by fifty-three officials. In a long memorial[91] Wang Shun and Liu Hsin argued that the contributions made to the dynasty by Wu ti and Hsüan ti were outstanding, and they were able to plead successfully for the retention of their worship. During P'ing ti's reign (AD 1–5) Wang Mang submitted that certain changes should be made to ensure that honours were being paid only where they were due. Each question must be judged in the full light of dynastic history, and he cited the case of the shrine to Hsüan ti's father which could not be justified, as he had never been Emperor.[92]

Once he was Emperor, Wang Mang took a number of steps in regard to the worship of ancestral spirits.[93] In AD 9 he bestowed nobilities on favoured individuals together with responsibility for making offerings to some of their ancestors.

[89] *HS* 73.14b, 15a.
[90] *HS* 9.12b (*HFHD*, II, 334); *HS* 73.16b.
[91] *HS* 73.17a.
[92] *HS* 73.20a. For this question see Fujikawa, pp. 91f.
[93] *HS* 99B.4b (*HFHD*, III, 274f.).

These included a number of heroic sovereigns known to Chinese myth, such as Yao and Shun; for Wang Mang purported to believe that the Wang family was descended from Shun. Wang Mang also established[94] a number of shrines which were dedicated to the service of the closer ancestors of his house, i.e. five to the founders of the line and four to his immediate ancestors together with their womenfolk. In the following year the Han ancestral shrines situated in the capital city were abolished.[95] But it was not until AD 20 that the order was given to build shrines to the ancestral house of Hsin, in honour of Wang Mang's own dynasty;[96] and two years later Wang Mang attended the inaugural ceremony.[97]

Heaven and Earth feature in a number of memorials or other Han documents before 31 BC. The references show an acknowledgement of their powers and of the need to venerate them, and there is some slight evidence of arrangements made for their sacrifice; but there is no evidence to show that an emperor took a personal part in worshipping Heaven and Earth.

In about 130 BC Wu ti agreed to order the directorate of prayer[98] to found services to the Grand Unity at the southeastern bounds of Ch'ang-an city. Shortly afterwards an unattributed memorial referred to the ancient practice whereby the Son of Heaven sacrificed to Heaven and Earth and the Grand Unity; and again Wu ti ordered the directorate of prayer to have services conducted. In neither of these instances is there reason to believe that the emperor took a personal part in the ceremonies. Sometime later (from 121) Shao Weng won Wu ti's favour by his claims to be able to attract the blessings

[94] *HS* 99B.5b (*HFHD*, III, 276).
[95] *HS* 99B.13b (*HFHD*, III, 303).
[96] *HS* 99C.8b (*HFHD*, III, 395).
[97] *HS* 99C.16a (*HFHD*, III, 422).
[98] A subordinate agency of the department of the *T'ai-ch'ang*; see note 72 above; *HS* 25A.23b.

of spiritual powers.[99] On his advice a terrace was constructed at Kan-ch'üan palace. Part of the structure was decorated with paintings of Heaven, Earth, the Grand Unity and other spirits, and furnishings used to make sacrifice were placed nearby so as to attract the spirits of Heaven.

Heaven and Earth are also mentioned on the occasions when services were inaugurated to other deities at Fen-yin and Kan-ch'üan. In the first instance[100] the officials who were advising about the proposed services to the Earth Queen observed that in the sacrifices to Heaven and Earth small bullocks were used as the victims. From this reference it would seem that sacrifices were already being made to those powers, but there is nothing to show that the Emperor took part, or that they ranked highly in the observances of state. On the second occasion the celebrant who formally announced the Emperor's personal participation in the service to the Grand Unity began his prayer by saying[101] 'Heaven has just bestowed the holy pledge of precious tripods on His Majesty the Emperor.' In the edict whereby the services at Kan-ch'üan were inaugurated, Wu ti referred to these and similar blessings, adding 'fearing as We do that We cannot fulfil Our duties, Our thoughts are bent on glorifying Heaven and Earth'.[102]

In 111 officials again alluded to the practices of the past, somewhat loosely.[103] Wu ti had noticed that while the popular services were accompanied by both dancing and music, there were no musical performances at the *chiao*. In reply officials said that in the past sacrifices to Heaven and Earth had always been accompanied by music. Much later (AD 5) Wang Mang cited the *Li-chi* to the effect that the Son of Heaven sacrificed

[99] *HS* 25A.24b.

[100] *HS* 25A.26b, *et seq.*; *MH* III, 475.

[101] *HS* 25A.33a; for the discovery of the tripod in 116, see *HS* 6.17b (*HFHD*, II, 71).

[102] *HS* 6.20b (*HFHD*, II, 77).

[103] *HS* 25A.34b.

to Heaven and Earth;[104] but in neither of these cases is there anything to show to what period the text is alluding.

Neither Heaven nor Earth are mentioned in the *Han-shu* in the list of deities worshipped since time everlasting at Yung. According to a fragment of the lost *Han chiu i*, which is ascribed to Wei Hung (*fl. c.* AD 25), the services held there were changed each year by rotation, in honour of Heaven, Earth and the Five Ti, respectively.[105] There is no suggestion that the Emperor took part in the sacrifices to Heaven and Earth, either in this context or in the two references for 111 BC and AD 5 just quoted.

Perhaps the greatest set of religious ceremonies in which Wu ti participated were those centring around the ascent of Mount T'ai and the performance of the *Feng* and *Shan* rites in 110.[106] The underlying motives behind these ceremonies lay in Wu ti's search for immortality, coupled with his reverence for the Power of Yellow (*Huang ti*), and in his service to the Grand Unity. The Power of Yellow was now personified, and Wu ti sacrificed at his tomb. And herein lay an anomaly, as Huang ti was conceived as an agent for attaining immortality who had done so himself and could thus make contact with the beings of the other, immortal world. Wu ti expressed surprise that, if Huang ti had indeed attained immortality by ascending to Heaven, a tomb should be preserved for his mortal remains. One of his attendants answered that at the time of his ascent his servants had buried his robes and hat. Earth was associated with these ceremonies in so far as, having completed his ascent of the mountain, Wu ti reached Liang-fu and made the requisite sacrifices to the master of the land (*ti chu*).[107]

Before considering other references to Heaven and Earth in the Western Han period it may be as well to compare these features of Wu ti's ascent of Mount T'ai with those of the

---

[104] *HS* 25B.19a.

[105] *HS* 25A.12b. The fragment is cited from the *So-yin* note to SC 28.46 (*MH*, III, 462).

[106] *HS* 25A.35a.   [107] *HS* 25A.36b.

ceremonies conducted there by Kuang Wu ti in AD 56. In neither case can a direct statement be made on the nature of the actual *Feng* and *Shan* services; for these were conducted in strictest secrecy and no account has been included in the Standard Histories or elsewhere.

Chavannes[108] traces the development of the concept of T'ai shan from a local power with limited influence to an intermediary being, who was subordinated to Heaven and through whom an emperor worshipped to Heaven. It seems that between the two ceremonies of 110 BC and AD 56 the role of T'ai shan may have developed somewhat significantly. While in 110 immortality had been the dominant motive,[109] at Kuang Wu ti's performance the emphasis was placed very distinctly on dynastic success. This may be seen from the text of a stone inscription which is preserved in the *Hou Han-shu*;[110] and the climax of the ceremonies seems to have been the declaration of achievement made by the Emperor at the summit of the mountain. The power to whom this declaration was addressed is not specified, but it seems very likely that the power of Heaven was intended. There is a distinct reference to Kuang Wu ti's acceptance of his mandate from Heaven; the notification was made by inscribing and depositing tablets made of jade. Before ascending the mountain and performing the *Feng* ceremony, the Emperor lit a pyre of brushwood, whose smoke was presumably intended to communicate with Heaven;[111] after the ceremony he conducted a service that was specifically dedicated to Heaven and which included rites with fire.[112] Later, at the *Shan* ceremony, he made sacrifice to Earth.[113] It would seem justifiable to conclude that, while there is nothing to show how far Kuang Wu ti paid reverence to Heaven or Earth at the

---

[108] *Le T'ai chan*, pp. 434f.
[109] This point is also stressed in *HHS* (tr.) 7.6b; see Chavannes, *ibid.*, pp. 160f.
[110] *HHS* (tr.) 7.9a; Chavannes, *ibid.*, pp. 308f.
[111] *HHS* (tr.) 7.10b.   [112] *HHS* (tr.) 7.11a.   [113] *HHS* (tr.) 7.12a.

Feng and *Shan* rites themselves, those powers received markedly greater attention at the ancillary ceremonies than had been the case in 110 BC.

There is a further clue that in 110 BC Heaven did not yet constitute the supreme object of imperial worship. In the ceremonies attendant on the adoption of the New Era in 104, the Emperor worshipped *Shang ti*, or the Supreme Power, whoever that may have been. Had Heaven already been accepted as the highest deity, it is unlikely that its worship would have been displaced on this important occasion.[114]

It has been suggested above that the changes that were introduced in the state cults of 31 BC marked the official adoption of the worship of Heaven and Earth in place of other deities, and that at the same time opportunity was taken to give greater emphasis to the powers of *Yin* and *Yang*. The general evidence of the edicts of the day tends to confirm the suggestion.

Tung Chung-shu (?179– ?104) is usually credited with formalizing the doctrine that the untoward phenomena that disturbed human life on earth or that appeared so dramatically in the skies were the warnings issued by Heaven of catastrophes that would follow poor government.[115] In fact the belief is mentioned some time before Tung Chung-chu's essays were completed. An edict of Wen ti which followed an eclipse that was reported for 178 BC specifically recognized the powers of Heaven in this connection: 'If the ruler of mankind lacks the requisite qualities and if his administration lacks impartiality, Heaven exposes this by means of calamities, in order to give due warning of a state of misgovernment'.[116] Later edicts which similarly reflect a belief in the powers of Heaven and Earth were again issued after the occurrence of untoward events, i.e.

---

[114] See *HS* 6.31a (*HFHD*, II, 98). For the significance of the events of 104 see Chapter 1.

[115] For a clear statement of this doctrine, see *HS* 56.3a.

[116] *HS* 4.9a (*HFHD*, I, 240).

the earthquakes of 70 and 48 BC.[117] But both here and in other edicts there is a marked absence of any compulsion to worship Heaven and Earth, and the same omission may be noted on two occasions when the Emperor wished to give thanks for incidents of a felicitous nature. In 109 the mushrooms of immortality sprouted in the inner part of the palace at Kan-ch'üan, and the edict of the day renders thanks to the Supreme *Ti*, but not to Heaven or Earth.[118] Similarly the appearance and behaviour of phoenixes and the fall of sweet dew were commemorated in an edict of 58;[119] and in response to these happy signs, worship had been renewed to the Grand Unity, the Five *Ti* and the Earth Queen; Heaven and Earth are only mentioned in the edict as the quarters whence the phenomena appeared. Similarly in the great edict issued after Wu ti's performance of the *Feng* and *Shan* sacrifices on Mount T'ai,[120] although reference is made to the gifts bestowed by Heaven and Earth there is no question of offering them worship; and in 107 BC an edict[121] refers to the imperial sacrifice made to the Earth Queen and to the appearance, but not the worship, of the spirit of the land.

In the case of *Yin* and *Yang*, the evidence of imperial edicts is even more striking. Between 178 and 30 a total of forty-six edicts referred to the appearance of phenomena or the conduct of worship. In nine of these the imbalance of *Yin* and *Yang* is mentioned as a feature or cause of disaster, and the dating of these nine indicates the development of the faith in *Yin* and *Yang* in the twenty years preceding 32 BC. Apart from the earliest of the nine edicts, which was dated in 65, the others were all issued between 48 and 35.[122] *Yin* and *Yang* are not

---

[117] *HS* 8.6b, *HS* 9.2a (*HFHD*, II, 213 and 303).
[118] *HS* 6.27a (*HFHD*, II, 91).
[119] *HS* 8.18a (*HFHD*, II, 244).
[120] *HS* 6.25b (*HFHD*, II, 88).
[121] *HS* 6.28b (*HFHD*, II, 93).
[122] i.e., 48, 47, 47, 46, 44, 42, 42 and 35; *HS* 8.12a; *HS* 9.3a, 3b, 4a, 5a, 5b, 8a, 8b and 11b (*HFHD*, II, 230, 305, 306, 309, 311, 312, 320, 321 and 332).

mentioned in the documents which inaugurated the worship of the Earth Queen and the Grand Unity in 114–13, but *Yin-yang* imagery and symbolism is seen in the arguments for the reforms of 32 and later.[123]

The religious reforms and political developments of Ch'eng ti's reign are also mentioned in the *Han-shu* in connection with strange phenomena and their interpretation. The references occur mainly in the *Wu-hsing chih* (*Han-shu*, chp. 27) which sets out to reproduce the explanations offered by Tung Chung-shu, Liu Hsiang and others for phenomena which occurred during the twelve reigns of the Han period up to Wang Mang; the chapter also notes the precedents that were recorded in the *Spring and Autumn Annals*.[124] Very often the treatment of incidents in this chapter is one of simple comparison: an occurrence is described, be it natural, freakish or catastrophic; there follows a narrative account of an historical event and the reader is left to draw his own conclusions regarding cause and effect. In five instances a deliberate association is implied in this way with the conduct of worship.

The incessant rains and landslide at Lan-t'ien of 161 BC were followed by the destruction of a large number of homes and the death of over 300 persons. The *Han-shu* observes[125] that, prior to this event, Wen ti had taken the advice of his favourite Hsin-yüan P'ing and set up shrines to the Five *ti* at Wei-yang, and he had also sacrificed there in person. The *Han-shu* goes on to record Hsin-yüan P'ing's fall from favour and the punishment of himself and his family.

In two other cases the *Han-shu* again implies that floods were a natural consequence of religious change, i.e. the floods of 39, which had been preceded by the abolition of ancestral shrines in the provinces and the floods of 30, following the move from Kan-ch'üan and Ho-tung and the suspension of

---

[123] For a vague reference to the sacrifice of animals to the spirits of *Yin* and *Yang* in the past, see *HS* 25A.24a.

[124] *HS* 27A.2a.   [125] *HS* 27A.21b, 22a.

services at Yung.[126] The remaining two cases were not concerned with the state cults.[127]

Of more immediate interest is a strange occurrence which was associated not only with the floods of 30 but also with the rise of the Wang family to political power. In all three events the power of *Yin* was conspicuously strong. A nine-year-old girl named Ch'en Ch'ih-kung was said to have made her way right into the Wei-yang palace of Ch'ang-an without being detected by the guards. The *Han-shu* comments:[128] 'The panic which overcame the population owing to the fear of floods marked the zenith of the power of *Yin*. The young girl's penetration into the halls of the palace was a symbol that, by exploiting the favours granted to a woman, the lower orders would be taking up residence in the buildings of the palace.'[129] The text then draws the attention of the reader to the rise to prominence of the Wang family which had been beginning at just this time. This again was a sign or result of the dominance of *Yin*.[130]

---

[126] *HS* 27A.22a. [127] *HS* 27B.26b. In 34 a regional inspector imposed a ban on the general erection of private sanctuaries; officials had hewn down a large pagoda tree (*huai*) at a site within his area, but the same night it raised itself on its former position. The second instance (*HS* 27C.1.22a) concerned the frightened and peculiar behaviour of the populace at a time of worship to the Queen Mother of the West. (3 BC). [128] *HS* 27C.1.21a.

[129] This phenomenon is recorded more briefly in *HS* 10.4a (*HFHD*, II, 381).

[130] See also: (i) *HS* 27A.15a. In 32 BC a fire broke out in the shrine dedicated to Hsüan ti's father (this shrine had been restored in 34, after the interruption of services six years earlier). (ii) *HS* 27B.1.26a. A popular boys' song of the Yüan ti period which referred to the overflow of spring waters was followed by the uncontrolled rise of a spring in the palace in 31. These occurrences were associated with similar events of the *Ch'un-ch'iu* period and taken as presaging the rise of *Yin* to the exclusion of *Yang*, as brought about by the Wang family. (iii) *HS* 27B.1.6a. In 32 brilliant lights were observed in the north-west, whence a typhoon arose; other climatic disturbances followed.

It begins to be comprehensible why K'uang Heng, Chancellor of the Han government, apparently voiced no opinions during the panic of 30 BC and why it was left to Wang Shang to steady the Emperor's nerves and allay the fears of the public. For K'uang Heng did not dare to speak. Recently he had been tampering with the religious practices of state, and it may be conjectured that, had he expressed a view about the floods, political detractors might have fastened upon him responsibility for exciting the wrath of the spirits and thus endangering the life of Ch'ang-an. It may be surmised that for K'uang Heng discretion lay in silence.

The end of the panic was marked by an imperial edict, issued in the ninth month (October to November) of 30 BC[131] 'The provinces of the empire have recently suffered disastrous floods and the flowing waters have brought death to persons in their thousands. Groundless rumours were rife in the capital city and men were saying that floods were drawing near. Officials and members of the public took fright, fleeing away or climbing the walls of the city.' The edict closed by ordering senior officials to conduct a commission of enquiry throughout the empire. But more than human gestures were needed for the welfare of government, and the hand of nature was soon to lend some credence to the fears expressed so forcibly.

The main problem presented by the Yellow River was that of directing the heavy press of water to the sea. If inundation of the surrounding country was to be avoided in the lower reaches, two principal channels were necessary. A major breach which occurred in one of these in 132 was not repaired until 109, when Wu ti attended personally at the work of erecting dykes.[132] It seems that the situation was improved considerably at some time between 95 and 69 by the formation of a secondary outlet as the Tun-shih ho;[133] this was of equal width and depth as the

---

[131] *HS* 10.4a (*HFHD*, II, 381).   [132] *HS* 29.6a, *et seq.*
[133] *HS* 29.13a.

main course of the river and followed the natural lie of the land. However, there were no dykes to constrain the waters, and the situation was still dangerous; some time between 69 and 66 artificial channels were dug to divert the stream.

In 39 BC the river burst its banks and the Tun-shih ho was disrupted. Early in Ch'eng ti's reign Feng Ch'ün, Commandant of Ch'ing-ho commandery, pointed out that while one channel was being forced to do duty for two, disaster could not be avoided. However, his plea to have the channels dredged before it was too late was rejected on the grounds of economy; and following the heavy rains of 30, the Yellow River duly burst its banks at Kuan-t'ao and Chin-t'i. Four prefectures were affected and 150,000 *ch'ing* of land were inundated, sometimes up to a depth of thirty feet.[134] This disaster occurred in the autumn of 29 BC; Yin Chung the Imperial Counsellor was blamed for taking ineffective action and was forced to commit suicide.

This chapter started with an account of a panic that took place in Ch'ang-an; it will close with an account of the successful action taken by Chinese officials in an emergency.[135] The situation of 29 was saved by the prompt action of Fei T'iao[136] in distributing relief in the affected areas. A fleet of 500 boats was assembled to evacuate the inhabitants and a total of 97,000 persons was moved. In addition Wang Yen-shih was appointed commissioner of the river dykes, with orders to have the breaches sealed. Bamboo canisters measuring forty feet long and nine girths[137] were filled with small stones; a boat was lashed to each side of the canister which was towed and lowered into position; and after thirty-six days the dykes were

[134] *HS* 29.14b; *HS* 10.5a (*HFHD*, II, 383).

[135] *HS* 29.14b.

[136] Fei T'iao was appointed *Ta-ssu-nung* in 42 BC (*HS* 19B.38a) and held the post until 27. He is very probably to be identified with the provisional (*shou*) *Ta-ssu-nung* T'iao who features in an undated strip found at Chü-yen (214.33A; TP 357; *Chia*, 1175a).

[137] *Wei*; it is not clear how this unit of measurement was defined at this period.

completed. To mark this successful achievement an edict ordered the regnal title to be changed for the following year to Ho-p'ing, 'Pacification of the River'. The work of the conscript labourers who had been engaged was recorded as being equivalent to six months' service away from home,[138] and Wang Yen-shih was rewarded with an official appointment, a minor nobility (i.e. that of *Kuan nei hou*) and a gift of gold. A practical measure of his achievement was shown two years later, when the damage inflicted by a further breach of the Yellow River was estimated at half the extent of that suffered in the early days of Ch'eng ti's reign.[139]

[138] I follow the interpretation of Yen Shih-ku.
[139] *HS* 29.15a.

CHAPTER 6

The Office of Music – c. 114-7 BC

It has long been recognised that the establishment of the Office of Music (*Yüeh fu*) as one of the agencies of state in Han imperial government played an important role in the development of Chinese poetry and nurtured the growth of particular genres of literature; and the precedent that was set at this time was followed at later stages of China's literary development with highly important results.[1] Less attention, however, has been paid to the work of the office in arranging musical performances, or to the circumstances in which the office was established and in which its activities were several times curtailed, prior to its eventual abolition. In addition historians have not always appreciated the connection that may be traced between the rise and fall of this office and other changes which occurred in the intellectual history of Han China.

In very general terms it may be said that the foundation of the Office of Music was one of several measures which were taken during the reign of Han Wu-ti (141–87 BC) as part of a policy of imperial expansion. Like the adoption of new observances in the religious cults of state and the Emperor's personal participation in those cults,[2] the foundation of this office was designed to provide the Han government with

---

[1] See Fang Tsu-shen, *Han shih yen-chiu* (Taipei, 1966), pp. 168f.; J. R. Hightower, *Topics in Chinese literature* (Cambridge, Mass., 1950), pp. 49f.; and J.-P. Diény, *Aux origines de la poésie classique en Chine* (*T'oung Pao*, Monographie, VI; Leiden, 1968).

[2] For the more regular attendance of emperors at these cults, beginning from 114 BC, see Chapter 5.

intellectual and spiritual authority; and it served to demonstrate that Han was acting as the dynastic successor to Ch'in. However, from *c.* 70 BC there set in a reaction against this trend which may be described as Reformist in character. Political decisions and the measures which affected intellectual developments were now directed to somewhat contrary principles, whereby Han was to be displayed as inheriting the constitutional authority and moral leadership that had been postulated of the kings of Chou. The measures taken by the Reformist statesmen of those days included important changes that were introduced in the state cults in 31 BC; simultaneously the steps taken to reduce the importance of the office of Music from about 70 BC culminated in its abolition in 7 BC just when the Reformists were achieving their final successes in other fields.

The abolition of the office was deemed necessary at this time as it was maintained that it had sponsored musical performances which had a disruptive moral effect; and it was thought necessary to concentrate attention on music of a type which was thought to be morally beneficial. At the outset of the dynasty Han had adopted many of the institutions of Ch'in, and with them Han had continued the recitation of the hymns of Ch'in in some religious practices[3]; but at the end of Western Han the Reformists hoped to purge the court of such influences and to replace them with the music that was traditionally associated with Chou.

The following passage from the *Han-shu*[4] gives the fullest account of the foundation of the office:

'After establishing his rule over the world, Kao-tsu was once passing through P'ei[5] and making merry with his former associates and old friends. Overcome by what he had drunk, he was filled with joy and then sorrow. He composed the song which is called "The winds rise" and gave orders for a choir of 120 young men from P'ei to

[3] See *HS* 22.12b, for Shu-sun T'ung's part in the adoption of Ch'in's spiritual incantations; *HS* 22.13b, for Han's use of Ch'in dances.
[4] *HS* 22.14a.   [5] Liu Pang's place of origin.

2. Recently discovered clay model of a musical performance, attended by seven spectators, and given by an orchestra of six musicians, their conductor, two dancers and four acrobats. Discovered in Chi-nan in 1969 (see note 10).

practise singing it. By the time of Hui-ti [195–188] the palace of P'ei was regarded as the original shrine[6]; the young men of the choir were trained to play wind instruments and to perform antiphonally, and there was a regular complement of 120 members. But during the reigns of Wen-ti [180–157 BC] and Ching-ti [157–141] these performances were given by the offices of ceremonial only.

When Wu-ti established ceremonies for the seasonal worship of the bounds, services were held in honour of the Grand Unity at the dedicated site that lay at Kan-ch'üan; and the Earth Queen received sacrifice at Fen-yin, on the square mound that lay within the lake.[7] It was now that the Office of Music was set up to make a collection of poems and to maintain a complement of choirs for the palace.[8] There were heard the strains of Chao, Tai, Ch'in and Ch'u. Li Yen-nien was appointed Master of Harmony, and often gave performances of the poems and of *fu* which had been composed by Ssu-ma Hsiang-ju and many others.'[9]

Although no precise date is specified for the foundation of the Office of Music, the passage associates it immediately with the establishment of religious cults of state that occurred in 114–113 BC, and the office certainly included a complement of

[6] This statement is somewhat enigmatic; see Yen Shih-ku's note for a different interpretation.

[7] For these sites and cults, see Chapter 5, pp. 166f.

[8] Alternatively 'and to collect those songs which did not circulate freely' (i.e. owing to their criticism of the Government). For the choice between these interpretations, see the notes in *HS* 22.14b ff.

[9] For other references to Li Yen-nien, see *HS* 25A.34b; 54.15a; 93.4a; 97A.13b. There is no record of this title being conferred on any other individual; I have coined the term 'master of harmony' for *Hsieh lü tu-wei* despite the usual rendering of *tu-wei* as 'commandant' (Dubs renders the expression as 'commandant of harmonies'). For Li Yen-nien's relationship to one of Wu-ti's consorts and his death during the crisis of 91–90 BC, see Chapter 2, especially pp. 53. For *fu*, see J. R. Hightower, *Topics in Chinese Literature* (Cambridge, Massachusetts, 1950), p. 26. See Y. Hervouet, *Un poète de cour sous les Han: Sseu-ma Siang-jou* (Paris, 1964), p. 63f., for the use made of Ssu-ma Hsiang-ju's compositions. As Ssu-ma Hsiang-ju died *c.* 117 BC he can hardly have been involved in producing poems specially for the ceremonies with which the Office of Music was involved.

some musicians who performed at those services.[10] Although the *Tzu-chih-t'ung-chien* enters the foundation of the office for the year 120, it seems likely that it took place some six years later;[11] and allusions to the existence of the office in the reigns of Hui-ti, Wen-ti, and Ching-ti may probably be regarded as anachronistic.[12] However, this reservation need not preclude the possibility that before the actual foundation of the office, some officials of government were already performing some of the work which was later to become its responsibility.[13]

[10] *HS* 22.35a. Considerable archaeological evidence illustrates the way in which musical performances were arranged during the Han period, but this dates mostly from Eastern Han. Figure 2 shows an exceptionally early example that has been found recently; see *Wen-wu* (1972), vol. 1, p. 82 and Plate XI; *Kaoku* (1972), vol. 1, p. 33, figure 7; *Wen-wu* (1972), vol. 5, pp. 19–23; and *Wen-hua ta ko-ming ch'i-chien ch'u-t'u wen-wu*, vol. I (Peking, 1972), p. 125.

[11] See *Tzu-chih-t'ung-chien*, 19.13b (SPTK ed.). In his note to *HS* 11.2a, Wang Hsien-ch'ien dates the foundation of the Office of Music in 120 BC, and this statement may be based on the entry of the *Tzu-chih-t'ung-chien* for that year. The entry associates the establishment of the office with the reported discovery of a Heavenly Horse which had arisen from the river Wo-wei. That event is dated variously at 120 (*HS* 22.26b), 113 (*HS* 6.19b; *HFHD* II, 75) or possibly 121 (*HS* 6.14a; *HFHD*, II, 60; in this passage the name of the river is given as Yü-wu); but there is no immediate evidence which supports Ssu-ma Kuang's tentative conclusion that the Office of Music was established at the time of the incident (see *Tzu-chih-t'ung-chien k'ao-i*, SPTK ed., 1.8a). The *Ch'ien Han-chi* does not report the foundation of the office for any of these three years in question. For the hymn on the Heavenly Horses, see p. 199 below, and A. Waley, 'The Heavenly Horses of Ferghana', *History Today*, vol. V, No. 2 (February, 1955), pp. 95f.

[12] *HS* 22.13b, reports that in 193 BC Hsia-hou K'uan, director of the Office of Music, was ordered to attend to certain musical instruments. In a somewhat shorter text, which corresponds with the passage that is cited from *HS* 22, above, the *Shih-chi* (24.6; *MH* III, 234) observes that 'during the reigns of Hui-ti, Wen-ti, and Ching-ti no additions or changes were made, and within the Office of Music there took place nothing more than the regular performances and rehearsals of old-time music'.

[13] See Fang, *ibid.*, p. 227, for the view that Wu-ti's action was not an inauguration of something new but an extension of existing practice.

The Office of Music was responsible for the collection of songs (in accordance with old tradition), the maintenance of orchestras and choirs, and for providing musical performances at certain occasions of state such as court audiences, banquets, and religious services; the office also provided martial music, in accordance with the old institutions of war. It will be seen later that, at the time of its abolition in 7 BC, the office was employing a total of 829 virtuosi to fulfil these duties. These included a formidable array of singers, instrumentalists, and craftsmen, who practised skills that had originated in all parts of the empire. While it is not possible to estimate the extent of the office's activities, the *Han-shu* fortunately carries the text of some of the songs for whose preservation the office may have been responsible. These include the seventeen-stanza hymn entitled *An-shih fang-chung*[14], and the nineteen hymns that were sung at the religious cults of state. In addition it is possible that the office had been responsible for collecting the religious hymns, military ballads, and songs which were associated with particular occasions or persons and for which entries were made in the catalogue of writings held in the imperial library of Ch'eng-ti (33–7).[15]

The *An-shih fang-chung* hymn is concerned with religious practices, ethical values, and the earthly blessings of good government. The music had been composed in the time of Kao-tsu, in the southern style of the state of Ch'u, for which he had a predilection. Originally the hymn had been called that of *Fang-chung*, and it had been renamed *An-shih* after certain changes that had been made in 193 BC.[16]

[14] *HS* 22.16a.

[15] *HS* 30.56b f. Fang (*ibid.*, p. 167) divides the material into (*a*) compositions of members of the imperial family and men of letters and (*b*) compositions of anonymous popular poets. He estimates that (*b*) amounted to four-fifths of the total, but points out that it is (*a*) that has mostly survived.

[16] *HS* 22.13b. The text is translated in *MH*, III, 605f. In a note to

The nineteen hymns reflect many aspects of contemporary belief.[17] There are general invocations to the holy spirits, whose presence on earth will assure happiness and prosperity and will eliminate calamities. There are references to music, dances, sacrifices, and other means of pleasing these spirits and persuading them to descend to the world of man. Some of the hymns were composed to commemorate conspicuous incidents which demonstrated the kind favours extended by such powers to mankind—incidents such as the discovery of the holy tripods (114 BC), the growth of the magical plant which conferred immortality[18] (109 BC), or the capture of the White Lin animal (122 BC) and the six scarlet geese (94 BC). Some of these incidents took place at sacred places which were associated with the worship of the Grand Unity, the Five Powers[19] or the Earth Queen, who are all mentioned in the invocations. At the same time there are references to Heaven and Earth, although the cults of state were not to be inaugurated in favour of these deities until 31 BC.

Other intellectual and spiritual influences to which the hymns allude include the forces of *Yin* and *Yang* and the cyclical alternation of the Five Elements; and there is a *cri de coeur* for the life of the immortals and for the joys of P'eng-lai. In two instances the *Han-shu* takes note of changes which were introduced in the text of the hymns by K'uang Heng along with the other reforms which he brought to the cults of state.[20] However, we may note one important aspect of religious activity that does not appear to be mentioned in the hymns; this is the use of intermediaries (*fang shih*) and shamans. Wu-ti had him-

---

Shih-chi, 24.6, the *So-yin* commentator mistakenly identifies the *An-shih fang-chung* hymns, allegedly in nineteen stanzas, with the nineteen stanzas which are stated to have been composed by Wu-ti (*SC, ibid.*).

[17] See *MH*, III, pp. 612f., for translations. See also Fang, *ibid.*, pp. 169f.
[18] *Chih*; see *MH*, vol. II, no. 7, p. 176.
[19] For the Five Powers, see Chapter 5, pp. 167f.
[20] See Chapter 5, pp. 170f.

self been engaged in seeking their services, but in one incident after another, which culminated in 109 BC, their claims had been shown up as bogus.[21]

Hymn No. 10 sings of the happiness attendant on the arrival of the Heavenly Horses,[22] and its composition is associated with two events. The first was the report that such a horse had emerged from the waters of the Wo-wei river in 120 BC; and the second was the acquistion of some of these animals as a result of the campaigns fought in the north-west from 104 to 101 BC. This is the only one of the nineteen hymns whose text is also carried in the *Shih-chi*,[23] and the passage there sheds some light on the contemporary attitude to music and its place in the emotions. Chi Yen, who held the post of Superintendent of the Capital,[24] protested that the song had been composed and that it had been performed in a religious context with the intention of commemorating the spectacular achievement of a reigning emperor. Not surprisingly, Wu-ti found such a criticism far from amusing; and it is said that Kung-sun Hung, the Chancellor, suggested that Chi Yen should be punished by the elimination of his family, on the grounds that he had dared to criticise a performance of a type that had been hallowed by the sage kings of old.[25]

The Office of Music is listed as one of the agencies which was

[21] The incident concerned Luan Ta and his execution for making claims that could not be substantiated; see *HS* 18.10b; 25A.27a; and *HFHD*, II, 19.

[22] See Waley, 'The Heavenly Horses of Ferghana'.

[23] *SC* 24.7.

[24] *Chung-wei*: Dubs—Commandant of the Capital. In 104 BC this title was changed to *Chih-chin-wu*.

[25] There are some difficulties about this incident, as Kung-sun Hung died in 121 (*HS* 6.14a; *HFHD*, II, 60; and *HS* 19B.18a), and his known views are such that he could have been expected to agree with Chi Yen's protest. Ssu-ma Kuang suggests that the proposal to punish Chi Yen may have emanated from elsewhere (see *Tzu-chih-t'ung-chien k'ao-i*, SPTK ed., 1.8b).

subordinated to the *Shao-fu* or lesser treasury.[26] During the Western Han period this department of state developed from being an office that was concerned with the Emperor's privy purse to become one of the two major financial organs of the Empire.[27] But simultaneously it retained responsibility for providing the imperial palace with the appurtenances of a civilized way of life and the latest luxuries that could be found to ensure the Emperor's comfort. The offices which were subordinated to the lesser treasury were charged with matters that ranged from medical attention to the upkeep of buildings, from the manufacture of textiles for the imperial robes to the supervision of the lakes in the grounds of the Shang-lin palace. Like many other subordinate agencies, the Office of Music was served originally by a complement of one director and one assistant. In 104 BC this complement was enlarged so as to comprise three assistants, and from stray references in the *Han-shu* we know the titles of two other of its members of staff.[28]

From about 70 BC there occurred a series of attempts to reduce the activities of the Office of Music, which were due both to principle and expedient. The activities of the office had become intimately associated with the court of Wu-ti, with its boasts of power, its display of imperial grandeur, and its vaunting of imperial prestige. However, these attitudes and the policies of expansion and rigorous controls with which they had been accompanied had become subject to criticism, even before the end of Wu-ti's reign (i.e. before 87 BC). During the succeeding hundred years the protests gathered momentum, so that the critics were eventually able to bring about the reversal of some of the policies that had been advocated by Wu-ti's

---

[26] *HS* 19A.15a. Dubs renders *Shao-fu* as Privy treasurer.

[27] See S. Katō, 'Kan dai ni okeru kokka zaisei to teishitsu zaisei to no kubetsu narabi ni teishitsu zaisei ippan', Shina keizai shi kōshō, *Studies in Chinese economic history*, vol. I (Tokyo, Tōyō Bunko, 1952), pp. 35f.

[28] *HS* 19A.17a; Fang, *ibid.*, 165. *HS* 59.12b mentions Ching Wu as *Yüch-fu yin chien* and Mang as *Yüeh fu yu-chiao*.

advisers. These included measures which concerned the control of the population, the aims of foreign policy, the promotion of intellectual ventures, and the nature of religious practices. In addition to reasons of principle, the Reformist critics urged a number of changes on the grounds of economy; for the extravagant foreign policy and luxurious way of life practised at Wu-ti's court had depleted the treasury somewhat drastically. The activities of the Office of Music and the type of performances that it sponsored were thus open to criticism on grounds of both theory and practice.

In 70 BC, therefore, the Office of Music was ordered to reduce the complement of its musicians; this step was but one of several measures of economy that were intended to curtail the extravagance and ostentation of the palace.[29] A subsequent reduction of the office's staff and employees which was ordered in 48 BC was likewise accompanied by measures to diminish the extravagance of the imperial banquets;[30] and it is of interest to note that this incident is mentioned in connection with I Feng, who is well known for his Reformist views in other connections.[31] Fifteen years later, when the Reformist view had gained considerable support, no less an official than the Superintendent of the Lesser Treasury himself, Shao Hsin-ch'en, proposed that some of the extravagant practices of the Office of Music should be discontinued. This too was but one of several measures designed to save expenditure, and Shao Hsin-ch'en was given due credit for his proposals.[32] In addition it was just at this juncture that another Reformist, K'uang Heng, was urging the adoption of similar changes on grounds of principle. In his proposals for the reform of the cults of state he specified a number of abuses of which the state's religion

---

[29] *HS* 8.6b; *HFHD*, II, 213.

[30] *HS* 9.2b; *HFHD*, II, 304.

[31] *HS* 75.15a.

[32] *HS* 89.13b. Shao Hsin-ch'en held the post of *Shao-fu* for two years from 33 B C.

should, in his view, be purged, including the attendance of female choirs at the services.[33]

These preliminary measures culminated some twenty-five years later in the much more drastic step of abolishing the Office of Music altogether. As will be seen below, a large number of the musicians who had been in its employ were dismissed, and the remainder, whose services were retained for certain specified purposes, were assigned to other agencies in the government.[34] This action followed a curt edict of the sixth month of 7 BC which observed that 'The sounds of Cheng are of a licentious nature; they disturb and disorder music and were left in abeyance by the sage kings. The Office of Music is to be abolished'.[35] Fortunately there is considerably greater detail in other passages of the *Shih-chi* and *Han-shu* which will be considered shortly and which bring out very clearly the ideological issues that were involved in this incident.

The abolition of the office took place at a time when a number of other changes that were also of a reformist nature were being introduced. Ai-ti had just acceded as Emperor, and his short reign was to witness critical stages in dynastic and political history.[36] In particular, the very same year saw the imposition of restrictions on landholdings and on the number of slaves who could legitimately be owned; although a call for such measures had been voiced for about one hundred years, they had never been put into practice. A further reform, in political usage, was seen this year in the removal of the privilege whereby senior officials could nominate their sons or brothers for office (*jen tzu*).[37] In addition, to reduce the extent

[33] See Chapter 5, p. 174; *HS* 25B.13a.

[34] The agencies are not specified; they may have included the office of the *T'ai-yüeh ling*, who was subordinate to the *T'ai-ch'ang* (*HS* 19A.6b).

[35] *HS* 11.2a; *HFHD*, III, 19; *HS* 19A.17a.

[36] See Chapter 8.

[37] See R. de Crespigny, 'The recruitment system of the imperial bureaucracy of the Late Han', *Chung Chi Journal*, vol. VI, No. 1 (1966), pp. 67–78, especially 68.

of imperial extravagance, the agencies which manufactured and supplied luxury textiles for the imperial wardrobes were discontinued; females kept in attendance in the palace who were aged thirty and below were dismissed from that form of service; and slaves in the employ of the palace who were aged fifty and above were given their freedom.[38] This was the year following the death of Liu Hsiang (79–8 BC); it was a time when his Reformist views regarding the validity of the Classical texts formed the intellectual aspect of changes which were being advocated and practised in politics and dynastic protocol.

Passages in the treatises on music of the *Shih-chi* and *Han-shu* help us to understand why the 'sounds of Cheng' were subject to criticism. And they show that the criticism was in line with the other opinions of the Reformist statesmen, who wished to replace the aims of Wu-ti (i.e. imperial expansion, control of the population, and the worship of certain cults that had been inherited from Ch'in) by ideals that were attributed to the kings of Chou and the Duke of Chou in particular (i.e. retrenchment rather than expansion, the reduction of controls over the populace, and the worship of Heaven and Earth).

In the introductory passage to the monograph on music, the *Shih-chi*[39] cites a saying to the effect that the tunes which accompanied the Ya and Sung poems of the *Book of Songs* lead to correct behaviour by the people; the sounds of cries and exhortations call warriors to deeds of valour; but the songs of Cheng and Wei, which derive from the *Kuo-feng* part of the *Book of Songs*, lead to licentiousness. Although no source is given for this very general saying, support for this view of the music of Cheng may be found in the *Lun-yü*.[40] For good measure the *Shih-chi* adds that the music of Cheng was promoted at a time when the principles of ordered government had been rendered nugatory or defective. Confucius himself had failed to halt the

[38] *HS* 11.3a, 3b; *HFHD*, III, 24.
[39] *SC* 24.4; *MH*, III, 232.
[40] See 'Analects', xv, x, 6, and Mencius, *Liang Hui wang*, II, i.

decline of music which had accompanied the misbehaviour of
the kings of the Spring and Autumn period and their subsequent forfeiture of independence at the hands of Ch'in; and
the description of the Second Ch'in Emperor's enjoyment of
debased music, despite Li Ssu's remonstrances, is presumably
intended as a warning of the dire effects that may result from
these indulgences. For music is an expression of the period in
which it was composed; and by insisting on the practice of a
particular type of music, so can a temporal régime demonstrate
the ideal view which it holds of the contemporary age. In the
same chapter the *Shih-chi*[41] gives unstinted praise to the
seventeen-stanza hymn whose composition was ascribed to
Wu-ti and whose preservation may have been due to the efforts
of the Office of Music.[42] These poems are lauded for their deep
allusions to the classical texts and for their literary elegance.

The greater part of the *Shih-chi*'s chapter on music consists
of a long passage that forms part of the *Li-chi*.[43] The passage
concedes that the practices of conventional behaviour (*li*) and
music may vary from one age to another and that even the
most praiseworthy of monarchs such as the 'Five Sovereigns'
or the 'Three Kings' are not obliged to follow their predecessors' examples blindly and without change. This important
principle, i.e. that the institutions of state should derive ultimately from expedient rather than from dogmatic acceptance
of past practice, is ascribed in the same chapter to the Ch'in
statesman Chao Kao in connection with the type of music in
which the Second Ch'in Emperor indulged.[44] But it is also a
view which is of far wider application and which distinguishes
those who upheld the expansionist policies of Ch'in and Wu-ti
from those statesmen who reacted against such measures. It
was the latter who suggested means of reforming current

[41] *SC* 24.6; *MH*, III, 235.   [42] See p. 197, note 16.
[43] *SC* 24.9 to 24.72; *MH*, III, 238–86; S. Couvreur, *Li Ki* (Ho kien
fou, 1913), vol. II, pp. 45f.
[44] *SC* 24.5; *MH*, III, 234.

political abuses and who believed in the fundamental and un-
changing value of the Classics, their precepts, and their
institutions.

The main lesson that is laid down in this part of the chapter[45]
concerns the differences that may be drawn between various
types of music on moral and utilitarian grounds. The value of
music, like that of the rules for conventional behaviour, lies in
the way by which it will guide the emotions correctly and lead
to a harmonious and orderly state of the world and its subsequent prosperity;[46] whereas improper music, such as the
songs of Cheng, lead to depravity and disorder. The moralist
purpose of music is emphasized in the final appreciation that is
appended at the end of the chapter and which presumably
derives from the hand of Ssu-ma Ch'ien.[47] Several scholars
have commented recently on the nature of the music of Cheng
and its contrast with traditional music owing to its irregularities
and its dependence, for effect, on excess. Cheng's music was
new rather than old; 'pop' rather than classical; and it could be
scorned as being derived from regions that lay outside the
cultural centre of Chou.[48]

At the time when this chapter of the *Shih-chi* was compiled
(i.e. before *c.* 90 BC), the Office of Music had been in existence for some twenty-five years only. As yet the policies of Wu-
ti's statesmen had been conspicuously successful, despite some
ominous military defeats of recent years; and the reaction
against those policies and all that the court of Wu-ti represented had hardly gathered strength. It is therefore not surprising that, although the *Shih-chi* carries the standard view of the
music of Cheng, it does not charge the Office of Music with
leading Wu-ti's court astray or assisting it to indulge in evil
practices by providing performances of this type of music. But

[45] *SC* 24.38, 44, 54; *MH*, III, 261, 264, 270.
[46] *SC* 24.36, 38; *MH*, III, 259, 261.
[47] *SC* 24.75; *MH*, III, 290.
[48] See Hervouet, *op. cit.*, p. 279; J.-P. Diény, *op. cit.*, pp. 17f., 28f.

by the time to which Pan Ku refers the situation was very different.

In the *fu* written in praise of the Two Capital Cities, Pan Ku pays due tribute to the place occupied by the Office of Music within the context of the cultural measures adopted by the government. The introduction to the *fu* includes the following statement:[49]

'When the Han dynasty was first founded there was no time for leisure. But by the time of Wu-ti and Hsüan-ti [74–49], the offices of ceremonial were held in high esteem and attention was paid to the promotion of literature. At the palace there was established the Gate of the Golden Steeds, where scholars would assemble, and the Tower of the Stone Conduit, where books were preserved; outside, the government promoted the activities of the Offices of Music and Harmony so as to bring to light what had been abandoned and to hold fast the threads of continuity with the past.'

There is a far fuller statement in the *Han-shu*. From the outset of its remarks about music[50] the chapter distinguishes between different types on the grounds of their effect on the emotions and on moral behaviour. The text notes[51] the rise of the music of Cheng and Wei at the time of political and moral decadence of the Spring and Autumn and Warring States periods. But the famous comment which is incorporated in the text on the soporific nature of traditional music and the excitement engendered by that of Cheng and Wei tells only too clearly why the popularity of the latter had grown during the centuries.[52]

The *Han-shu*'s main criticism of certain types of music follows the verses of the nineteen hymns which have been

[49] *Wen-hsüan*, I.1a f. (SPTK ed.).

[50] *HS* 22.7b; the text incorporates a number of passages which are also seen in the *Shih-chi* and *Li-chi*.

[51] *HS* 22.12a.

[52] *HS* 22.12b. This well-known comment also appears in *SC* 24.56; *MH*, III, 272.

discussed above.⁵³ The text reads as if it were part of a memorial which had been submitted to the throne, and it seems to refer to a practice that was contemporary with the writer. In temporal sequence this part of the text is placed between the reigns of Wu-ti and Ch'eng-ti, and it is appended to the statement that king Hsien of Ho-chien (155–129 BC) had been collecting some of the ancient and traditional music for presentation to the throne. The critic recounts the long history of various musical forms of the past, going back to the Yin dynasty, and observes the foundation and extension of that tradition. By contrast the poems and songs of 'today' have no ancestry, and there is no proper tuning in their performances. Music is presented by virtuosi of the women's quarters in the palace and by the Office of Music in the Shang-lin palace, and in all these respects the sounds of Cheng are given a wide hearing at court. This statement is supported elsewhere.⁵⁴

During the reign of Ch'eng-ti an attempt was made by P'ing Tang, who is described as counsellor and academician,⁵⁵ to recover the traditional music such as had been collected at the court of the king of Ho-chien. In making this attempt he drew attention to the cultural enrichment that derived from such music and reminded the Emperor that it had been approved by notable statesmen such as Kung-sun Hung and Tung Chung-shu, and that it had been linked with the name of Confucius. It may be noted that Kung-sun Hung and Tung Chung-shu were two of the earliest writers to criticise the highly practical measures of Wu-ti's expansionist government. P'ing Tang was trying to reinstitute older forms of music in place of the forms that were being currently practised by the Office of Music and which were characterised by the 'sounds of Cheng'. In making

⁵³ *HS* 22.33a.
⁵⁴ See Fang, *ibid.*, 167, for the revival of the 'harmonies' under Hsüan-ti and the popularity of the music of Cheng during the reign of Ch'eng-ti (*HS* 64B.8b).
⁵⁵ i.e. *ta-fu po-shih*; *HS* 22.34a. (Dubs—grandee, erudit).

this attempt he was deliberately associating the different types of music with the different attitudes to government.

At the time P'ing Tang's attempt met with no response. The music of Cheng was very popular at the court of Ch'eng-ti and some of its performers had achieved a considerable notoriety. The *Han-shu* writes[56] that the resulting extravagance and licentiousness were excessive, and such that the ruler of mankind himself became involved in making a bid for the services of some of the performers. But matters changed on Ch'eng-ti's death in 7 BC. Even before his accession (in the fourth month of 7 BC) the new emperor had thought contemporary practice unseemly; but it must also be added that he allegedly had no ear for music. Within two months he had issued the edict abolishing the Office of Music in the circumstances which have already been described. The edict coupled the popularity of the music of Cheng and Wei with the extravagance of the times, and observed that the two tendencies would lead to the poverty of the state and the depravity of daily life. The edict noted the difficulty experienced in maintaining the integrity and self-sufficiency of the populace if the source of corruption was not stemmed; and after citing Confucius' injunction to abandon the depraved music of Cheng, the edict ordered the abolition of the office. At the same time it provided for the retention, under the auspices of other offices of state, of facilities for the performance of music at the religious services of the bounds; of the martial music of the traditional instututions of war; and of such music as existed within the canonical tradition and which was not identified with the sounds of Cheng and Wei.

The distinction drawn between different types of music on ethical grounds is paralleled by a distinction drawn by Yang Hsiung (53 BC–AD 18) between different types of poetry; and Yang Hsiung was one of the reformer thinkers protesting against current extravagances at this time.[57] Ai-ti's edict was followed by the submission of a long and detailed memorial by

[56] *HS* 22.34b.   [57] *HS* 30.59a.

K'ung Kuang and Ho Wu. Of these two senior statesmen, K'ung Kuang had been appointed Chancellor on the very day of the former Emperor's death, and Ho Wu, who had held the post of Imperial Counsellor had recently been given the title of *Ta-ssu-k'ung*.[58] The two statesmen were concerned with deciding which members of the office's staff should be dismissed and which should be retained for the purposes which had been specified. They suggested that of the total of 829 members, the services of 388 should be retained, while those of 441 members, whose performances and skills did not accord with canonical institutions or which were concerned with the music of Cheng and Wei, should be discontinued.

This proposal was accepted; the musicians who were kept on the strength of government, albeit in other offices, included the sixty-two who played at the seasonal services of the bounds; an orchestra of 128 who were paraded at the palace during audiences of state; and a number of other specialists or solo performers on various named instruments. All but one of the four teams, totalling sixty-two members, who played the music of Cheng were dismissed; the exception being the single member who also played old-style music; and many other musicians who were associated with the music of Cheng and with other local traditions were included among those who were declared redundant.[59]

The final passage in the *Han-shu*'s treatise on music[60] spells out without equivocation the principles that were involved in the abolition of the Office of Music. The passage concerns 'the present time', i.e. the time in which the authors lived, after the restoration of the Han dynasty; by then a new beginning had

[58] Dubs renders *Yü-shih ta-fu* 'Imperial Counsellor' as 'Imperial Clerk Grandee'. For the significance of the change of title to *Ta-ssu-k'ung* and for Ho Wu and K'ung Kuang see Chapter 8.

[59] For the full list, which still awaits critical examination, see *HS* 22.35a.

[60] *HS*, 22.37a.

been made and the population had returned to their proper basic occupations and way of life after the disturbances of civil war. It was claimed that material prosperity and moral standards were being evidenced in the growth of the population and the reduction of punishments, and cultural standards were being improved in respect of schooling, the rules of behaviour, and the performance of music. These blessings were due to the existence of a heritage of past tradition and the models that it provided. As Confucius had said, history showed how succeeding dynasties, such as the Yin and the Chou, had accepted and adapted the institutions of their predecessors; and in so far as Han had acted as the successor of Chou, it had been a matter of profound regret, as had been expressed by men such as Chia I, Tung Chung-shu, Wang Chi,[61] and Liu Hsiang, that so long a time had elapsed before the dynasty had been able to establish the correct forms of behaviour and music.

However marked the evolutionary changes of the succeeding centuries have been, these principles have persisted throughout China's cultural history. One of the clearest statements to this effect, which was destined to affect the course of Chinese education for generations, may be seen in Chu Hsi's introduction to the *Book of Songs*, where he writes of the relationship between ethical values, political success, and the various types of poetry that are included in that collection.

---

[61] For Wang Chi, see *HS* 72.3a. His Reformist attitude was expressed in protests against the type of government practised under Hsüan-ti, which was based on expedient and legal sanction rather than on principle and ethic. He called for the abolition of the *jen-tzu* privilege, and of state games, the reduction of the Office of Music and the abolition of the agencies which provided luxuries for the use of the palace. See Chapter 4, p. 140.

CHAPTER 7

The Punishment of Chih-chih – 36 BC

In 36 BC a comparatively junior official named Ch'en T'ang executed a bold stroke of action such as had rarely been seen in Chinese military history. He was serving on the north-west frontier in a military capacity; and leading a force of men drawn mostly from the communities of central Asia, together with some Chinese farm settlers, he marched deep into the far west and laid siege to the headquarters of Chih-chih. Chih-chih was one of the two principal leaders of the Hsiung-nu, and whereas his rival had succeeded in gaining acceptance at the court of Ch'ang-an, Chih-chih's overtures had been rejected; as a result he had turned for sympathy, refuge and support to Sogdiana (K'ang-chü). In these remote regions he established his headquarters, and he forged a matrimonial alliance with the king, whose ambitions of winning suzerainty over the states of central Asia found a ready sympathy in Chih-chih's bitterness against the Han court. From this position of strength, and thanks to the long distance which separated him from the seat of Chinese government, Chih-chih was able to interfere with Han activities, to the point of capturing or killing Han envoys by the hundred;[1] and the extent of his activities became known,

---

[1] *HS* 70.11a. This figure need not necessarily be regarded as excessive, as the 'envoys' should be taken as including all members of the diplomatic and trading missions sent out by the government. According to *SC* 123.24, 25 as early as *c.* 111 BC up to ten caravans set out to the west annually, sometimes being manned by hundreds of men.

above all, to officers such as Ch'en T'ang, who were serving
in the north-west. After a siege and fight which was sufficiently
bold to stir the imagination of contemporary artists, Ch'en
T'ang succeeded in defeating his enemy; and in the course of
the battle Chih-chih was slain.

So ended a somewhat difficult situation in Chinese relations
with the Hsiung-nu and the states of central Asia; and had the
prevailing feeling at the court of Ch'ang-an been somewhat
different, it might have been possible for the Chinese government to exploit this success and to establish a newer and
stronger form of Chinese influence in those regions. However,
other views prevailed in the offices of Chinese government; and
those statesmen who were basically opposed to a policy of
Chinese involvement in Asia were able to point to the circumstances in which the action had been taken so as to prejudice
the cordiality of the reception extended to Ch'en T'ang on his
return. For in order to proceed with his plan, he had had to
issue orders which would authorise the call-up of certain
forces; and, realising that such documents would never be
forthcoming from the central government, he had acted
entirely on his own initiative and had drawn up the imperial
edict that he required. In this measure, and in subsequently
passing off the edict as if he had received it from Ch'ang-an,
Ch'en T'ang had eventually secured the co-operation of Kan
Yen-shou, Protector General of the West.

Thus, while the unquestioned success of Ch'en T'ang's
military action warranted his treatment as a hero, it could
equally be held by some that his initiative had been criminal and
that he deserved to face legal processes. After considerable
discussion, Ch'en T'ang was pardoned for his misuse of authority and rewarded for his success, and after a somewhat che-
quered career he died peacefully in Ch'ang-an.

Ch'en T'ang's action stimulated argument over the major
principles of Han foreign policy towards central Asia; and in
order to understand these issues it is necessary to review the

course of Chinese expansion there during the Han dynasty. From *c.* 110 to *c.* 65 BC Chinese policy had been expansionist, militarist and even aggressive; from *c.* 65 to *c.* 40 it was characterised by the attention paid to colonial activity and the establishment of sponsored farms; and from *c.* 40 onwards it was marked by an avoidance of involvement and by a preference for keeping Chinese servicemen and civilians free from burdens, expense or danger. This final attitude lay behind the policy to be adopted by the first of the emperors of Eastern Han. Very much the same stages may be traced in Chinese relations with the Hsiung-nu. However, in view of the grave danger with which those peoples could confront and invade China, the Han governments were ready to take precautionary measures or even positive steps to check their energies more forcefully than was necessary with other peoples of central Asia.

These changes, which may be traced in a series of diplomatic and military moves, show the transition from Modernist to Reformist policies; and as in other matters of policy the principles at stake and the main arguments that were put forward are clearly discerned in the *Yen-t'ieh lun*. In so far as that document may be regarded as an accurate record of the debate held in 81 BC, it must be considered as a review of policy which was undertaken at a time when some statesmen were only too well aware of the need to defend Chinese integrity against the Hsiung-nu. Thus in some passages of the debate the speakers advocated Han initiative and even aggression in central Asia, as forming an essential element in China's protection.[2] Elsewhere statesmen saw the necessity of separating the various peoples who could threaten China most effectively, and referred to the value of the commanderies of the north-west in so far as they split the Hsiung-nu from the Ch'iang-tribes.[3] In addition one speaker expressed the belief, or hope, that China would benefit by promoting trade with the states of central

[2] See the speech of the Counsellor (*ta-fu*) in *YTL* 44 (291).
[3] See the speech of the Counsellor in *YTL* 46 (297).

Asia.[4] But spokesmen for the Reformist point of view believed that the very large expense and effort of mounting Chinese initiative and launching military campaigns in the far west could not possibly be repaid by any benefits that would accrue; and that the only goods which would be forthcoming from such trade would be the few baubles and luxuries that were used in the palace.[5] In addition they argued that it was virtually impossible to inflict real harm on an enemy such as the Hsiung-nu by military means. For while those peoples were free to move around at will in very large areas, to engage them by military expeditions would be like 'fishing in the Yangtse River or the Ocean without nets'.[6]

The reign of Hsüan ti (74–49 BC) witnessed the last stages of one and the initial stages of another policy. The transition to colonial in place of military measures marks a more sophisticated approach to foreign relations and a more expert appreciation of the practical issues of the day. For it had been realised that the use of military force alone against a highly mobile opponent would be frustrating and ineffective, and its results could not be long-lasting.[7] Instead it was hoped to establish Chinese influence on a permanent footing, to co-ordinate the diplomatic and commercial activities of the Chinese explorers and to implant a more solid type of Han prestige among the communities of central Asia.

It was comparatively late in Wu ti's reign that the Government was able to turn its attention to central Asia. So far as foreign

---

[4] See the speech of the Counsellor in *YTL* 2 (12).

[5] See the speeches of the man of learning (*wen-hsüeh*) in *YTL* 2 (12–3) and *YTL* 46 (298).

[6] See the speech of the man of learning in *YTL* 46 (297).

[7] This principle had in fact been realised, but not adopted, at an earlier stage. See, e.g. the memorial submitted by Sang Hung-yang urging the establishment of colonies at Lun-t'ai (south-east of Ku-cha) in *HS* 96B.15b, *et seq.*

and military affairs had been concerned, the prime pre-
occupation of government hitherto had been to provide security from the potential enemies of the north; and the campaigns
which had been initiated for this purpose since *c.* 133 BC were
brought to a successful conclusion in 119.[8] Thereafter it became
necessary to refrain from any ventures which would demand
the expenditure of labour, resources or money, and it was not
until 112 that the Han armies could again take the field. For the
next few years they were engaged in campaigns in the north-
east and the south, and the successful results of Chinese initiative resulted in the establishment of ten new commanderies
between 112 and 108.

Since about 125 BC, however, Chang Ch'ien and other
travellers had been telling exciting tales about central Asia;
and their stories had concerned the strength and riches of those
areas and the value of trading with communities such as Ta-
yüan (Ferghana), Wu-sun and K'ang-chü.[9] However, it was
not until *c.* 110 that the Han Government felt able to turn its
attention directly to those communities. This was the year
following the victory parade and display of force in the north,
and in which a series of religious observances had been held at
Mount T'ai and elsewhere within Chinese home territory.
From now until *c.* 65 Han statesmen, soldiers and diplomats were
engaged in taking the initiative so as to foster relationships with
the peoples of central Asia and establish Han prestige in a
position of dominance over the Hsiung-nu. Their action concerned states such as Wu-sun, Chü-shih (Turfan), Ta-yüan and
So-chü (Yarkand). They wished to win and retain the friendship of such states and to benefit from their control over the

---

[8] See Chang Chun-shu, 'Military aspects of Han Wu-ti's northern and
north-western campaigns' (*Harvard Journal of Asiatic Studies*, vol. 26,
1965–6, pp. 148f.); and Loewe, 'The campaigns of Han Wu-ti', in a
forthcoming volume to be entitled *Chinese Ways in Warfare* (Harvard
University Press).

[9] *HS* 61.3a, 7a; *HS* 96A.37b; *HS* 96B.2b.

oases of the desert; they also wished to deny to the Hsiung-nu the services which those states could render as allies and guides. Han statesmen, or some of them at least, wished to secure certain unique products of the north such as horses and perhaps furs and woollens; they may also have wished to satisfy certain religious impulses.[10]

By about 110 BC the leaders of Wu-sun, a community situated in the valley of the I-li River, had realised the need to come to terms with both Han and the Hsiung-nu. For although the latter had been effectively deterred from invading China, they were still strong enough to threaten and overpower some of the smaller communities of central Asia. Wu-sun took the initiative in asking Han for the hand of a princess, whose marriage to their leader would set the seal on an alliance and would demonstrate to other parties that Wu-sun could rely on the support and friendship of the Han Empire. The Chinese statesmen were attracted by the idea of having an ally at the far end of the trade routes which were then being developed, and they may have looked upon the offer as an opportunity to promote trading ventures. In the very formal exchange which took place with Wu-sun, the Chinese received 1,000 head of horse; and in return they sent Wu-sun a princess of the imperial blood with a full retinue of attendants and imperial equipages, and a lavish supply of gifts. Not to be outdone, the Hsiung-nu simultaneously sent a girl to be a consort to the leader of Wu-sun.[11]

These moves were essentially diplomatic by nature and commercial by motive; but they were accompanied by military or administrative measures in which the Han Government took the initiative so as to expand its influence in central Asia. General Chao P'o-nu succeeded in defeating Chü-shih (Turfan) and capturing the king of Lou-lan, and for this display of force and its effect on the lesser communities he was rewarded with

[10] See Waley in *History Today* (February, 1955), pp. 95f.
[11] *HS* 96B.1a, *et seq.*

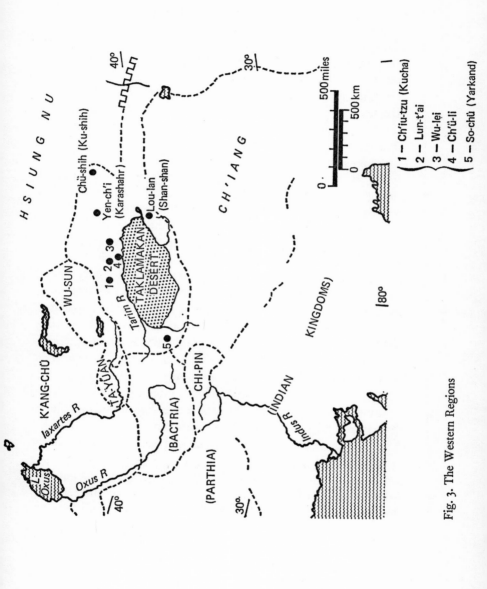

Fig. 3. The Western Regions

1 — Ch'iu-tzu (Kucha)
2 — Lun-t'ai
3 — Wu-lei
4 — Ch'ü-li
5 — So-chü (Yarkand)

a nobility (108 BC).[12] By now the 'Silk Roads' were becoming securely established. Government officials were posted at a whole series of stations, which were defended by Chinese garrison troops and which stretched as far west as the Jade Gate (Tun-huang). Trading caravans, sponsored by the Chinese government, took the arduous roads as far as Tun-huang, and thereafter left the protection of Han troops as they plied their way further west; and by 104 the two new commanderies of Chiu-ch'üan and Chang-i were founded so as to consolidate the Chinese administration of the area.[13]

In the same year the Chinese government despatched Li Kuang-li on a campaign against Ta-yüan.[14] The expedition marked the highest point reached in Chinese ambitions so far, in view of the very large numbers of the forces who were engaged, the distance at which their objective lay from China, and the concept of the enterprise. In the event the Chinese casualties were enormous; the campaign lasted for four years, allowing for the commanding general to return to Tun-huang and set out again for a further attempt. Finally Li Kuang-li had succeeded in imposing Chinese will on Ta-yüan, whose king had been put to death. A Chinese nominee was declared King; a few of the finest horses and over 3,000 of the lesser breeds were sent back to China, and peace was declared.

By these means the Chinese had embarked on imperialist ventures; and they had also entered into obligations from which they were going to find it difficult or even impossible to withdraw. By striking deep into Asia and seeking to establish

[12] *HS* 17.11a and *HS* 96A.11b. This was the nobility of Cho-yeh. He had previously held the title of noble of Tsung-p'iao, but he had forfeited this honour in 112 BC, along with many other holders of nobilities (*HFHD*, vol. II, pp. 126f.). For the identification of Ku-shih with Chü-shih, see *HS* 96A.7a note.

[13] These were later extended by the foundation of Tun-huang commandery (after 104 BC and before 91) and Wu-wei commandery (between 81 BC and 67); see *RHA*, vol. I, pp. 59f.

[14] *HS* 61.9b; *HS* 96A.37a.

Chinese power as against that of the Hsiung-nu, the Chinese laid upon themselves a duty of no mean extent; for if they failed to maintain their prestige, they would pay the price of weakness and invite the Hsiung-nu to threaten Chinese territory once again. In addition there were further complications of a different and exacting nature which applied to China's relations with Wu-sun. For so long as Han's relations with another party depended solely on military force, Han accepted no obligations; but once these relations had been strengthened or sealed by the despatch of a princess or by the acceptance of foreign hostages in Ch'ang-an, there arose mutual obligations of good faith and protection. The Emperor of China could not abandon an imperial princess to a fate which might be considerably worse than death; Han was therefore unable to withdraw from an alliance which had been contracted and reinforced in this way. Indeed, Han could on occasion feel obliged to support Wu-sun against an enemy, if only to protect her own interests there; and Wu-sun, or certain other parties, were not above exploiting such a situation so as to demand Chinese military help. Moreover, Han was subject to ethical pressure; the government was bound by the principle that once a promise had been made to a foreigner, Han would not sever relations simply for reasons of expediency. For these reasons, in the following decades it was not always possible for Han to extricate itself from an involvement as easily or as quickly as some of its statesmen might have wished.

Some years passed after Li Kuang-li's expedition before a Chinese government felt able to take the initiative again. When it did so, it was in an attempt to reinforce Chinese prestige and to strengthen the Chinese position in the west. But instead of using large bodies of troops such as had been assembled from all parts of the Empire for the campaigns of 104 to 101 BC, the government began to be more sparing and to rely on a more effective and direct use of smaller bodies of picked men; at the same time Chinese commanders were calling on men from the non-assimilated communities of the north-west in greater measure than hitherto. By these means the Chinese maintained a policy of expansion and even aggression in their relations with Chü-shih (Turfan), Lou-lan (also called Shan-shan), Ch'iu-tzu (Ku-cha), Wu-sun, So-chü (Yarkand) and the Ch'iang tribes.

In 99 there was a slight and unsuccessful attempt to attack Chü-shih; ten years later the Chinese induced the troops of six other states in the west to renew the offensive, and this resulted in the surrender of the king of Chü-shih to Han (89).[15] Sometime during Chao ti's reign, the Chinese Princess who had been married into the ruling family of Wu-sun reported that the Hsiung-nu were colonising Chü-shih, and planning to attack Wu-sun with its help.[16] A Han decision to launch a counter attack on the Hsiung-nu was deferred owing to Chao ti's death in 74, but shortly after Hsüan ti's accession a large punitive expedition was despatched, under the command of five generals (71). Whether or not the despatch of force at this juncture suited Han policy, the government had no option, for it had become necessary to do so in order to protect the person of an imperial princess who had appealed for help. At the same time the services of an officer named Ch'ang Hui, who held the rank of colonel, were lent to Wu-sun.[17] Thanks to his part in the splendid results achieved by the forces of Wu-sun against the Hsiung-nu, Ch'ang Hui was rewarded with a nobility (70);[18] the colonists of the Hsiung-nu were expelled from Chü-shih; and after a further setback in 68 BC Chinese influence was re-instated. On that occasion the forces included a majority of

[15] *HS* 96B.29b. The venture of 89 took place as a by-product of Ma T'ung's attack on the Hsiung-nu. For Ma T'ung, see Chapter 2, pp. 43f.

[16] *HS* 96B.5a.

[17] *HS* 8.5b (*HFHD*, vol. II, p. 211); *HS* 70.3a; *HS* 94A.29b; *HS* 96B.5b. For the relative seniority and appointment of generals and colonels, see the Appendix p. 313, and *RHA*, vol. I, pp. 74f.

[18] *HS* 17.28b.

men from the local communities, with a mere handful of Chinese.[19] The commanding officer of the force was one Cheng Chi, whose name will recur later in this story. At this juncture he was promoted to the rank of Guards' Major, with orders to protect the more southerly of the two routes that led west, i.e. the one which lay by Shan-shan.[20]

Shan-shan was the name which the Chinese obliged the state of Lou-lan to assume in 77 BC. From about 100 BC Lou-lan had been prepared to act for the Han court in supplying information about the movements of the Hsiung-nu.[21] Hostages from Lou-lan were lodged in Ch'ang-an as an earnest of Lou-lan's good intentions, and on the death of the king in 92 the Han government was able to control the succession to its own satisfaction. Thereafter, however, Lou-lan's attitude became somewhat ambivalent. The strength of the state lay in the commanding position that it occupied on the Silk Road; it could provide or deny essentials such as water and supplies and the services of guides and escorts, and by exercising such powers the state could make or break the success of Chinese trading missions. Sometimes Lou-lan acted in favour of Han, sometimes in favour of the Hsiung-nu; and in 77 a Chinese officer named Fu Chieh-tzu went out to upbraid Lou-lan, and also Ch'iu-tzu, for providing these facilities for the Hsiung-nu. Fu Chieh-tzu had suggested to Huo Kuang that he should look for an opportunity to have the king of Lou-lan put to death; and with the help of a handful of bold followers he succeeded in doing so, having first got the king drunk at a banquet. Huo Kuang and the government approved these actions, as was signified by the bestowal of a nobility on Fu Chieh-tzu, when he had safely despatched the king's head to Ch'ang-an.[22] It

---

[19] *HS* 96B.30b specifies over 10,000 men from the walled towns of the localities and 1,500 Chinese agriculturalists.

[20] *HS* 70.4a.   [21] *HS* 96A.12b, *et seq.*

[22] *HS* 70.1a, *et seq.*; *HS* 96A.13a; see also Chü-yen strip 303.8 (*RHA*, vol. I, p. 66).

was at this juncture that the Chinese consolidated their position of dominance by changing the name of the state to Shan-shan and providing the new king with the title and insignia of a Chinese office.

Huo Kuang's willingness to take the initiative is also seen in connection with Wu-huan, a people who operated on the north-eastern side of China's borders.[23] As in the west, there was no particular advantage to be gained by the Chinese in occupying the areas where these nomads roamed, but it was necessary to prevent the Hsiung-nu from gaining control and proceeding thence to harass the farms and cities of China. When Huo Kuang learnt (78) that the Hsiung-nu were about to attack Wu-huan, he consulted two senior officers, Chao Ch'ung-kuo, who was later to take a leading part in the campaigns against the Ch'iang tribes,[24] and Fan Ming-yu, his own son-in-law.[25] Chao Ch'ung-kuo advised that no attack was necessary, in the belief that the barbarians should be left to wear one another out by fighting and thus free China from the danger of raids. As in later years, Chao was anxious to reduce the strain on Chinese soldiers and to find a better way of settling border problems than the despatch of Han armies. However, Huo Kuang accepted the advice tendered by Fan Ming-yu, which was to attack; and that officer was despatched with orders to cross the Liao River, with a force of 20,000 cavalry. His appearance was sufficient to induce the Hsiung-nu to withdraw, and, acting under Huo Kuang's orders to bring back some material benefit from the campaign, Fan Ming-yu used his forces to defeat the Wu-huan, who were already suffering from the attacks of the Hsiung-nu. For these successes he was given a nobility.

From this point onwards a change may be discerned in the out-look of the Han government; there are signs of misgivings about an expansionist policy, and, indeed, opinion had already

[23] *HS* 7.8a (*HFHD*, vol. II, pp. 168–9); *HS* 94A.28b.
[24] See p. 224 below.   [25] See Chapter 4, p. 117.

been divided regarding Han's relations with Ch'iu-tzu.[26] As
has been mentioned (see p. 220) in 71 BC Ch'ang Hui had successfully mobilised Wu-sun's help against the Hsiung-nu; and he
then asked permission to attack Ch'iu-tzu, on the grounds that
that state had contrived the death of a Chinese envoy. Although
Hsüan ti refused his approval, Huo Kuang hinted to Ch'ang
Hui that he should take whatever action the situation required;
and with a force of 500 officers, Ch'ang Hui collected some
47,000 men from the states of the western regions and delivered
his attack, successfully. Huo Kuang's approval at this time of a
positive policy which was based on principles of expediency
may be compared with his consent to Fu Chieh-tzu's under-
hand plot to have the king of Lou-lan slain six years earlier.[27]
But his attitude forms a sharp contrast with the sentiment of an
imperial edict that was proclaimed two years later (69). Here
the Emperor harked back to the more noble motives of earlier
idealised sovereigns, writing 'We are informed that Yao loved
the nine clans and thereby brought harmony to the imperial
states of the world. . .'.[28]

The question of Han's relations with Wu-sun came to a head
in 64 BC, when a request was sent for the hand of another
princess; on this occasion some reluctance was voiced against
accepting further involvement in central Asia.[29] This was the
opinion of Hsiao Wang-chih, superintendent of state visits, who
stressed the distance which separated Wu-sun from China and
the practical difficulties of maintaining a secure relationship in
such circumstances. However, these warnings were ignored
for the moment, although they were to gain some acceptance
at a later stage of Han history. The preparations made for the
despatch of a princess included the detachment of over 100
attendants to study the language of Wu-sun, and eventually the
party set out on their way, after a display of wrestling and
musical entertainment. But internal troubles soon broke out in

[26] *HS* 70.3a.   [27] *HS* 70.1a, *et seq.*
[28] *HS* 8.7a (*HFHD*, vol. II, p. 215).   [29] *HS* 96B.6a.

Wu-sun, and the project was cancelled. Hsiao Wang-chih was able to point to the unreliability of the men of Wu-sun and to the failure of matrimonial ties that were of forty years standing and which were now about to be renewed.

At much the same time Chinese action in So-chü (65) was characterised by determination and vigour; but this was due to the initiative of a single officer rather than the central government. On the death of the king, one of the sons of the Chinese princess of Wu-sun had been put on the throne of So-chü. The new king had been living in China, and his accession was brought about with Han approval; but unfortunately he soon developed oppressive habits, and he was put to death by one of his uncles, who also took the opportunity to kill the Chinese envoy. From the Chinese point of view the situation was grave, and it could become very dangerous indeed if this event were to be interpreted as a sign of Chinese weakness and followed by the defection of the small neutral communities to the Hsiung-nu. A junior officer named Feng Feng-shih, who happened to be escorting visitors from Ta-yüan back to their home, realised that the situation called for bold action. Without delay he assembled a force of 15,000 men from the non-Chinese states, and after a successful attack on So-chü he had the new king's head sent back to Ch'ang-an;[30] this prompt action served to restore Chinese prestige to the western regions. These events occurred in 65 BC, but they were by no means universally applauded. As will be seen below,[31] the propriety of Feng Feng-shih's action did not pass unquestioned.

The same degree of determination was seen in the campaigns led by Chao Ch'ung-kuo against the Ch'iang tribesmen, which resulted in their surrender and the establishment of the Dependent State of Chin-ch'eng (61).[32] Very large forces, which were

[30] *HS* 96A.41a reads that he had the king put to death; *HS* 79.2a that he killed himself.

[31] See p. 232.

[32] *HS* 8.17a (*HFHD*, vol. II, p. 241); *HS* 69.2b, *et seq.*

drawn from many different parts of China and included non-Chinese, were used in these campaigns[33] which, however necessary they were, were not regarded as the most profitable measures that policy could devise. Chao Ch'ung-kuo's contribution to the Han Empire lay not only in his leadership of these forces, but also in his realisation that imperial interests could be served better by the establishment of permanent colonies than by mounting short and sharp campaigns against a mobile enemy. His opinions show clearly the transition from a policy of military aggression to one of settled colonialism.

A proposal to establish Han military colonies at Lun-t'ai had been put forward by Sang Hung-yang in *c.* 90 BC.[34] At the time this had been rejected, owing to the exhaustion of the Chinese effort in the recent campaigns; but during Chao ti's reign an officer had been appointed to operate the scheme,[35] and military colonies had certainly been founded further east, in Chang-i commandery, as early as 85.[36] Twenty-five years later Chao Ch'ung-kuo was able to adduce more cogent arguments than his predecessor and to link them to a systematic plan.[37] This aged officer,[38] who was a native of western China, was by now the acknowledged expert in the affairs of the west. He had seen service in Li Kuang-li's campaign against the Hsiung-nu (90)[39] which had ended disastrously for Han arms. In subsequent expeditions he had proved himself to be a most able officer with a keen eye for logistics, and he had successfully insisted that, despite his seventy years of age, he should be

[33] See *RHA*, vol. I, p. 78.

[34] *HS* 96B.15b; *RHA*, vol. I, p. 57.

[35] *HS* 96B.20a. This did not take place before 81 BC, as the refusal to plant colonies at Lun-t'ai was cited as still being operative at the time of the debate of that year; see Chapter 3, p. 97.

[36] See *RHA*, vol. I, p. 56.   [37] *HS* 69.1a, *et seq.*

[38] According to *HS* 69.16b, he died at the age of eighty-six in 52 BC. At the time of the campaign against the Ch'iang he was aged seventy-seven

[39] *HS* 8.37b (*HFHD*, vol. II, p. 115).

given command of the expedition sent to suppress the rebellion of the Ch'iang tribes in 61. Shortly after the successful conclusion of the campaign, Chao Ch'ung-kuo submitted proposals for a long-term solution to the problem of preventing these tribes from raiding Han territory; and in place of the repeated despatch of task forces he suggested the permanent establishment of sponsored farming settlements.

He began his memorial[40] by pointing out the dangers of relying on military force, and stressed that very extensive supplies of food were needed to keep an army on the march. That his estimates were not exaggerated may be shown by comparison with the rations provided for the garrison troops who lined the wall further north.[41] In addition he noted that the Ch'iang were not the only tribes who were likely to give trouble; and while the Ch'iang themselves could easily be conquered by dexterous scheming, it was difficult to defeat them with armed forces. Attack was therefore inexpedient. The memorial continued:

'I calculate that there are over 2,000 *ch'ing*[42] of land which have been left uncultivated by the inhabitants; these are fields previously belonging to the Ch'iang and open fields [*kung t'ien*] which lie east of Lin-ch'iang and extend as far as Hao-men. In this area many of the posts and stations of Chinese officials have fallen into disrepair; however, there are some 60,000 pieces of hewn timber of all sizes which were cut by the forces under my command on an earlier expedition to the hills; and these are now lying stacked by the river. I suggest that the cavalry should be disbanded and a force should be left there numbering in all 10,281 men, and comprising convicts on easy service,[43] volunteers, infantrymen from Huai-yang and Ju-nan, and officers' private retainers. Their monthly consumption of grain and salt would amount to 27,363 and 308 *hu*, respectively[44], and they

[40] *HS* 69.10a.   [41] See *RHA*, vol. II, p. 70.

[42] The *ch'ing* (100 *mu*) was equal to 11.39 English acres.

[43] i.e. *ch'ih hsing* or convicts under amnesty; see Hulsewé, pp. 241–2; and *RHA*, vol. I, pp. 79, 150, note 24.

[44] For the use of the *shih* or *hu* as the standard unit of capacity for

should be divided into detached garrisons posted at important points of control. When the ice melts the timber may be brought downstream for the repair of government stations and the construction of water-courses. The bridges on the roads west of the Huang River gorge may be repaired in seventy places, so that communication will be possible about as far as the Hsien River. [In the spring] the men should be sent out to work their turn in the fields,[45] each man being allotted 20 *mu*; and when, by the fourth month, the crops begin to sprout, a force should be despatched to the farms to act as protective patrols. Such a force should include 1,000 cavalrymen from the commandery and 1,000 non-Chinese cavalry volunteers from the Dependent State, with two auxiliary horses being provided for every ten head of horse in the force. The produce of the fields should be brought into Chin-ch'eng commandery to supplement stocks and reduce expenditure, for the quantity of grain at present transported there by the Superintendent of Agriculture is sufficient to supply the needs of 10,000 men for a year. I beg leave to submit details of the land in question together with a schedule of the equipment needed; and I leave it to Your Majesty to reach a decision.'

Considerable discussion followed in which Chao Ch'ung-kuo supported his case with cogent arguments,[46] and won the support of Wei Hsiang, the Chancellor. In the end he succeeded in having his principle accepted, and an edict was proclaimed ordering the disbandment of the main forces and concentration on military colonies of the type that Chao had advocated.[47]

---

measuring grain and salt, see Loewe, 'The measurement of grain during the Han period' (*T'oung Pao*, XLIX, 1961, pp. 64f.) The *shih* or *hu* was equivalent to just under 20 litres. For the extent of the standard rations issued to the Han garrison forces, see *RHA*, vol. II, pp. 65f.

[45] *HS* 69.11a; for this interpretation, see the note of Yen Shih-ku. For the identification of the Hsien River, see the notes to *HS* 69.6a.

[46] *HS* 69.11b Chao is reported as listing twelve arguments to support his proposals. [47] *HS* 69.14b.

The transition from one policy to another is seen clearly in a study of the work and achievement of Cheng Chi.[48] His name has already appeared as that of the officer who took command of the successful expedition against Chü-shih in 68 BC, and who was given orders to protect the more southerly of the Silk Roads. A significant change in the Han attitude may be seen in 60 or 59[49] in the recognition that it was necessary to co-ordinate the activities of the Chinese on both the northern and the southern routes; and the conferment of the title of Protector General on Cheng Chi for this purpose is described as a climax which followed marked Chinese successes.[50] Certainly it seems that Han statesmen were now taking a more sophisticated view of their relations with the West, which was doubtless partly due to experience and a better knowledge of those regions. In addition, the moment seemed ripe for attempting a peaceful settlement from a position of strength, as Cheng Chi had just accepted the surrender of one of the minor kings of the Hsiung-nu; and his effective action in Chü-shih had allowed him to set up farming establishments under the control of 300 officers and men. For these services he received a nobility.[51]

The title of Protector General was conceived as that of a co-ordinator who would do his best to maintain Chinese influence in a state of strength and steadiness. Preferably he would settle all difficulties by peaceful means, but if necessary he could use force. One of his main tasks was to retain Han control of the fields that could be worked profitably at the oasis of Chü-shih and to deny their use to the Hsiung-nu[52]; Cheng Chi soon

[48] *HS* 70.3b, *et seq.*

[49] According to *HS* 96A.7b, the title Protector General was not adopted until after certain events of 59 BC, but *HS* 8.17b (*HFHD*, vol. II, p. 243) uses the term with reference to 60 BC. Probably the latter use is anachronistic. The statements in *HS* 19A.23b and *HS* 70.21a that the title was first used in 68 are probably erroneous.

[50] *HS* 96A. 7b, *et seq.*   [51] *HS* 17.30a and *HS* 96B.31a.

[52] *HS* 96B.31a, *et seq.*

showed himself capable of achieving this result. Later he was
sufficiently strong to threaten the use of force in order to bring
pressure to bear on Wu-sun.[53]

Strictly speaking, the term Protector General (*tu-hu*)[54] was
an honorary title which carried no defined stipend or duties, but
which was conferred as an extra mark of honour or responsibility on an officer who was already serving with an appointment in the north-west. Thus the first recipient of the honour,
Cheng Chi, was Commandant of Cavalry and Political
Counsellor at the time; and the new title was given with the
injunction that he should proceed on a mission for the protection of the thirty-six states of the western regions.[55] In effect,
however, he was soon acting in a newly conceived administrative capacity. He established his headquarters at the town of
Wu-lei, which was situated close to the agricultural grounds of
Ch'ü-li and lay centrally within the western regions.[56] Quite
soon a Colonel of Agricultural Colonies was established as one
of his subordinates;[57] and when, twenty years later, Ch'en
T'ang accompanied the Protector General on his mission to the
west, he served as his deputy, with the rank of colonel.[58] Other
officers who were subordinate to the Protector General included an assistant, two majors, captains and company leaders;[59]
and it is probably due to the staff of the Protector General and
their assiduous collection of information that the *Han-shu* could
draw on statistical accounts of the states of the western

[53] *HS* 96B.8a.

[54] *Tu-hu*: Dubs—Protector General.

[55] *HS* 19A.23b. Dubs renders *ch'i tu-wei* (Commandant of Cavalry) as
chief commandant of cavalry and *chien ta-fu* (Political Counsellor) as
Grandee Remonstrant.

[56] *HS* 96A.8a.

[57] *HS* 96A.7b. Dubs renders *t'un-t'ien hsiao-wei* as Colonel of the
Agricultural Colonists.

[58] *HS* 70.5b.

[59] Dubs renders *ch'eng, ssu-ma* and *hou* as assistant, major and captain,
respectively, and *ch'ien-jen* (company leader) as millenary.

regions.[60] According to one source[61] offices in the north-west were held for periods of three years only before the incumbent was changed. Altogether ten men are known to have held the title of Protector General, beginning with Cheng Chi in 59, and ending with Li Ch'ung, who disappeared at about the time of Wang Mang's death.[62]

The emphasis on agricultural settlements was taken one stage further in 48 BC, when the post of Wu and Chi colonel was established. While it is not known how regularly the post was filled, it is at least certain that there was an incumbent in AD 16, and that the officer was supported by a staff of assistants. His duties were to found and operate colonies in the lands which had hitherto been occupied by the community of Chü-shih, and which lay open to occupation and exploitation by either the Chinese or the Hsiung-nu.[63] To fulfil his task adequately, the officer disposed of a limited number of troops, and it was on just such a force that Ch'en T'ang and Kan Yen-

[60] i.e. the precise figures of distance, population, etc., which are given in *HS* 96 for all the states of the western regions. The inclusion of this information is unique to this chapter, and does not feature in chapters of the *Han-shu* that are concerned with the non-Chinese peoples of other regions, where there was no official equivalent to the Protector General.

[61] *HS* 70.19a, note by Ju Shun (*fl.* 221–265). This remark remains undisputed by other commentators.

[62] The following are known holders of the title of Protector General, with dates taken from Huang Wen-pi, *Lo-pu-nao-erh k'ao-ku-chi* (Peiping, 1948), pp. 179f.: Cheng Chi (60–49 B C); Han Hsüan (48–46); Kan Yen-shou (36–34); Tuan Hui-tsung (33–31); Lien Pao (30–28); Han Li (24–22); Tuan Hui-tsung (21–19); Kuo Shun (12–10); Sun Chien (A D 1–3); Tan Ch'in (4–13); Li Ch'ung (16–23). (According to *HS* 70.19b, Tuan Hui-tsung's second term of duty with the title of Protector General was dated during the period 24–21; see p. 247.)

[63] See *HS* 96A.8a and *HS* 96B.32b for the establishment of the post and *HS* 96B.36a for the existence of a Wu and Chi colonel in AD 16. For the title of the post and the question whether it implied a complement of one or two colonels, see *HS* 19A.23b, notes of Yen Shih-ku and others; and Lao Kan, in CYYY 28, vol. 1 (1956), pp. 485f.

shou called in the fight against Chih-chih in 36 BC.[64]

Probably these men were conscript soldiers who were serving their regular tour of duty and had been detached for work as farm labourers. Conscripts were certainly used in this way on the sponsored farms which had been established in Tun-huang and Chang-i commanderies, where they worked under the supervision of the regular officers of the garrison or else under special commissioners.[65] Presumably, but we do not know for certain, some of the local native inhabitants were able, or even encouraged, to join in the work; and the earliest scheme for founding colonies at such a distance from China may well have envisaged long-term emigration to the new farms by civilians from inside China.[66] There is some evidence to indicate that the conscripts who were set to work on the sites of the garrisons stayed there for comparatively long periods of time,[67] and it is likely that the same conditions applied to service at the sponsored farms of Chü-shih.

From the beginning of Yüan ti's reign (*accedit* 49) there were signs that the Han government was reluctant to become involved in foreign ventures, and that it would be ready to engage in action only when previous undertakings made this necessary. This new attitude conformed with other principles that are described here as Reformist, e.g. that the people of China were not to be put to labour or service unnecessarily; that the rule of

[64] *HS* 96A.33b, 34a.

[65] e.g. the *Nung tu-wei* and *T'ien kuan*; for these posts see *RHA*, vol. I, pp. 56, 61, 70, 144, note 26.

[66] This appears to have been behind Sang Hung-yang's scheme; see *HS* 96B.15b.

[67] See the evidence of the strips collected as document MD 9 (*RHA* vol. II, pp. 82f.), for the settlement of men at Chü-yen with their families; it is unlikely that such arrangements were made on a short-term basis. For reasons for supposing that officials and officers were posted at Chü-yen for long-term periods, see documents, UD 1 and UD 2 (*RHA*, vol. II, pp. 169f., 176f.) and *RHA*, vol. II, p. 73, note 7.

the Empire depended not on the exercise of force but on the qualities of the Emperor and his example, and that the expansionist ambitions associated with the Ch'in Empire and the years of Han Wu ti's reign were to be abandoned in favour of a passive policy which could be attributed to the kings of Chou. Such views commended themselves to Yüan ti in person, if we are to believe an account of a conversation which he had with his father;[68] they had already been expressed in connection with foreign ventures by Hsiao Wang-chih[69] and they were soon to be reiterated by other statesmen.

It is noticeable that on an occasion when Yüan ti's government was forced into taking action it was Feng Feng-shih who was concerned, and in order to understand the issue fully it is necessary to revert to an earlier point of time. Feng Feng-shih[70] was one of the last statesmen of western Han to sponsor the cause of action and expansion, having first risen to an official post in Wu ti's reign. He served in the highly successful campaign which was fought against the Hsiung-nu in 71 BC and was sent as an envoy to the western regions.[71] It was in that capacity that he took immediate and strong action to prevent disaffection against Han spreading from So-chü (65)[72] and he subsequently achieved the further success of acquiring some of Ta-yüan's special breed of horses for the Han court.

These events had taken place in 65 BC, and on Feng Feng-shih's return to Ch'ang-an the Emperor raised the question of rewarding his achievement with a nobility. The ensuing discussions reveal the differences of opinion that were prevailing in high places at that time and they have some bearing on the events of 36. Wei Hsiang, the Chancellor, and the generals of the Han armies supported the idea of giving Feng a nobility. They cited a principle of the *Spring and Autumn Annals*,[73] to the effect that those whose achievements outside Chinese

[68] See Chapter 4, pp. 151.   [69] See p. 223.   [70] *HS* 79.1a, *et seq.*
[71] See p. 220.   [72] See p. 224.
[73] The precise source for this is untraced.

territory had resulted in bringing peace to the dynasty should be singled out for reward. However, this view was disputed by Hsiao Wang-chih, who was at that time Superintendent of the Lesser Treasury.[74] He reminded his colleagues that Feng Feng-shih had received specific orders when he had set out on his mission to the west. But he had exceeded his instructions in so far as he had drawn up an imperial edict, without the requisite authority, in order to mobilise troops from the communities of the western regions. Hsiao Wang-chih recognised that Feng Feng-shih's achievement had been highly successful, but he argued that it should not be allowed to be taken as a precedent. For, if Feng Feng-shih were to be rewarded for his exploits with a nobility, subsequent envoys would wish to emulate his example; and if they in their turn were to mobilise troops and strive to win credit by engaging an enemy at such a distance from China, they would without question expose the dynasty to the dangers of embroilment with foreign tribes.

Hsiao Wang-chih presented his arguments so successfully that although Feng Feng-shih was appointed Counsellor of the Palace and Superintendent of Parks and Lakes,[75] he did not receive the honour of a nobility. Nearly twenty years later, when he was about sixty-five years old, he rose to become general of the right (46), Superintendent of the Dependent States (43) and Superintendent of the Palace (41). By that time his daughter had been admitted as one of Yüan ti's consorts.[76]

The issue of involvement or withdrawal came up for discussion in 45 BC.[77] In this year Chih-chih made direct overtures to the Han government, seeking the same terms of amity and

[74] *Shao-fu*; Dubs—privy treasurer.

[75] *Kuang-lu ta-fu* and *Shui-heng tu-wei*: Dubs renders these terms as Imperial Household Grandee and Chief Commandant of Waters and Parks.

[76] This was in 48 BC; see *HS* 97B.20b. *Tien shu-kuo* and *Kuang-lu-hsün* are rendered by Dubs as Director of Dependent States and Superintendent of the Imperial Household.

[77] *HS* 70.5a.

friendly treatment that had been accorded to his rival Hu-han-hsieh. Some years earlier both Chih-chih and Hu-han-hsieh had sent their sons to act as hostages in Ch'ang-an; and Hu-han-hsieh's position had been strengthened both formally and materially by the honourable reception that had greeted him on his own visit to Ch'ang-an in 51. In trying now to establish better terms, Chih-chih asked for the return of his son, and the particular issue that lay before the government was the extent of the escort that he should be granted.

There were those who favoured escorting Chih-chih's son right back to his home. In this way Han would declare itself as being fully involved in the relationship with Chih-chih and would need to accept the further consequences of such a relationship. The protagonists in favour of this whole-hearted gesture included Ku Chi and Feng Feng-shih. Ku Chi was a guards' major at the time; he was the father of Ku Yung who was later to make his name as an interpreter of strange phenomena.[78] Ku Chi believed that it would not be right for Han to break with ties which had already been made by the acceptance of a hostage; and he thought that the risk of exposing a single Chinese envoy to danger by sending him to escort Chih-chih's son home was justified by the hope that such a step might ensure the security of the dynasty.

While Feng Feng-shih agreed with Ku Chi's views, they were opposed by two notable men of Reformist views; these were Kung Yü, who was at that time Imperial Counsellor, and the academician K'uang Heng. Kung Yü had it in mind that not so long ago Chih-chih had deliberately insulted a Chinese envoy named Chiang Nai-shih, and he thought it quite improper to risk exposing China to a similar act of degradation. However, his fears were disregarded and Ku Chi duly set out on his mission, only to be put to death by Chih-chih in a fit of rage.

These events were to lead directly to the moves made by

[78] *HS* 85.1a, *et seq.*

Ch'en T'ang and Kan Yen-shou in 36; for, realising that he had now incurred Han's deepest enmity, Chih-chih threw in his lot with the kingdom of K'ang-chü (Sogdiana) and with its help attacked China's traditional ally Wu-sun. Emboldened by his success he proceeded to behave with the utmost arrogance and violence, not only against the Chinese envoys in the west, but also against the rulers of K'ang-chü on whose help he had so recently relied.

Three years later (42) Feng Feng-shih was once more involved in foreign affairs, this time in connection with some of the Ch'iang tribesmen who had revolted against Han authority.[79] In this incident, the Han government was eventually obliged, despite its unwillingness, to mount a large-scale expedition in order to maintain its position among alien peoples. It happened to be a year of famine, and the senior ministers who were consulted were anxious to conserve China's resources and to avoid heavy outlays at a time of hardship. Feng Feng-shih insisted, however, that if Han authority were to be upheld, the revolt must be crushed, and he offered to lead a punitive force in person. To achieve speedy and effective results, he asked for 40,000 men, and he promised to bring the campaign to a decisive conclusion within a month. The reaction of the government, which was to offer him a mere 10,000 men, betrays their reluctance to expend resources in the interests of supporting a Chinese effort away from home. Feng Feng-shih argued that the despatch of a small force could only end in a failure that would provoke a stiffer resistance among the dissidents and induce other tribes to join them; but his urgent plea for a larger force fell on deaf ears, and he set out with a mere 12,000 men.

Feng Feng-shih's prediction of failure was soon justified only too well, and he had to report that his senior officers had been killed by superior forces. At the same time he submitted a detailed acount of the topography and a further estimate of the

[79] *HS* 79.3a, *et seq.*

size of the force needed to ensure success. This time his request was answered by the despatch of no less than 60,000 men, with whom he was able to defeat his enemy soundly; and he forced the surviving dissidents to withdraw into the Tibetan hills. He was then ordered to disband his forces with the exception of a few garrisons who were left to establish agricultural colonies at certain strongpoints.

The reluctance of the government and its subsequent shabby treatment of Feng Feng-shih discloses once again its anxiety to avoid involvement. On a previous occasion he had been refused the nobility which his success surely deserved (65);[80] and on his return to Ch'ang-an in 41 BC, after the vindication of his views and a military success to his credit, he was rewarded with the lesser honour of a metropolitan nobility,[81] together with some material gifts. The treatment to which he was subjected is of interest in view of the government's later behaviour towards Ch'en T'ang and Kan Yen-shou. Feng Feng-shih died in 35,[82] but the case for giving him a nobility was to be reopened a few years later.[83]

Two features of the incident of 36 BC deserve particular attention, the part played by K'ang-chü (Sogdiana) in the venture and the treatment of the two protagonists Kan Yen-shou and Ch'en T'ang.[84] K'ang-chü, it will be recalled, had been glad enough to receive Chih-chih in 45 and to offer him friendship and protection. Subsequently as his strength had grown he had behaved with considerable arrogance, violence and oppression.

[80] See p. 232.

[81] *Kuan-nei-hou*, Dubs—Marquis of the Imperial Domain; for this order of honour, see *Aristocratic Ranks*, pp. 152f., and Chapter 4, note 18.

[82] *HS* 79.5b, 6a. He died two years before Kan's ennoblement; see p. 243.

[83] See p. 243.

[84] *HS* 70.6a, *et seq.*; see also *HFHD*, vol. II, pp. 279f. It is possible that some of the fragments found at Chü-yen may be concerned with this incident (see *RHA*, vol. II, pp. 245f., document UD 9).

He had killed one of the king's daughters; forced local labour to build defensive walls; and extracted annual tribute from Ta-yüan and other states. Needless to say he had rejected with contumely a request made by the Chinese for the return of the mortal remains of the envoys who had met their deaths at his hands.

Ch'en T'ang fully realised the dangers that might occur with the further growth of Chih-chih's prestige and power. He foresaw a time when Chih-chih would be able to attack as far afield as Arsacid Persia; and if these fears were somewhat exaggerated, he was certainly right to envisage Chih-chih's effective domination of the states that lay east of the Pamir. When Ch'en T'ang broached the subject with Kan Yen-shou, the Protector General, the latter's instinct was to report back to Ch'ang-an and seek instructions; but Ch'en T'ang pointed out that the home government would be quite incapable of realising the gravity of the issues at stake and he thought that their own plan to attack Chih-chih would never be approved. At this point Kan Yen-shou fell ill; and, acting entirely on his own responsibility, Ch'en T'ang drew up the documents without which he would lack the necessary authority to call out the neighbouring forces, i.e. the agricultural settlers who were subordinated to the Wu and Chi colonel, and troops belonging to the communities of the west. In all, the force that he was able to collect mustered 40,000 men.

Kan Yen-shou was still anxious to avoid taking any positive action without due authorisation, but Ch'en T'ang succeeded in overcoming his scruples, allegedly at the point of the sword. Once the die was cast, the two officials reported their plans to Ch'ang-an. They could reckon that it would take several weeks[85] for the delivery of their message and the receipt of

[85] The exact time required can hardly be calculated. It took about fifty days for the routine delivery of documents from central China (Shansi) to one of the headquarters' posts lying east of Tun-huang, i.e. Taralingin-durbeljin (see *RHA*, vol. I, p. 44).

subsequent orders; and in these circumstances they included in
their report a confession that they had proceeded to mobilise
troops, even going so far as to proclaim an edict without due
authority to do so. As the campaign proceeded, Ch'en T'ang
picked up help from some of the leaders of K'ang-chü, who
were now anxious to be rid of Chih-chih's presence and attentions, and in the final battle the Chinese enjoyed the active
support of K'ang-chü's troops. Chih-chih died bravely enough
in the thick of the fight and the Chinese were able to recover
the insignia of the deceased Han envoys, together with the
presents of silk taken by Ku Chi on his ill-fated mission of
45 BC.[86]

Kan Yen-shou and Ch'en T'ang now had to report their
success to their superiors, and in doing so they took care to pay
respect to the current attitude and beliefs of the court.[87] They
compared Han with the ancient regime of Yao and Shun; they
claimed that they had been conducting a punitive campaign on
behalf of Heaven against a rebel, and that their victory had
been due to the Emperor's spiritual qualities, to the active co-
operation of *Yin* and *Yang*, and to the purity of Heaven's
energetic force. Such arguments would hardly have had much
appeal had they appeared in military reports presented during
the days of Wu ti's Modernist statesmen.

The first test of the government's reaction to this exploit
occurred quite soon. The head of Chih-chih had been sent back
to Ch'ang-an as a trophy, and Ch'en and Kan suggested that it
should be suspended in that quarter of Ch'ang-an which was
made over to the lodges of foreign visitors. The idea was doubtless '*pour encourager les autres*', and it raised the whole question
of foreign policy and the motives of Han's relations with other
peoples. The suggestion was opposed by the Reformist
Chancellor K'uang Heng and the Imperial Counsellor P'o Yen-

---

[86] See p. 234; Duyvendak in T'oung Pao vol. XXXIV (1938), pp. 249f.;
HFHD, vol. II, pp. 281f.; and *Everyday Life*, pp. 80–1.

[87] *HS* 70.10a.

shou, but it was supported by some of the generals;[88] both
parties cited canonical writings to support their arguments. But
opinion was apparently running against Kan Yen-shou and
Ch'en T'ang. Kan had refused the hand of the daughter of Shih
Hsien, Leader of the Secretariat,[89] and had thus incurred his
enmity; and some of Ch'en T'ang's officers were accused of
misappropriating booty that had been taken during the campaign. These men had actually been arrested, and they were
only released on the personal orders of the Emperor, after
Ch'en T'ang's intervention on their behalf. There now arose
the question of assessing the degree of merit that had been
earned during the exploit and of conferring suitable rewards
for service, and it was on this matter that the real discussion
centred.

The suggestion that the two officers should be rewarded for
the successful conclusion of the campaign against Chih-chih
was opposed bitterly by Shih Hsien and K'uang Heng, and the
reasons which they adduced bore a close affinity to those voiced
by Hsiao Wang-chih against the proposed ennoblement of
Feng Feng-shih.[90] To raise the troops the two men had issued
imperial orders on their own authority, and they were lucky
not to face a charge and suffer punishment on this account. Any
further bounty that they might receive, be it as an order of
honour or as a grant of land, would encourage subsequent
envoys to run undue risks in order to win a reputation for
bravery; and they would thus be tempted to provoke incidents
with foreign peoples and involve China in difficulties.

Yüan ti himself wished to reward Kan and Ch'en, but he felt
obliged to defer to the opinion of his advisers. For a long time

---

[88] These included Wang Shang (no relation of Wang Mang); see
Chapter 5, p. 155.

[89] *Chung-shu-ling*; this term was used in place of *Shang-shu-ling* when a
eunuch was ordered to lead the secretariat.

[90] In another passage (*HS* 79.6a) the *Han-shu* implies that K'uang Heng
had the example of Hsiao Wang-chih's speech in mind.

no decision was taken, until Liu Hsiang, formerly Super-intendent of the Imperial Family,[91] submitted a memorial on the subject. In general Liu Hsiang was of a Reformist frame of mind, but his intellectual stature was such that he could afford to adopt an independent attitude if he thought it right to do so. In the present instance he found himself arguing against his close colleagues. Chih-chih, he wrote,[92] had murdered Chinese envoys and officers by the hundred [*sic*]. His activities were widely known abroad and served to reduce Chinese prestige and power, and the Emperor had determined to have him punished. This was precisely what Kan Yen-shou and Ch'en T'ang had achieved, by gathering together the support of the local chieftains and their forces. Despite all the hazards, they had succeeded in taking the town, in capturing the enemy's banners and in executing Chih-chih; and by these measures they had restored Chinese prestige in the west and removed the stain of Han's disgrace, that had been incurred by the murder of Ku Chi. These successes had inspired all the other communities with a fear of Han, and Chih-chih's rival Hu-han-hsieh was ready to adopt a subservient attitude at the Han court, which could be expected to be maintained for generations. No officers had done more or achieved greater merit in their efforts to establish a long-lasting settlement.

Liu Hsiang then cited instances from the time of the kings of Chou. The effective punishment of certain tribes had resulted in the allegiance of many of the others, and such feats had been held up to praise in the *Book of Songs* and the *Book of Changes*. The present achievement was greatly in excess of those exploits. In addition, when meritorious service was being assessed, minor misdemeanours are disregarded. There was excellent reason to act with speed in the conferment of re-wards, and the recent successes had been all the more remark-able for the great distance at which the campaign had been

[91] *Tsung-cheng*: Dubs—*Superintendent of the Imperial House.*
[92] *HS* 70.11a.

fought from China. To deny Kan Yen-shou and Ch'en T'ang a reward and to subject them to legal processes was hardly the way to encourage men to serve the state or to stimulate their valour.

In addition Liu Hsiang wrote that there was historical precedent in pre-imperial China whereby a military officer's successes had been such that his criminal acts were tacitly forgotten. There was also the case of Li Kuang-li who had commanded a force of 50,000 men and spent untold resources in a four years' campaign. For such an outlay, he simply had a few fine chargers to show, together with the exhibition of the dead king's head in Ch'ang-an. In addition, very serious crimes had been committed by some of his officers during the course of the campaign. Nevertheless Wu ti had taken into account that it had been fought at an immense distance away from home; he had had no record made of the misdemeanours of the officers and had rewarded them liberally. In this way, two had become nobles, three rose to be ministers of state, and over a hundred had been appointed to senior posts in the government.[93] Now, in the present case, K'ang-chü was a stronger state than Ta-yüan; Chih-chih's fame had been more renowned than that of the King of Ta-yüan; and Chih-chih's crime of murdering Chinese envoys had been far more serious than Ta-yüan's misdemeanour of refusing to let the Chinese have some horses. Kan Yen-shou and Ch'en T'ang had not involved Chinese troops in arduous service nor had they consumed Chinese stocks of food, and their achievements were an hundred-fold greater than those of Li Kuang-li. More recently Ch'ang Hui and Cheng Chi had been ennobled, in the one case for accompanying a foreign force which was anxious to take the offensive, and in the other for receiving the surrender of a king who had made over spontaneously to the Chinese cause.[94] It could

[93] i.e., *chiu ch'ing* (ministers of state) and *erh ch'ien shih* (posts graded at a stipend of 2,000 *shih*); see Appendix pp. 309f.

[94] For Ch'ang Hui's activities in 71, see p. 220; for Cheng Chi's

thus be shown that the achievements of Kan Yen-shou and Ch'en T'ang were superior to those of their predecessors in every respect; it would be deplorable if their great services were to pass by unrecognised while their minor faults were brought to light. It was only proper to drop any charges that had been levelled against the officers and to reward their services with appropriate honours.

Possibly as a result of Liu Hsiang's appeal, Yüan ti granted a pardon to the two officers and ordered his advisers to consider their ennoblement. They advised that the two men should be rewarded in accordance with the provisions of military law for those who had arrested or killed a leader of the status of *Shan-yü*. But K'uang Heng and Shih Hsien objected that, by fleeing from his own country, Chih-chih had fortfeited any claim to such status; and they further disputed Yüan ti's idea of rewarding them according to the precedent set in the case of Cheng Chi. However, Kan Yen-shou received a full nobility, and Ch'en T'ang a metropolitan nobility, with the further gifts of estates and gold. They were also appointed to hold the rank of colonel.

Shortly afterwards Kan Yen-shou died in office. At the accession of Ch'eng ti (33), K'uang Heng seized an opportunity to renew the accusation that Ch'en T'ang had misappropriated captured goods, and he was duly brought up on a charge and dismissed from his post. Moreover, still further trouble awaited him. For he sent in a report to the throne, stating that the attendant at the palace who had been passed off as the son of the king of K'ang-chü and was thereby acting as a hostage, was in fact no son of the king at all. Ch'en T'ang's allegation was investigated and found to be false; and he was judged guilty of a crime that was punishable by death. He was saved from his fate by the intervention of Ku Yung, son of that Ku

---

acceptance of the Jih-chu king, at his defection from the Hsiung-nu, see *HS* 96A.7b.

Chi who had been put to death by Chih-chih in 45 BC. Ku Yung repeated some of the arguments already adduced by Liu Hsiang, stressing the magnitude of Ch'en T'ang's achievement and the popular esteem in which he was held. As a result Ch'en T'ang was released from prison and punished by reduction to commoner status. At a later stage, Ch'en T'ang was exiled to Tun-huang, whence he was moved to An-ting. Finally he was recalled to Ch'ang-an and died in full recognition of his services.[95]

The reluctance to reward Ch'en T'ang and the treatment to which he was subjected reflect the distaste felt in government for his venturesomeness and their unwillingness to engage in further foreign undertakings. The same conclusion may be drawn from a later incident in which the achievement of Feng Feng-shih was invoked.

As has been seen, Liu Hsiang tried to persuade the government to confer a nobility on Kan Yen-shou by showing that his services were greater than those of some of the heroes of an earlier age who had gained full recognition for their work. Once Kan Yen-shou had received his nobility, in 33 BC, a similar plea was put forward on behalf of the late Feng Feng-shih, who had been denied a nobility after his successful chastisement of the King of So-chü in 65.[96] The plea was voiced by Tu Ch'in who will be mentioned later in connection with China's relations with Chi-pin (Kashmir). On this occasion he argued that if, notwithstanding his fabrication of orders, Kan Yen-shou had been judged worthy of a nobility, so too did Feng Feng-shih merit that honour, despite his irregularities of a similar nature. Moreover, if the achievements of the two officers were compared, those of Feng were considerably greater than those of Kan. Chih-chih's crimes were less heinous than those of the king of So-chü, whose forces had been stronger. Feng,

[95] *HS* 70.14a and *HS* 70.18a.
[96] See pp. 232f; *HS* 17.31a; and *HS* 79.6a.

however, had had fewer forces at his disposal than Kan. It was highly inequitable that while Kan Yen-shou had received his reward, Feng's achievements had not been distinguished in the same way; equal rewards should be given for equal services rendered, or else confusion would ensue and the system of the rewards and punishments of state would fall into disrepute. However, despite his eloquence, Tu Ch'in's plea was not accepted. Ch'eng ti, who had just acceded to the throne, declined to take any action, on the flimsy pretext that the suggestion concerned events of a previous reign.

Several other incidents during Ch'eng ti's reign reveal the government's desire to disengage and to avoid unnecessary involvement in central Asia. Slight and somewhat unsatisfactory attempts had been made since Wu ti's reign to open negotiations with Chi-pin (Kashmir),[97] and these had culminated disastrously for Han, in the murder of a Chinese envoy with seventy members of his staff. This crime had been committed by a native of Chi-pin who had actually established himself as king with the blessing of the Han Emperor; but despite this insult and injury, Yüan ti's government had decided that the great distance which separated Chi-pin from China precluded retaliation. Early in the next reign, Chi-pin made overtures to Ch'eng ti, asking for a pardon and for the establishment of relations but the request was refused, after a powerful speech made by Tu Ch'in.[98] He said that Chi-pin was only too ready to exploit the distance at which it lay from Han for its own purposes; the behaviour of the king was servile enough if he was begging for privileges or facilities, but otherwise he displayed arrogance and behaved with abandon. It was in such circumstances that the Han envoys had been put to death, and the overtures sprang from motives that were anything but

[97] *HS* 96A.25a.
[98] See the speech made by Tu Ch'in to Wang Feng at the time when the latter held the title of Supreme General (i.e. between 33 and 22 B C).

honourable, being directed solely towards commercial ends. Tu Ch'in then discussed the arduous nature of communications between China and Chi-pin, describing the precipitous mountain passes, and the dangers of climbing the hills with their attendant exposure to sickness and robbery. He thought it quite improper to expend Chinese effort or to risk Chinese lives in order to maintain relations with so unsatisfactory and distant a party.

Tu Ch'in's advice was eagerly accepted by the government and a consideration of the man and his forbears reveals something of the transformation that had overcome Chinese politics during the previous hundred years or so. Tu Ch'in's grandfather, Tu Chou, may be described as a Modernist of extreme views which he did not hesitate to put into practice. He was appointed Superintendent of Trials in 109 BC, and it was alleged that in that capacity he had acted arbitrarily and harshly, rather than in conformity with established practice and principle.[99] Such methods must surely have appealed to the contemporary attitude which favoured government in accordance with expedient rather than tradition; but eventually his conduct of justice was thought to be so cruel that he was relieved of his post and demoted (98). However, this was no more than a temporary setback, and we find that he was shortly promoted to become Imperial Counsellor, and that he held that post until his death four years later.[100]

---

[99] *HS* 60.1a, *et seq.* See also the criticism in *YTL* 28 (194).

[100] *HS* 19B.21b, 24b; and *HS* 60.2b. As Ku Yen-wu points out there appear to be discrepancies in the passages of the *Han-shu* which relate to the dating of these appointments. While *HS* 19B dates Tu Chou's appointment as *Yü-shih ta-fu* in 98 B C and his death in 94, according to *HS* 60 the appointment took place after the arrest of Sang Hung-yang and the judicial processes in which the empress Wei and the heir apparent were involved; and on the face of it *HS* 60 is here referring to events that took place in 80 and 91 B C respectively. Wang Hsien-ch'ien solves the problem by suggesting that *HS* 60 is referring to events that took place during the 'Great Search' of 99 B C (see *HS* 6.34a, *HFHD*, vol. II, p. 105). For other examples of a 'search', see Chapter 2, p. 38 and note 1.

Tu Chou thus held views which conformed with the Modernist ideal of government which was based on the strict control of the population and which was directed towards the enrichment of imperial resources. His son, Tu Yen-nien, showed some dissatisfaction with other aspects of this attitude, as has been shown above;[101] for he distrusted the contemporary affluence of the court; he asked Huo Kuang to introduce economies and he requested a reconsideration of the principle of the state monopolies. Like his father he rose to hold the post of Imperial Counsellor (55–52).

In Tu Ch'in the move towards the Reformist point of view was complete, as may be seen in the views which he expressed about Chi-pin. Tu Ch'in was one of the younger sons of Tu Yen-nien, and the only one who did not achieve high office; but he was by far the best known, principally in connection with the interpretation of strange phenomena.[102] It may be noted that, like Liu Hsiang, he was a man of sufficient independence to judge questions on their own merits, as has been seen in the plea that he entered to honour the memory of Feng Feng-shih.[103]

At much the same time as Chi-pin's overtures were being rejected, the Han government was pondering the question of relations with K'ang-chü. In this instance it is noteworthy that no less an expert and senior official than the Protector General advised disengagement.[104] This was Kuo Shun, who submitted a number of reports urging that Han should sever its relations with the state. He saw little prospect that K'ang-chü would be able to forge an effective alliance with the Hsiung-nu and Wu-

---

[101] See Chapter 4, pp. 122, 146.

[102] I am hoping to examine Tu Ch'in's part in intellectual history and his attitude to phenomena in a forthcoming study.

[103] See p. 243.

[104] *HS* 96A.34a. In this passage the *Han-shu* apparently reproduces a summary of several submissions that were made by Kuo Shun.

sun which would act to the disadvantage of Han; for the three states were mutually antagonistic. The traditional alliance between Han and Wu-sun had been bound by matrimonial ties, but so far from being of advantage to Han it had cost the government dearly; nevertheless, in view of the undertakings of the past, this alliance could not now be abrogated. However, matters stood very differently with K'ang-chü, which was accustomed to relegate Han envoys to lower places of honour than those accorded to the representatives of other states. The only reason why K'ang-chü wished to maintain relations with Han were commercial; and from the point of view of the Han government, the expense of escorting envoys and hostages to and fro, over the very long distances involved, could not be justified.

However frequently they were re-iterated, Kuo Shun's views proved to be of no avail, and for reasons which are not altogether clear, the Han government retained its relations with K'ang-chü. Possibly the court felt obliged to do so in view of the help rendered by K'ang-chü in the fight against Chih-chih, but Han certainly refrained from entering on a matrimonial alliance with this state.

Another Protector General, Tuan Hui-tsung, was also concerned with the affairs of K'ang-chü. He had first held this title in 33 BC, and he was re-appointed for a second term during the period 24 to 21.[105] On the occasion of his re-appointment, his friend Ku Yung took the opportunity to warn him not to emulate the examples of men such as Fu Chieh-tzu, Cheng Chi, Kan Yen-shou or Ch'en T'ang, for the days were long past when such ventures had been suitable. Nevertheless, Tuan found it difficult to avoid taking the initiative. In general he met with a friendly reception among the states of central Asia; and he soon had to report that the heir apparent of K'ang-chü wished to make over to Han with a large number of followers,

[105] *HS* 70.19a, *et seq.*; for the dates of his appointment, see note 62 above.

and wished for Han's protection. Han agreed to accept the offer and sent out a Guards' Major to meet the prince, but the incident was marred by two events. Tuan Hui-tsung called out the troops stationed under the Wu and Chi colonel to assist in providing the escort for the prince and when his tour of duty was over, he found himself facing the very same charge with which Feng Feng-shih and Ch'en T'ang had been confronted, i.e. of the misuse of authority. However, he does not appear to have been punished for such a misdemeanour.[106] The offer of the heir apparent of K'ang-chü in fact came to nothing, owing to a foolish mistake on the part of the Guards' Major. This officer was frightened by the large number of those aliens who were to be brought over to the Han cause, and possibly failed to appreciate the real situation; he therefore ordered them to be bound in fetters. Not unnaturally this gesture provoked the anger of the heir apparent, who promptly withdrew with all his followers.

As a result of the matrimonial ties which had first been formed a century previously,[107] Han was still intimately involved in the affairs of Wu-sun—too intimately in the opinion of some statesmen. The leadership of this state had been subject to bitter internal rivalries, and it had eventually been split between two protagonists, who were known as the Greater and the Lesser K'un-mi (from 53 BC). But whatever the inclinations of the government might be, it was obliged by earlier commitments to support the established leaders against the claims of pretenders; and as such claims were sometimes pressed home with violence, Han found it necessary not only to provide moral support by conferring titles of honour on the recognised native leader, but also to intervene forcefully should the situation so demand. It was for these reasons that Tuan Hui-tsung found himself in central Asia once again in the years 12–11 BC, this time with full permission to call on the troops that were subordinated to the Wu and Chi colonel. Faced with an

[106] *HS* 70.16a, *et seq.*   [107] *HS* 70.19b; *HS* 96B.2b, *et seq.*

awkward situation and potential dissidence, Tuan Hui-tsung completed his mission of pacification with marked success, using a minimum number of troops and exerting his powers of persuasion and his force of character. He died at the age of seventy-five in Wu-sun and was generally mourned among the communities of the west. About ten years later (1BC), the strength of the ties between China and Wu-sun were such that one of the leaders of Wu-sun came to present himself in Ch'ang-an.

Many of the measures taken by Wang Mang may be understood as part of his deliberate pose as a latter-day Duke of Chou, and they accord with the Reformist principles of the statesmen who acted as advisers to Yüan ti and Ch'eng ti. However, other considerations entered into the complex dynastic situation of the time, with the result that some of Wang Mang's policies were in conflict with that attitude. Believing that Kan Yen-shou and Ch'en T'ang had been insufficiently rewarded for their success, he increased the value of the nobility which had been given to Kan and which was at that time held by his grandson. He conferred a nobility posthumously on Ch'en T'ang and allowed his son to bear the title; and he also gave a nobility to the junior officer who had actually decapitated Chih-chih on the field of battle.[108]

In central Asia, Wang Mang seems to have been set on making a show of force in the hope of establishing his prestige on a strong basis.[109] During the period AD 1–5, while he was effectively in control of the government, he had two kings of the central Asian states executed, so as to discourage disaffection. Unfortunately, similar action which he ordered two years after his assumption of the throne (10) had precisely contrary results. This was the beheading of a popular king of

[108] For the honours paid to Kan's grandson, see *HS* 70.19a; *HS* 17.31a implies that this act was dated in AD 7. See also *HS* 18.32b.
[109] *HS* 96B.33b.

Further Chü-shih, in the course of an expedition which had been sent to the west. The result of this foolhardy act was to drive the inhabitants of that kingdom to seek refuge with the Hsiung-nu, and before long the Chinese position fell into collapse amid general antagonism. Tiao Hu, who was the Wu and Chi colonel, was killed by his subordinates, who thereupon made over to the Hsiung-nu; Tan Ch'in, the Protector General, was killed by anti-Chinese dissidents of the state of Yen-ch'i (Karashahr). An attempt (AD 16) to reduce Yen-ch'i ended in failure, and with the disappearance of Li Ch'ung, the last of the Protectors General, Chinese relations with central Asia were severed effectively.

The appreciation at the end of that chapter of the *Han-shu* which is concerned with the states of central Asia[110] was written with the benefit of hindsight and in full recognition of the somewhat negative policies of the first half of the first century AD—i.e. before the emperors of Eastern Han had embarked on a vigorous foreign policy that was possibly comparable with that adopted under Wu ti. While observing that Wu ti's activities had been initiated partly as a defensive measure against the Hsiung-nu, the writer protested at some of the consequences, such as the extravagance of indulging in foreign luxuries at court; the great expenditure involved in equipping diplomatic missions; the consequent need to levy imposts on the people of China; and the disaffection which broke out in the provinces. The appreciation re-iterated views which were expressed by the King of Huai-nan, Tu Ch'in and Yang Hsiung,[111] to the effect that natural barriers effectively separated a Chinese regime from those regions wherein it had no business; and it belittled the advantages and disadvantages that the states

[110] *HS* 96B.36b.

[111] For Tu Ch'in, see p. 244; for Yang Hsiung, see *HS* 94B.12a. See *HS* 64.2a for the king of Huai-nan's attempt to dissuade Wu-ti from starting a campaign against Min-yüeh.

of the west were capable of bringing to bear on the govern-ment of the Han Empire. In such circumstances the first of the Eastern Han emperors was to be congratulated for his refusal to extend Chinese commitments to the west; and the apprecia-tion ends with a sentiment that would have been dear to the heart of the Reformists, by observing that by this refusal he had emulated the noble example of the Duke of Chou.

CHAPTER 8

The Reign of Ai ti – 7-1 BC

The *Han-shu* records the occurrence of two somewhat strange events in 5 BC. Chu Po, whose background and point of view was utterly different from those of contemporary statesmen and officials, was appointed Chancellor; and the government adopted a regnal title which immediately evoked memories of the one that had been chosen exactly one hundred years previously, at the height of Chinese pride and prestige and at a time when Modernist policies were in high favour. Neither of the two events of 5 BC bore a long-lasting result. Within four months of his appointment Chu Po had committed suicide; and after a mere two months the new regnal title was withdrawn by edict. But transient as these events were they deserve consideration in the major context of dynastic history; for while they derived from the intellectual developments and political attitudes of the past, they serve to illustrate the force of the dynastic rivalries that coloured the reign of Ai ti (7-1 BC).

Imperial consorts and their families were involved in the dynastic and political destinies of the Han Empire almost since its foundation; and three families may be singled out[1] as exercising a critical influence on the conduct of affairs during the last years of Ch'eng ti (33-7 BC) and throughout Ai ti's reign. These were the families of Wang, Fu and Ting, who had come to prominence originally in the persons of Wang Cheng-chün

[1] For a fuller account of the consorts' families and reference to some families which do not feature here, see *HFHD*, vol. II, pp. 366f. and vol. III, pp. 1f.

Table 5. Principal office holders from 8–4 BC (in chronological order)

Year	Month	Emperor	Chancellor	Marshal of State	Imperial Counsellor
Sui-ho 1	1				
(11 February 8 BC to 30 January 7 BC)	2				Ho Wu appointed *Yü-shih ta-fu* (a)
	3				
	4			Wang Ken re-appointed (b)	Ho Wu appointed *Ta-ssu-kung*
	5				
	6				
	7				
	8				
	9				
	10			Wang Ken dismissed (c)	
	11			Wang Mang appointed (d)	
	12				
Sui-ho 2	1				
(31 January 7 BC to 18 February 6 BC)	2		14 March Chai Fang-chin died		
	3	17 April: death of Ch'eng ti	17 April K'ung Kuang appointed		
	4	7 May: accession of Ai ti			
	5				
	6				

(a) *HS* 19B.47b dates this on a day whose term did not fall within the month specified, i.e. the third month, which ran from 11 April to 9 May.

(b) *HS* 19B.47b dates this on a day whose term did not fall within the month specified, i.e. the fourth month, which ran from 10 May to 8 June.

(c) For the dating and its difficulties, see notes in *HS* 19B.48a.

(d) *HS* 19B.48a dates this on a day whose term did not fall within the month specified, i.e. the eleventh month which ran from 3 December 8 BC to 1 January 7 BC.

Year	Month	Emperor	Chancellor	Marshal of State	Imperial Counsellor
	7			27 July Wang Mang dismissed; (*e*) 30 July Shih Tan appointed	
	Intercalary 8				
	9				
	10				30 November Shih Tan appointed *Ta-ssu-kung*
	11				
	12				
Chien-p'ing 1	1				
(19 February 6 BC to	2				
7 February 5 BC)	3				
	4			Fu Hsi appointed (*f*)	
	5				
	6				
	7				
	8				
	9				
	10				23 November Chu Po appointed *Ta-ssu-kung*
	11				
	12				
Chien-p'ing 2	1				
(8 February 5 BC to 27 January 4 BC)	2			28 March Fu Hsi dismissed Ting Ming appointed	
	3				

(*e*) This dating is doubtful; see *HS* 19B.48b notes.

(*f*) *HS* 19B.49a dates this on a day whose term did not fall within the month specified, i.e. the fourth month, which ran from 19 May to 16 June.

Year	Month	Emperor	Chancellor	Marshal of State	Imperial Counsellor
	4		[19 May] K'ung Kuang dismissed (*g*) Chu Po appointed		8 May Chu Po appointed *Yü-shih ta-fu* 19 May Chao Hsüan appointed *Yü-shih ta-fu*: (*g*)
	5				5 June–4 July: Chao Hsüan imprisoned
	6				
	7				
	8		21 September Chu Po committed suicide		
	9				
	10				
	11				
	12		30 December P'ing Tang appointed		

(*g*) *HS* 19B.49a dates K'ung Kuang's dismissal and Chu Po's appointment on a day whose term does not fall within the fourth month as specified. A slight emendation allows the date corresponding to 19 May, i.e. the day when Chu Po's previous post of *Yü-shih ta-fu* was filled by Chao Hsüan.

(empress of Yüan ti and mother of Ch'eng ti), the lady Fu (secondary consort of Yüan ti and grandmother of Ai ti) and the Lady Ting (mother of Ai ti). But despite the liberal arrangements for providing the Emperor with consorts, the future of the dynastic line was far from secure, as none of Ch'eng ti's principal consorts had succeeded in bearing him a son; and to allay the jealousy of one of those consorts, the Emperor had arranged for the murder of two boys who had been born to him by lesser women.[2]

[2] See *HFHD*, vol. II, pp. 369f.

During the reign of Ch'eng ti the Wang family had safely maintained its dominant position, and five of its members had succeeded one another as holders of the title Marshal of State.[3] As yet this title did not carry with it a staff of subordinate officials, but the holder was in effect head of the 'Inner Court', whose significance will be described shortly. He acted as Leader or supervisor of the Secretariat[4] and was in a position to control the conduct of imperial business. A change took place immediately after the accession of Ai ti, when the new Emperor wished to redress the balance of the court and to replace the influence of the Wang family by that of the Fu and Ting families.[5] As will be seen, this objective was achieved with some success; but two very different types of critic were soon to express strong opposition to the interference in politics by the family of any consort. These were respectively the statesmen of staunch Reformist views and the Emperor's favourite Tung Hsien. The latter had gained a commanding influence over the young Emperor from *c.* 5 BC; Ai ti had taken his love for the young man[6] to the point of abandoning his reliance on the Fu and Ting families, and he had even proposed that he should abdicate in Tung Hsien's favour. Ai ti's sudden death, in 1 BC, left Tung Hsien somewhat isolated and unable to consolidate his position against potential rivals; and in such circumstances the aged Empress Dowager Wang and her nephew Wang Mang were quickly able to re-assert their strength and drive Tung Hsien to suicide.

It was against this background that controversies arose during the reigns of Ch'eng ti and Ai ti regarding the titles and

[3] *Ta-ssu-ma* is rendered by Dubs as Commander-in-Chief. The five holders of the title were: Wang Feng (33–22), Wang Yin (22–15), Wang Shang (15–11), Wang Ken (11–7) and Wang Mang (7 B C).

[4] *Shang-shu*: Dubs—Office of the Masters of Writing.

[5] *HS* 86.15b.

[6] See *HFHD*, vol. III, pp. 8f., for Tung Hsien's rise, his homosexual relations with Ai ti and for the permission given to his wife and children to take up residence in the palace.

concept of the senior posts of government; the nomination of Liu Hsin to be Heir Apparent; the adoption of Reformist measures which concerned the state cults, land tenure and other problems; the part taken by the Empress Fu and her kinsmen in government; the grant of honorific titles to the Empress Fu and the Empress Ting; the style of burial provided for the Empress Ting; Chu Po's appointment as Chancellor; and the introduction of the regnal title *T'ai-ch'u yüan-chiang* in 5 BC.

The structure of imperial government, which had been inaugurated by Ch'in and inherited by Han, provided both for the division of the highest authority of state between several statesmen and for its devolution according to a recognised hierarchy. Thus, while final authority for the conduct of government rested with the Chancellor,[7] responsibility for appointing civil servants and for taking executive action to implement imperial edicts rested with the Imperial Counsellor,[8] who ranked immediately below the Chancellor; and the command of the armed forces was invested, initially at least, in the third of the most highly ranking of the officials, the Supreme Commander.[9] In this way it was hoped that no single one of the three most senior officials of state would be able to take effective action that would threaten the throne; for he would need to secure the co-operation of his two colleagues in order to achieve success.

At the same time it was necessary to retain degrees of seniority and status, so as to encourage men to compete for the highest forms of service, and to allow senior officials to take disciplinary measures in respect of their juniors. It shortly came about that the post of Supreme Commander was allowed

[7] *Ch'eng-hsiang*: Dubs—Lieutenant Chancellor. For this rendering, see Hulsewé, p. 14.

[8] *Yü-shih ta-fu*: Dubs—Imperial Clerk Grandee.

[9] *T'ai-wei*: Dubs—Grand Commandant.

to lapse; and while some of the highest functions of government were left as the prerogative of the Imperial Counsellor, the Chancellor retained superior status, stipend and prestige as the head of the government. The fixed hierarchies were continued to the next levels by filling subordinate posts with civil servants who held specified appointments, graded stipends, and defined responsibilities. These executive offices came to be known as the 'Outer Court', as distinct from an unofficial organ that had grown up in the palace and which was known as the 'Inner Court'. This unofficial organ had come into being as the result of two causes; the reliance that the emperor placed on officials, and sometimes eunuchs, who served in a low-level agency called the Secretariat;[10] and the conferment of certain titles of honour as adjuncts which marked a recognition of services rendered to the state by a senior official or a general. The most highly coveted and senior of these titles was that of *Ta-ssu-ma*, or Marshal of State; and when a *Ta-ssu-ma*, or a holder of one of the other titles, was charged with the duty of leading or supervising the Secretariat, he was able to take control of the government effectively out of the hands of the recognised organs of the outer court, i.e. the Chancellor, the Imperial Counsellor and their subordinate executives.

This development had occurred in the first instance during the reigns of Chao ti (87–74 BC) and Hsüan ti (74–49), when Huo Kuang had stabilised a critical dynastic situation, led a triumvirate of state, and effectively controlled the government by virtue of his title of *Ta-ssu-ma*. Later, Hsüan ti achieved his majority and began to take a personal hand in government; Huo Kuang died (68) and his family suffered elimination;[11] and the style of government reverted to normal for a few decades. During Ch'eng ti's reign, however, it became possible for the

[10] See note 4 above. This was a subordinate agency to the *Shao-fu* (lesser treasury). For the Inner and Outer courts, see Wang Yü-ch'üan, *The central government of the Former Han Dynasty*, pp. 161f., and pp. 313 below.

[11] See Chapter 4.

Wang family to follow Huo Kuang's example to even greater effect, and to arrange for the title of *Ta-ssu-ma* to pass successively to five of their own members. Meanwhile the offices of Chancellor and Imperial Counsellor were dutifully filled, and the structure of imperial government, as established by Ch'in and inherited by Han, was formally preserved.

This situation aroused protest and opposition on the part both of those statesmen who believed in Reformist ideals and those who had fallen out with the Wang family on personal grounds. It was suggested by Ho Wu,[12] with the support of Chang Yü, that supreme responsibility for government should be invested in officials who bore the titles of the *san kung* of the Chou period, i.e. *Ta-ssu-ma*, *Ta-ssu-k'ung* and *Ta-ssu-t'u*. By this means it would be possible to revert to the models of a glorious age, and by its example to eliminate contemporary abuses. The government would be set up in imitation of the three luminaries of Heaven; each of the three officials would bear his defined duties; and instead of the hierarchic structure which had led from Chancellor to Imperial Counsellor, the three senior statesmen (*san kung*) would co-ordinate government from positions of equal status.

Ho Wu had received a regular training from the academicians and was well versed in the *Book of Changes*. He owed much to the members of the Wang family, in so far as both Wang Yin and Wang Ken, who had each held the title of *Ta-ssu-ma*, had recommended him for office. He had served in the capacity of Regional Inspector, assistant to the Chancellor, and Superintendent of Trials (10 BC); and his proposal for the change of structure and titles was probably made at the time of his promotion to Imperial Counsellor (third month, 8 BC).[13] Chang Yü, who supported Ho Wu, had likewise received a grounding in works such as the *Book of Changes* and the *Analects* and he had been praised by Hsiao Wang-chih, the

[12] *HS* 81.11a; *HS* 83.13b; and *HS* 86.1a, *et seq.*
[13] *HS* 19B.48a.

leading Reformist statesman of Yüan ti's reign.[14] Early in Ch'eng ti's reign, Chang Yü had co-operated closely with Wang Feng in the leadership of the Secretariat, and from 25 to 20 BC he had held the post of Chancellor.

However, Chang Yü was evidently more in favour with the Emperor than with certain members of the Wang family. He had earned the resentment of Wang Ken, after acquiring some coveted land from Ch'eng ti, and Wang Ken had countered by slandering him openly. Nevertheless Chang Yü continued to act as Ch'eng ti's consultant during the years 16 to 9 BC. On one occasion Ch'eng ti visited him in person to ask his advice. Certain calamities had been attributed to the domination that the Wang family were exercising in politics, and the Emperor wanted to hear Chang Yü's views. Chang Yü gave a circumspect and evasive reply, suggesting that the reasons for calamities cannot be fathomed; and that as there was little point in discussing miraculous phenomena, it would be better to attend to the affairs of state.

Ho Wu, then, who had been appointed Imperial Counsellor in the third month of 8 BC duly became *Ta-ssu-k'ung* a month later.[15] For the first time a complement of officials was established to support the *Ta-ssu-ma* in his duties, and what had hitherto been an honorary title became the designation of a post which carried an official seal and ribbon and a stipend.[16] But this change, which was based on Reformist principles, lay open to question by a number of officials, including Chu Po.

Chu Po is described[17] as a man of integrity and thrift who was not given to material indulgences. He rose from the humblest of positions to attain great wealth and honour, but he still kept to his frugal habits; and he differed from his colleagues in government in so far as there is no record of his training by masters of the books of the canon. In his youth he became known as a

[14] *HS* 81.11b.   [15] *HS* 19B.48a.   [16] *HS* 83.14a.
[17] *HS* 83.9b, 15b.

man of daring, ready to face any hazard in the pursuit of friendship and fun. In one of his feats he successfully impersonated a doctor, in order to make his way into prison and there visit one of his patrons;[18] and in this way he managed to save him from the death penalty. As a result, Chu Po was recommended for service; he was put on the staff of Wang Feng, and during the latter's dictatorship (33–32) he passed through a number of provincial posts, to become a Regional Inspector.[19]

Basically, Chu Po was a military officer who was not well versed in civil affairs or state institutions. His character enabled him to get the better of his subordinates, who tried to play on his ignorance; and his rigorous administration became feared throughout the area which he inspected. The same characteristics appear later, when he was governor of Lang-yeh commandery, and took strenuous action to prevent his subordinates from malingering. He was known as a martinet for discipline with a firm grasp on his staff, and as Metropolitan Superintendent of the Left[20] (from 15 BC) he employed informers to acquaint himself of what went on at the lower levels of the administration. Chu Po held the post of Superintendent of Agriculture for about a year (14 BC), and later became governor of Chien-wei Commandery, and then Superintendent of Trials (11).[21] Being general of the rear (10) he was dismissed for complicity in crimes of which a noble stood accused.

At the time when Ho Wu successfully introduced the changes of title and structure that are described above, Chu Po was not holding a high office of state. At some point after his dismissal as General of the Rear he became a Counsellor of the Palace;[22] and it was in that capacity that he was promoted

[18] Ch'en Hsien: he held the post of Superintendent of the Lesser Treasury from 16 to 14 (*HS* 19B.45a).

[19] *Tz'u-shih*: Dubs—Inspector of a Circuit.

[20] *Tso-p'ing-i*: Dubs—Eastern Supporter.

[21] *Ta-ssu-nung*: Dubs—Grand Minister of Agriculture; *T'ing-wei*: Dubs—Commandant of Justice; *T'ai-shou*: Dubs—Grand Administrator.

[22] *Kuang-lu ta-fu*: Dubs—Imperial Household Grandee.

Metropolitan Superintendent of the Right[23] in 7BC. It is therefore not clear whether he was one of the many counsellors who voiced misgivings at Ho Wu's change. The criticism which they offered was based on Modernist principles; for they believed that different times demand different institutions of state, and that a simple change in the titles or in the scope of duties of the most senior officials would not suffice to benefit the needs of the administration. It so happened that natural events came to the aid of the critics; the wells dried up in the courtyard of the Imperial Counsellor, or rather *Ta-ssu-k'ung*'s office; and the migrant birds, who used regularly to return in their thousands to nest in the oak trees that grew there failed to appear. In an age which was prone to pay attention to the signs of Heaven and Earth, such events cannot have failed to excite astonishment and alarm, and it is very likely that these phenomena were related by some observers to the recent changes perpetrated by man.

It is not known whether Chu Po was able to make use of these occasions to express his views, but he was certainly able to do so two years later when he had himself been appointed *Ta-ssu-k'ung*.[24] In a memorial to the throne he repeated that there was no call to follow tradition blindly in ordering the institutions of state, and that each case must rest on the expedients and demands of the times. He pointed out that the institution of a Chancellor and an Imperial Counsellor who ranked next below him had worked very well for 200 years of Han history; and he saw considerable advantage in a system whereby a man rose to become Chancellor after the experience of serving in the immediately junior post.

Ai ti accepted Chu Po's advice, and he was duly appointed Imperial Counsellor.[25] However, four years later Chu Po's work was to be undone, when the title of *Ch'eng-hsiang* was

[23] *Ching-chao-yin*: Dubs—Governor of the Capital.
[24] *HS* 19B.49a; this was dated on 4 December 6 BC.
[25] *HS* 19B.49a; this was dated on 8 May 5 BC.

replaced by that of *Ta-ssu-t'u*; and *Yü-shih ta-fu* was replaced by *Ta-ssu-k'ung*; this was in 1 BC, at a time when the title of *Ta-ssu-ma* was conferred first on Tung Hsien and later on Wang Mang.[26]

These changes indicate different concepts of government and different views of the functions of the senior officials of state. The posts of the *san kung*, which were associated with Chou, were attractive to the Reformists; the titles of Chancellor and Imperial Counsellor, which were inherited from Ch'in, were preferred by the Modernists. At the same time similar changes were introduced in respect of certain provincial posts. The regional inspectors (*tz'u-shih*) had been established in 106 BC,[27] to examine the work of officials in the commanderies, including the governors (*t'ai-shou*), and to report directly to the central government if they found evidence of corruption, oppression or official misconduct. One of the characteristics of these posts was that they were graded at a low stipend, far beneath that of the governors whose work they inspected.

Shortly after his nomination as *Ta-ssu-k'ung* (fourth month of 8 BC), Ho Wu had taken the opportunity to advise that the title *tz'u-shih* should be replaced by that of *mu*, or shepherd of the people; and the position of the *mu*, he hoped, would be commensurate with the senior nature of their duties.[28] The new officials would be superior to the men whose work they were assessing and whose consequent promotion or demotion lay in their hands; and as in the case of the *san kung*, so would the establishment of the *mu* be in accord with pre-Han practice of the glorious past. The change was effected in 8 BC and the stipend of the new officials was raised to the level of the governors of the commanderies. However, in 5 BC Chu Po succeeded in having the change revoked and the system of regional inspectors restored. Along with most of the senior

[26] *HS* 11.8a (*HFHD*, vol. III, p. 37); *HS* 19B.51a.
[27] *HS* 19A.26b, *et seq.*   [28] *HS* 83.14b.

officials of the central government, this practical man of affairs preferred a competitive hierarchical system, whereby those who had served successfully as regional inspectors could be promoted to become governors, and whereby low status and stipend stimulated men to greater effort and better service. A reversion to the use of the title shepherd of the people was effected in 1 BC.

The question of the imperial succession[29] formed a further matter of controversy which came into open discussion in 8 BC. Ch'eng ti had been reigning for twenty-five years but as yet he had no direct heir; and the nearest relatives who would form the obvious candidates to succeed him were his younger half-brother, Liu Hsing, king of Chung-shan, and his half-nephew, Liu Hsin, king of Ting-t'ao. Liu Hsin was said to be a man of some scholastic ability whose character fitted him for the imperial throne. His grandmother, the Dowager Empress Fu, took a number of steps, including bribery, to canvass on his behalf, and she was able to secure the support of Ch'eng ti's consort Chao,[30] and Wang Ken who held the title of *Ta-ssu-ma*. Ch'eng ti finally yielded to pressure and summoned a council to discuss the question. This involved, not only the rivalries between different families, but also the formal principle of whether a half-brother or a son of a half brother had a stronger claim to near kinship and therefore to the imperial succession.[31] The council was attended by Wang Ken, Chai Fang-chin (who had been Chancellor since 14), K'ung Kuang (Imperial Counsellor since 15), Lien Pao (General of the Right), and Chu Po (General of the Rear).[32] With one exception the advisers recommended the nomination of the king of Ting-t'ao.

[29] *HS* 81.16a; *HS* 97B.16b.

[30] i.e. *Chao Chao-i* (where *Chao-i* is the title for that particular grade of concubine; see *Aristocratic Ranks*, p. 162).

[31] For this question, see Fujikawa, pp. 139f.

[32] *HS* 81.17a; *HS* 84.1a, *et seq*. Lien Pao held the title of Protector General from 30 to 28 BC (see Chapter 7, p. 230, note 62).

This was Liu Hsin, the son of the Emperor's half-brother, and to support their case they cited the dictum of one of the books of proper behaviour, to the effect that the son of a brother is comparable with a son.

The exception was K'ung Kuang, who will appear in other discussions during the course of Ai ti's reign. He was a descendant of Confucius in the fourteenth generation and he had acquired a profound understanding of Han institutions. Under Ch'eng ti he had served as Director of the Secretariat and had taken care to avoid open contradiction of the Emperor's views. His sense of discretion was extreme, reaching possibly to a point of absurdity; for he is said to have refused to tell his family what trees had been planted in the palace grounds, for fear of infringing the demands of security. In upholding the cause of Ch'eng ti's half-brother, the king of Chung-shan, K'ung Kuang pointed out that the books of proper behaviour laid down that the nearest of kin should succeed; and that the King of Chung-shan, as well as being the brother of the reigning Emperor, was also the son of the previous Emperor. He also invoked a very ancient precedent from the kingdom of Yin. However, his arguments proved to be of no avail against the pressures to which Ch'eng ti was subject, and the king of Ting-t'ao was duly nominated heir apparent. K'ung Kuang paid the price of disagreement with the Emperor or with those who dominated him and was demoted to be Superintendent of Trials (8 BC). However, he was shortly able to retrieve his position: before the year was out he held the posts of Superintendent of the Lesser Treasury and General of the Left, and on the death of Chai Fang-chin (14 March 7 BC) he was appointed Chancellor.[33] The actual investiture of K'ung Kuang as Chancellor took place on the very night after Ch'eng ti's sudden death (17 April 7 BC), and Liu Hsin's formal accession as Emperor (Ai ti) followed some three weeks later (7 May). In

[33] *HS* 10.16a (*HFHD*, vol. II, p. 417); *HS* 19B.48a, b. For the discussion regarding the succession see *HS* 81.17b, *et seq.*

time the son of the rejected candidate was to accede and reign as the Emperor P'ing ti (1 BC–AD 5).

The changes that concerned the titles of officials may be seen to follow a pattern. In 8 BC new titles were introduced in conformity with Reformist principles, but these were withdrawn in 6 or 5 BC, under the influence of the more realistically minded statesman Chu Po; in 1 BC they were re-introduced, when the government was once more favourably inclined towards Reformism. A similar pattern may be observed in regard to the services of state, whose earlier changes are described more fully in Chapter 5.

In brief, from the foundation of the Han dynasty onwards, the state had maintained the worship of various deities at the sacred sites of Yung, in accordance with the practices of some centuries and the precedent set by the Ch'in empire. In Wu ti's reign, when Modernist principles were being pursued with renewed vigour and enthusiasm, worship of this type was reinforced by the foundation of further shrines at Kan-ch'üan and Fen-yin and the importance attached to these state cults was demonstrated by the more frequent attendance of the Emperor in person. A highly important change was introduced in 31 BC, when statesmen of Reformist views controlled state affairs. The existing practices were suspended and replaced by services of a simpler type, which were addressed to Heaven and Earth; and these were conducted at newly dedicated sites which lay at the outskirts of Ch'ang-an city. The change took place in the face of some criticism, and in 14 BC it was revoked, in the hope that the restoration of services of the old religion at Yung, Kan-ch'üan and Fen-yin would result in the birth of an imperial heir. However, Ch'eng ti died[34] without accomplishing this, and immediately before his interment and the formal accession of his successor, the Empress Dowager Wang ordered the

[34] *HS* 10.16a (*HFHD*, vol. II, p. 417); *HS* 11.6b (*HFHD*, vol. III, p. 33); *HS* 25B.18b.

restoration of the observances to Ch'ang-an (7 April 7 BC).

However, steps were soon taken to revert to practices which were associated with Modernist opinion. Ai ti's illnesses provided reason enough to summon to court masters of magic or other arts, and men of the type who had been in favour at Wu ti's court. As part of the reforms of Ch'eng ti's reign, 475 of a total of 683 provincial shrines had been abolished, and services had been suspended at all but fifteen of the 203 shrines of Yung. These were now restored, probably in 5 BC, and a total number of 37,000 services were said to have been conducted within the space of a year. In the following year (4 BC) the state cults were returned once again to Kan-ch'üan and the other traditional sites,[35] and it was left to Wang Mang to bring the worship back to Ch'ang-an, after his resumption of political power.

A further decision which was taken early in Ai ti's reign and which was based on Reformist principles of government might well have constituted a major innovation in the administrative practice of the Empire; and had it been fully implemented it could have been of prime importance in China's subsequent history. This was the attempt to introduce restrictions on land-ownership, which formed a controversial issue between the Modernist and Reformist points of view. The Modernist states-men were ready to allow, or even to encourage, free ownership to develop in response to private enterprise; for in this way the state would become richer as larger areas were put under the plough and revenue increased correspondingly. By contrast the Reformists took a grave view of the disparities of wealth that

[35] The restoration of worship at Kan-ch'üan is recorded for the year following the re-opening of the large number of sites elsewhere, and three years before the death of Ai ti (*HS* 11.6b, *HFHD*, vol. III, p. 33; *HS* 25B.18b, 19a). It would be of considerable interest to know the precise point of time at which the first of these changes was made in 5 BC, and whether it should be linked with other changes of that year directly.

had ensued from the unrestricted acquisition of land, and they would have liked to introduce controls so as to prevent the consequent distress and oppression of the poorer classes. Although Tung Chung-shu (*c.* 179 – *c.* 104 BC) had advocated such measures, it is hardly surprising that nothing had been done to this effect during Wu ti's reign or the ensuing decades; and it was not until the seventh month, or a little later, in 7 BC that proposals were actually put forward.

These proposals were made by Shih Tan,[36] who had received a training and enjoyed a patronage that prepared him for a career as a statesman of Reformist views. He had served K'uang Heng[37] and had been an academician at the end of Yüan ti's reign and under Ch'eng ti; and he had been recommended by K'ung Kuang and others by virtue of his great wisdom. He was appointed Counsellor of the Palace, and then senior tutor to the heir apparent,[38] i.e. the future Ai ti; and on Wang Mang's dismissal as *Ta-ssu-ma* (7 BC), Shih Tan was given the appointment in his place.[39]

In framing his proposals Shih Tan expressed the somewhat dubious statement that none of the holy kings of old had failed to practice the *ching-t'ien* system, with the result that their administration had always been equable. He continued by observing that no restrictions had been necessary on the owner-

---

[36] *HS* 11.2b (*HFHD*, vol. III, 21); *HS* 24A.20a (Swann, p. 200); *HS* 86.16a.

[37] See Chapter 4, p. 172.

[38] *Kuang-lu ta-fu*: Dubs—Imperial Household Grandee. *T'ai-tzu t'ai-fu*: Dubs—Grand Tutor to the heir apparent.

[39] There is some difficulty in dating Shih Tan's appointment precisely, as the figures that are given for the dates in *HS* 19B.48a, b are inconsistent and erroneous. Probably Wang Mang's dismissal and Shih Tan's appointment took place in the seventh month, and Shih Tan's tenure lasted until the tenth month. It seems unlikely that Shih Tan, who was General of the Left immediately before his appointment, would have had an opportunity to introduce his proposals for land reform until after his appointment as *Ta-ssu-ma*. See *HFHD*, vol. III, p. 132, note 3.1.

ship of land or slaves during the reign of Wen ti (180–157), when all energies had been devoted to increasing the yield of the land and to reducing expenditure; and as yet the growth of large landed estates under single ownership had not developed. However, in the succeeding years of peace, the rich had grown wealthier and mightier, while the poor had become poorer and more distressed. Certainly, in their conduct of government, statesmen should respect tradition and view the introduction of change very seriously, but the alleviation of suffering formed a just motive for such initiative, and restrictions on land ownership would now be appropriate.

Shih Tan's proposal to control the legal extent of land-holdings and of the number of slaves was referred for discussion to K'ung Kuang and Ho Wu; and as a result it was decided to introduce restrictions in varying degrees, according to the status and rank of the owner. In the event, however, the edict ordering these measures was not implemented, owing to the opposition of the Fu and Ting families and of Tung Hsien, who stood to lose heavily by Shih Tan's proposals.[40]

Other measures which were ordered by decree at much the same time as Shih Tan's proposals for restrictions on land ownership may be compared with the actions that had been taken by Reformist statesmen *c.* 47 and 44 BC.[41] These included steps to reduce the extravagance practised in the palace and to eliminate ways of oppressing the public. Thus, the production of luxury textiles for the palace was to be discontinued; the complement of staff serving in the palace was to be reduced; manumission was to be granted to slaves in government ownership; the stipends of junior officials were to be increased; cases of official oppression were to be investigated with a view to dismissing the officials who were responsible; and the Office of Music was abolished.[42] Two years later a further order of a

[40] *HS* 24A.20b (Swann, p. 203).   [41] See Chapter 5, pp. 159f.

[42] *HS* 11.3a (*HFHD*, vol. III, pp. 23f.) for the abolition of the Office of Music, see Chapter 6.

Reformist nature was announced (seventh month of 5 BC). It was decreed that, in order to avoid unnecessary disruption of the civilian population, migrations of the population should not be ordered to accompany the construction of imperial tombs.[43] This measure was in marked contrast with the civil disruption caused but a month earlier for the construction of the tomb for the Empress Ting;[44] previously Modernist governments had not hesitated to exploit occasions when labour was needed for this work to increase the control which they could exercise over civil occupations.

We may now consider the way in which the Fu and Ting families wielded their power to influence dynastic and political issues; the relative importance of the Emperor Ai ti himself; and the views of statesmen such as K'ung Kuang, Chu Po, Shih Tan and Tung Hsien. The immediate points of controversy were the tenure of the post of *Ta-ssu-ma*; the provision of the proper titles and of residences for the consorts of deceased emperors, and the style of burial for an imperial consort. By way of summary it may be said that at Ai ti's accession an attempt was made to instate the Fu and Ting families in power to the detriment of the Wang family. The attempt was opposed by Shih Tan, K'ung Kuang and Fu Hsi (who was actually the cousin of one of the two empresses who were involved); and owing to the efforts of the Empress Wang, who was supported by Chu Po, it did not achieve long-lasting success. It was left to Wang Mang at a later date to accord due honours to Fu Hsi for the part which he had played in these events.

Ai ti was in his eighteenth year at the time of his accession. He was no younger than several of his predecessors had been at a corresponding moment in their lives[45] but he had suffered

---

[43] *HS* 11.6a (*HFHD*, vol. III, p. 31).

[44] *HS* 11.5a (*HFHD*, vol. III, pp. 28–9).

[45] e.g. Wu ti (acceded in his sixteenth year; *HS* 6.1a, *HFHD*, vol. II, p. 27); Chao ti (in his eighth year; *HS* 7.1a, *HFHD*, vol. II, p. 151);

from poor health for many years.[46] From the outset of his reign
he took a personal part in government, and being thrifty in his
habits he tried to reduce the expenditure of the palace. In both
of these respects he formed a contrast with Ch'eng ti, whose
tastes lay more in gaming and amusements than in the work of
government, and whose palaces were by no means sparing in
their indulgences. During his youth, Ai ti had observed the
indolent way in which the previous Emperor had delegated the
cares of state to the members of the Wang family, and how that
family's fortunes had prospered; and he was determined to
remove such abuses at his accession. It was for this reason, in
an attempt to wrest control from the Wang family, that he
immediately conferred nobilities on members of the Ting and
Fu families.[47]

However, the success of these two families was short-lived.
In the words of the *Han-shu*[48] 'The Ting and Fu families rose to
sudden prominence for the space of a year or two and enjoyed
extraordinary success. But the authority and power which Ai ti
entrusted to them was not excessive and it was not comparable
with that which the Wang family had possessed in the days of
Ch'eng ti'. Early in Ai ti's reign Shih Tan[49] had foreseen the
dangers that might arise if the Emperor persisted in raising these
families to high positions as a means of reducing the strength
of the Wangs; and he had begged him to remember that the care
of the world rested with the Emperor's own kin. In addition he
expressed himself forcibly, in a style which would have done
credit to any of the Reformist statesmen of Yüan ti's reign,
against the suggestion that more honourable titles should be

Hsüan ti (in his eighteenth year; *HS* 8.3a, *HFHD*, vol. II, p. 204); Ch'eng
ti (in his nineteenth year; *HS* 10.1b, *HFHD*, vol. II, p. 373) and P'ing ti
(in his ninth year; *HS* 12.1a, *HFHD*, vol. III, p. 61, note 1.1).

[46] *HS* 75.32a; *HS* 81.17a; *HS* 86.15b.

[47] i.e. Ting Ming, Ting Man, Fu Yen, Fu Hsi and Fu Shang; *HS*
18.24a, b; 25a; 26a.

[48] *HS* 97B.18b.   [49] *HS* 86.16a, *et seq*.

granted to the Emperor's grandmother (the Dowager Empress Fu) and his mother (the Dowager Empress Ting).

'The institutions of our holy kings', he wrote, 'took their models from Heaven and Earth; as a result the prescribed distinctions of status were clear and the ethical relationships of man were set straight. In this way the polar opposites of the cosmos attained their correct stations, the powers of *yin* and *yang* followed their regular alternations, and the ruler of mankind and his myriad subjects together were blessed with good fortune. The distinctions of status provide a means of regulating the respective situations of Heaven and Earth and will not brook disruption.'

From these principles, Shih Tan argued against the grant of further titles; and he based his objections on the grounds of propriety and the need to maintain the correct hierarchies and marks of status of the cosmos. In this respect his arguments differed markedly from those that a Modernist might have put forward; for the Modernists regarded social and political hierarchies from a utilitarian point of view, as a means of regulating and disciplining the different classes of the community.

In all probability Shih Tan could only have raised these objections from a position of considerable strength; and it is likely that he expressed himself in this manner after his appointment as *Ta-ssu-ma*, which probably occurred in the seventh month of 7 BC. K'ung Kuang, the Chancellor,[50] added his voice in support of Shih Tan, as also did Fu Hsi, cousin of the Empress Fu; but as the issue is likely to have arisen and to have been discussed on several occasions, it is not possible to ascertain the sequence of events with certainty.

Fu Hsi's opposition to the conferment of the extra titles on the two Empresses shows that family solidarity did not always transcend other issues; and the subsequent story rests largely on the animosity that existed between the Empress Dowager and her cousin.[51] Fu Hsi had been a member of Ai ti's house-

---

[50] *HS* 81.18a. [51] *HS* 82.7b.

hold while the latter was heir apparent, and on his accession he was appointed Superintendent of the Guards[52] and then General of the Right. However, he evidently took exception to his cousin's intention to control her grandson and thus the Empire. Ai ti may have been informed of the difference of opinion, and, to avoid further friction, he offered Fu Hsi an honourable retirement. This was on the occasion of Shih Tan's appointment as *Ta-ssu-ma* (?seventh month of 7 BC); but some months later, when Shih Tan was demoted to become *Ta-ssu-k'ung*, Fu Hsi was appointed *Ta-ssu-ma* in his place (fourth month of 6 BC). At the time Ho Wu and others had impressed on Ai ti that, if he did allow Fu Hsi to retire, he would be represented as pandering to the will of the two Empresses Fu and Ting.

Fu Hsi's appointment as *Ta-ssu-ma* was followed by the Empress Fu's renewed claims for a title which would provide her with the marks of status and dignity that were comparable with that of the Empress Wang, Ch'eng ti's mother. Her expostulations were sufficiently strong to force Ai ti to dismiss Fu Hsi after less than a year in office; and in the second month of 5 BC the appointment was given to Ting Ming, older brother of Ai ti's mother the Empress Ting.[53] Ai ti was able to prevent the deprivation of Fu Hsi's nobility, that the Empress Fu had also requested; but it was not until the reign of P'ing ti, and Wang Mang's resurgence to power, that Fu Hsi was re-instated in a position of honour. Wang Mang was clearly rewarding Fu Hsi for his attempt to thwart the ambitions of the rivals to his own family.

There was another reason why Shih Tan was unable to sustain his position, apart from his opposition to the Empresses and their ambitions;[54] he was shown to have contradicted himself in the advice that he offered over the coinage; and after being accused of disclosing items of imperial business indiscreetly, he was dismissed from his post as *Ta-ssu-k'ung*.

In the meantime a further issue had arisen which concerned

[52] *Wei-wei*: Dubs—Commandant of the Palace Guard.
[53] *HS* 97B.18b.   [54] *HS* 86.18a.

the status of the Empresses and in which K'ung Kuang was involved and his career halted.[55] Shortly after Ai ti's accession, it became necessary to consider the problem of a suitable residence for the Grand Dowager Empress Fu. Being the grandmother of the Emperor, she had brought him up from infancy; and she still exercised a powerful influence on him in manhood. But while the Grand Empress Dowager Wang (i.e. the mother of Ch'eng ti) lived in the Ch'ang-lo palace in Ch'ang-an, the Empress Fu lived in a far less imposing way. Her son and grandson had in their time been kings of Ting-t'ao, but on her grandson's elevation to become Emperor, that kingdom had lapsed. The Empress Fu was therefore housed in one of the lodges that had been provided for the periodic use of those kings when they were paying homage to the throne.

K'ung Kuang realised the acute dangers that would arise if the Empress Fu were to be allowed to enjoy such close proximity to the imperial throne and thus to interfere in matters of state; and he therefore advised that a palace should be built for her, presumably some distance away from the centre. However, the Emperor took the advice of Ho Wu, and the Empress was allowed to live in the Northern Palace, from which there was direct and private access to the Emperor; by these means she was able to protect members of the Fu family from punishment or dismissal.

Both K'ung Kuang and Shih Tan raised vain protests against this type of favouritism; and both of the Empresses could call on the support of Chu Po. As has been seen, Chu Po had been appointed Metropolitan Superintendent of the Right in 7 BC;[56] and shortly after his appointment as *Ta-ssu-k'ung* (tenth month, 6 BC) he had called for the re-establishment of the title of Imperial Counsellor. He now put in a memorial suggesting the reduction of Shih Tan to the rank of commoner, and his suggestion was duly accepted. Acting in very close collaboration with the Empress Fu he had a bill of indictment drawn up

[55] *HS* 81.17b.   [56] *HS* 81.18a; *HS* 86.19b.

against K'ung Kuang, the Chancellor. He accused him of failure to scotch brigandage and to prevent the indolence of officials in the face of disaster; and he charged him with general incompetence as Chancellor. Kuang's dismissal followed immediately, and Chu Po was appointed in his place, in circumstances that will be described below (fourth month, 5 BC). In the same month the much coveted titles of honour were granted to the two Empresses.

Unfortunately the Empress Ting only survived these honours by two months. The orders that were given for the arrangements for her burial included a reference to the Emperor's desire to fulfil the duties that behoved a truly filial son, and to his wish to follow the precedents set in the Chou period.[57] However, this pious wish was not respected for long. Just as Wang Mang later took steps to re-instate Fu Hsi for his attempt to prevent the Empresses' acquisition of power, so too did he take steps to degrade the Empresses themselves. After P'ing ti's accession he had their graves opened, their insignia removed, and their remains re-interred in a style that was suitable for commoners. Shih Tan's detractors and opponents were reduced to the rank of commoner, and Shih Tan himself was ennobled, just a month or two before he died (AD 3).[58]

Chu Po was appointed Chancellor in the fourth month of 5 BC, and at the same time the post of Imperial Counsellor was given to Chao Hsüan.[59] It is clear that the appointments did not

[57] *HS* 11.5a (*HFHD*, vol. III, pp. 28–9); *HS* 18.25a; *HS* 97B.18b.
[58] *HS* 18.25a.
[59] Different versions are given for the dates of the appointments. *HS* 19B.49a gives *i wei* for Chu Po and *i hai* for Chao Hsüan; *HS* 27B(2).16a, b gives *i hai* but apparently omits the term for the actual day of the appointment. It is most likely that the two men were appointed on the same day and that this was *i wei* (19 May). In addition there is some doubt regarding the post formerly held by Chao Hsüan; *HS* 19B.49a gives this as *chung-wei*, but this post did not exist under that title in 5 BC; see *HS* 19B.49a, note by Wang Hsien-ch'ien; *HS* 27B (2).16b reads *shao fu*.

meet with general approbation, in view of the accounts of a strange phenomenon that occurred at the time and the reactions of at least two scholars who commented on the meaning of such incidents. As the two officials were waiting to receive their documents of appointment, a loud noise was heard, as of bells ringing, but no source of the disturbance could be detected. The sound was audible to all the courtiers and those who stood to arms at the ceremony, and the Emperor called for an explanation from Yang Hsiung and Li Hsün.

Yang Hsiung is well known for his literary work and for his contribution to China's intellectual development. He expressed views that may properly be described as Reformist, and in many ways he appears as the pre-cursor of Wang Ch'ung's rationalism of the first century AD; it is hardly surprising, therefore, that Wang Mang could rely on his support.[60] But for the particular occasion with which we are concerned, the *Han-shu* gives a fuller account of Li Hsün's reply than of Yang Hsiung's.

Li[61] specialised in the interpretation of phenomena and he followed strictly in the tradition set by Tung Chung-shu, seeing symbolic meanings in the motions of the sun, the moon and the stars. He related these movements to the actions taken by the leaders of men, and looked therein for signs of the warnings of Heaven.

Li Hsün had been trained in the *Book of History*, in astronomy and in the science of *Yin-yang*. In the world of politics, he had served under Chai Fang-chin and he had been well treated by Wang Ken (Marshal of State, 11–7 BC), who consulted him in connection with a number of strange phenomena. In a lengthy reply Li Hsün followed the usual pattern of referring to events which had actually taken place in the past; to their prognostication by certain phenomena; and to the consequent verification that such phenomena were the warning voice of Heaven. In this

[60] For Yang Hsiung, see T. Pokora, 'The necessity of a more thorough study of the philosopher Wang Ch'ung and his predecessors' (*Archiv Orientální*, 1962, pp. 243f.).　　[61] *HS* 75.21a.

way the threat of floods which had caused a panic in Ch'ang-an in 30BC[62] should not be regarded as a disaster but rather as a sure sign that Heaven was still maintaining the divine protection which it afforded to the Han dynasty; and he advised that a search should be made for new talent, that lay hidden from the public eye, and that certain advisers whose influence was evil should be eliminated. After Ai ti's accession, Li Hsün was again consulted in connection with floods, earthquakes and certain peculiar movements of the heavenly bodies. He repeated his belief in the efficacy of prognostication and verification, and warned the throne of the danger of becoming embroiled by the importunities of the women of the palace.

Li Hsün was ready to raise a protest against the influence of the Inner Court; and he stood in direct antagonism to men such as Chu Po, who were reacting against current abuses by seeking to impose a stricter control over the population, and by favouring Modernist methods of government. In his clear cut call for reform, Li Hsün associated the movements of the heavenly bodies with the actions and success of the sovereign, and he thought it essential to conduct the administration in accordance with the prescriptions and prohibitions that were proper to each of the seasons.[63] It is of considerable interest to note that he drew nostalgically on the examples of the Reformist statesmen Kung-sun Hung (died 122) and Kung Yü (died 44).[64] Kung-sun Hung had called for a rectification of mores, but he had been disregarded; and in the time of Kung Yü men had been ready to speak their minds, and had not been intimidated by the women of the palace.

If Li Hsün was bold enough to remind his readers of these precedents, it is hardly surprising that he made full use of the untoward incident that had occurred at Chu Po's investiture to protest against his appointment. He quoted[65] a dictum of the

---

[62] See Chapter 5.   [63] *HS* 75.24b, *et seq.*

[64] For Kung-sun Hung see *HS* 58.1a, *et seq.*, and Chapter 1, p. 20; for Kung Yü, see *HS* 72.9b and Chapter 5, p. 159.   [65] *HS* 27B (2).16b.

Hung-fan and recalled certain other occurrences to show that the sovereign was in danger of being misled. 'When a man whose reputation has no substance achieves advancement, then there are heard sounds without bodily form, and their origin cannot be comprehended'. He asked bluntly for the dismissal of the new Chancellor and Imperial Counsellor, so as to conform with the phenomena that had been manifested by Heaven. If they were not dismissed, he warned, before a full year had elapsed they would be overcome by calamities of their own seeking.

Yang Hsiung likewise took the view that the sound of undetected bells was a sign of error.[66] He regarded Chu Po as a man of strong determination who was given to the exercise of power and to scheming, and as a man who was more suitable for appointment to a military than to a civil post; and he predicted difficulties and disaster.

These predictions were only too true.[67] In the eighth month of 5 BC, i.e. only four months after his appointment as Chancellor, Chu Po was accused of treason and committed suicide; and Chao Hsüan, who also lay open to a charge, was fortunately able to secure a reduction from the extreme penalty. The crime for which they stood arraigned was that, rather than maintain the Emperor's full privileges and prerogatives, they had chosen to form a close association with the relations of the imperial consorts, thereby prejudicing the conduct of the Government.

Perhaps the most important event that occurred while Chu Po held the post of Chancellor was the introduction of the regnal title T'ai-ch'u-yüan-chiang from the sixth to the eighth months of 5 BC.[68] This came about at the suggestion of Hsia Ho-liang

[66] *HS* 27B (2).17a.

[67] *HS* 11.6a (*HFHD*, vol. III, p. 32); *HS* 19B.49a; *HS* 83.16a.

[68] *HS* 11.5a, *et seq.* (*HFHD*, vol. III, 29f.); *HS* 75.31a, *et seq.*; see *HFHD*, vol. III, pp. 6f.; and Tjan Tjoe Som, *Po Hu T'ung* (Leiden, 1949), pp. 124f.

and a few other men who had been pupils of a certain Kan Chung-k'o, of Ch'i. During the reign of Ch'eng ti, Kan Chung-k'o had been engaged in the study of calendrical reckoning; in a book that extended for twelve chapters,[69] he claimed that the 'Lord of Heaven' (*T'ien ti*) had sent Ch'ih ching tzu with a revelation. Ch'ih ching tzu, the essential spirit of Red, was made of truth and integrity, and he disclosed that the juncture reached by the Han dynasty formed the closing point of the cycle of Heaven and Earth, and that it faced the need to receive a renewal of the mandate from Heaven.

Kan Ch'ung-ko had first voiced this prophesy during Ch'eng ti's reign, and the matter had been referred to Liu Hsiang (79–8 BC). That great man of learning had pronounced that Kan Chung-k'o was laying a false claim to making contact with the spirits, thereby deceiving the emperor and bewildering mankind; and Kan was promptly thrown into prison where he died. Nevertheless, his pupils, who included Hsia Ho-liang, continued to propagate his doctrine, and saw that it was brought to official notice after Ai ti's accession. On this occasion Liu Hsin was consulted. He concurred with his father's view, observing that Kan's belief did not conform with the Five Books of the Canon and that it should therefore not be publicised. However, there were some at court who were able to discredit Liu Hsin over certain other matters; and Li Hsün and some others saw fit to encourage Hsia Ho-liang to continue with the propagation of his doctrine. In 5 BC Hsia Ho-liang was bold enough to inform the court that the Han dynasty had now reached the end of its allotted span and stood in need of renewal. Because Ch'eng ti had failed to respond to this need, he had not been blessed with a direct heir; the continued illness of the Emperor and the phenomena that had been reported recently were further signs of Heaven's warning. Only by the immediate adoption of a new regnal title and new imperial titles would it be possible to achieve prosperity, to procure the

[69] i.e. *chüan*; the book was called *Pao yüan t'ai p'ing ching*.

birth of an imperial heir and to avert further phenomena.

Hoping for a cure for his illness, Ai ti followed Hsia Ho-liang's advice, and in a long and carefully worded edict[70] he ordered a general amnesty, the immediate adoption of the regnal title T'ai-ch'u yüan chiang for the current year, and the change of the Emperor's own title to *Ch'en sheng Liu T'ai-p'ing huang-ti*. At the same time it was ordered that the dials of water clocks should in future be graduated in 120 divisions.

Unfortunately there was no abatement in the Emperor's illness. Thwarted in the furtherance of their ideas, Hsia Ho-liang and his friends made a vain attempt to have Li Hsün and others who were sympathetic to their cause appointed to high places in the government; but this suggestion went too far, and Hsia Ho-liang and his collaborators were imprisoned for their pains. An edict of the eighth month blamed Hsia for failure to substantiate his claims, and for infringing the ethical principles of the Canon and of the traditional institutions of state. All the measures adopted in the sixth month were revoked, except for the general amnesty. Hsia Ho-liang was put to death on a charge of disobeying moral principles, of misleading mankind and of behaving treacherously. Li Hsün was fortunate enough to secure a reduction of the death penalty and to be punished by removal to Tun-huang commandery.

The choice of the term T'ai-ch'u yüan-chiang[71] for the regnal title may perhaps show a conscious desire to evoke the memories of an earlier title, T'ai-ch'u. This had been introduced exactly one hundred years previously, for the year 104 BC; and the adoption of this title 'The Grand Beginning' had been but one of several measures which bore an important symbolic significance and which were intended to display the successful way in which the dynasty had been enjoying divine blessings.[72]

---

[70] *HS* 11.5a (*HFHD*, vol. III, p. 29); *HS* 75.32a.

[71] For this expression and the loss of the words *yüan-chiang* in some passages, see *HFHD*, vol. III, p. 30, note 5.8.

[72] For the adoption of this regnal title, see Chapter 1.

This had taken place at a time when the policies of Modernist statesmen had reached their most successful point, and when the grandeur of imperial prestige had never been higher. Whether or not it was intended to call this achievement to mind in 5 BC cannot be determined. No mention is made of that occasion in the edict which ordered the adoption of *T'ai-ch'u yüan-chiang*, although it does refer to the 200 years that had elapsed since the foundation of the dynasty.

The reason why it was decided to divide the period of the day into 120 parts is again not certain. Since Ch'in it had been the practice to divide the twelve hours into a total of 100 divisions, and that system is maintained on the two surviving examples of time-pieces of the Han period.[73] However, it is possible that the change to 120 parts for a few months in 5 BC was connected with the choice of the patron element of the dynasty. Until 104, this had been determined as Water but it had then been changed to Earth; the favourite numbers associated with these elements were six for Water and five for Earth. The decision to divide the day into 120 instead of 100 parts may conceivably be interpreted as a means of calling to mind the importance of six and the element Water; for it was under the aegis of that element that Modernist policies such as Chu Po advocated had been most in favour.

Later on the changes of 5 BC may have been associated with the theory of the Five Elements in a different and more significant way. According to Modernist opinion, the Five Elements followed one another according to the order of 'Mutual Conquest',[74] but according to the Reformist view they did so by way of 'Mutual Production'. To secure popular support and conviction for the legality of his regime, Wang

[73] See *RHA*, vol. I, pp. 126, 160, note 1 and vol. II, p. 20 and references there to works by Lao Kan and Needham; see also *Everyday Life*, p. 103 and fig. 33.

[74] See Needham, *Science and Civilisation in China*, vol. 2, pp. 255f.; and Chapter 9, p. 302f, below.

Mang, as in other respects, sponsored the Reformist view; and he tried to show that his own dynasty, which lay under the blessing of Earth (yellow), followed in proper sequence from a dynasty which had been blessed by Fire (red); for Fire produces Earth. For these reasons, Wang Mang clutched at the few indications that he could find to show that the Han dynasty had been founded under the aegis of Fire. Consequently, the prophecy which had rested on revelations of the essential spirit of red and which had been quoted in 5 BC had a particular attraction for Wang Mang. It may be noted that this prophecy, which had led to the abortive introduction of a new regnal title in 5 BC also figured in a memorial which Wang Mang presented in AD 8, in preparation for his assumption of the imperial throne.[75]

Tung Hsien was two years younger than Ai ti.[76] The favours which he acquired from the Emperor included appointments for his relatives, presents drawn from the imperial treasures, the authority to keep arms, the use of imperial transport and a mausoleum which was being constructed on an imperial scale of splendour. But these privileges were not extended until two years after Ai ti's accession, i.e. from perhaps 5 BC; and it was not until 3 BC that Ai ti was able to fabricate a reason for granting Tung Hsien a nobility. This was not achieved without protest, with which Ting Ming, *Ta-ssu-ma* since 5 BC, manifested considerable sympathy. By 1 BC the Emperor was able to issue a decree replacing Ting Ming by his favourite, who thus achieved the distinction of the title *Ta-ssu-ma* at the tender age of twenty-two. Members of the Tung family found themselves in receipt of greater honours and privileges than those that had been enjoyed by either the Fu or the Ting families; and on his visit to Ch'ang-an in 1 BC the Shan-yü of the Hsiung-nu expressed surprise that anyone so young should take so prominent

[75] *HS* 99A.34b (*HFHD*, vol. III, p. 251).
[76] *HS* 93.8a, *et seq.*; *HS* 97B.16b, *et seq.*

a place among the great ones of the court. Ai ti ordered his interpreter to explain that, young though he was, the *Ta-ssu-ma* occupied his position thanks to his very great ability and wisdom. The Shan-yü dutifully bowed his head and congratulated the Han Emperor on obtaining the services of able ministers of state. But Ai ti was shortly to go yet further by making a gesture to his favourite that had been unparalleled in imperial history. He suggested—apparently while under the influence of alcohol —that he should follow the precedent set by the blessed Yao and Shun, and abdicate in favour of Tung Hsien. It was left to Wang Hung[77], nephew of Wang Mang, to insist on the principle of hereditary succession and to beg the Emperor not to jest. Ai ti was forced to accept the rebuke and to abandon his scheme.

Ai ti's death (15 August, 1 BC) precipitated a complete change in the fortunes of those who had been concerned with the destiny of the dynasty.[78] A few months before the event, Tung Hsien had taken it as a bad omen that the outer wall of his splendidly built mansion had collapsed without visible cause; and he soon had reason to believe that his fears were only too well grounded. Almost immediately after Ai ti's death, the Grand Empress Wang summoned him to discuss the arrangements for the funeral, and she was able to claim that his incompetence was such that she had no alternative to dismissing him out of hand. Unable to face the disgrace, Tung Hsien and his wife killed themselves (16 August). The next day the Grand Empress summoned Wang Mang and appointed him to be *Ta-ssu-ma*, with orders to supervise the Secretariat. A month had still to pass before arrangements were made for the imperial succession to pass to Liu Chi-tzu, son of that very brother of Ch'eng ti who had been by-passed for the succession in 7 BC.[79] And as the two Empresses Ting and Fu had already died, in

[77] *HS* 93.11a, b; *HS* 18.19b.
[78] *HS* 11.8a (*HFHD*, vol. III, p. 37); *HS* 12.1a (*HFHD*, vol. III, p. 61); *HS* 19B.51a; *HS* 93.11b.
[79] *HS* 12.1a (*HFHD*, vol. III, p. 61); *HS* 14.23b.

5 BC and 1 BC, respectively[80] the way lay open for the Wang family to re-establish and consolidate its fortunes with greater strength than ever.

Reference has been made above to the steps taken by Wang Mang to degrade the Ting and Fu families; at the same time Wang Mang sought to reward with high honours one particular official who had struggled to prevent those families from acquiring dominion. This was K'ung Kuang who, even in Ai ti's time, had been appointed Chancellor immediately after the death of the Empress Fu.[81] He was now given the title of *T'ai-fu*, Senior Tutor, and then *T'ai-shih*, Senior Teacher.[82] These constituted the most honourable posts that a senior statesman could hold in an official hierarchy that followed the models of the Kings of Chou.

By way of summary, it may be remarked that Ai ti's reign formed an interlude in which the fortunes of the Wang family suffered a set-back at the hands of the Fu and Ting families and Tung Hsien. At the same time the Reformist point of view, ably represented by statesmen such as Ho Wu, K'ung Kuang and Shih Tan, became subject to opposition, mainly from Chu Po. But in neither case was the effect long-lasting. The interests of the Fu and Ting families and of Chu Po were not sufficiently closely identified to make a long-term alliance against the Wang family feasible, although there were occasions when Chu Po was willing to act on behalf of the Empress Fu. However, Chu Po could be no match for his political opponents, who enjoyed the advantages of a scholastic training, a social background and political manipulation which Chu Po had not personally experienced. While men such as K'ung Kuang and Shih Tan were probably anxious to eliminate all female influ-

---

[80] *HS* 11.5a, 7b (*HFHD*, vol. III, pp. 28, 37).

[81] *HS* 11.8a (*HFHD*, vol. III, p. 38); *HS* 19B.50b.

[82] *HS* 19B.51a; Dubs renders *T'ai-fu* as Grand Tutor, and *T'ai-shih* as Grand Master.

ence from the palace and the government, Ai ti, either for his own reasons or owing to the pressure that was brought upon him, wished to remove the Wang family's influence and transfer ti to the Fu and Ting families; and in this venture he was able to enlist the support of Chu Po. When, finally, the Wang family staged a come-back, they were immediately able to scotch any threat of rivalry from Ai ti's favourite Tung Hsien; and the further success of the Wang family may well have been built on moralist pretensions. For they claimed that they were restoring stability and normality to the political and dynastic scene, and so could pose as the representatives of the Reformist point of view.

CHAPTER 9

The Support for Wang Mang – AD 9

If the mood of those who stood around waiting for the ceremony to begin on the day of the winter solstice in 105 BC[1] had been one of loyalty, pride and hope, it may be asked what was the dominant feeling of those who attended the ceremonies of court in AD 9, when solemn acts of state signified the inauguration of the Hsin dynasty of Wang Mang.[2] It may be surmised that some at least of the courtiers and officials who had witnessed the decay of the house of Liu in the previous decades and the collapse of the loyalties that it had commanded for over two centuries were filled with unease, disillusion or bewilderment. Others perhaps were ready to accept that in the prevailing weakness and dynastic failure of the Han Empire a new dispensation would be better fitted to maintain the principles of a traditional order and to cherish those values that formed the essential element of the rule of the son of Heaven.

Perhaps there was a sense of bewilderment at the apparent contradiction between the claims made by the new government and the facts as they were known to most people; although the time had long gone by since spokesmen of government had insisted that appearance and reality, or the claims of government and their verification,[3] must coincide, there were

---

[1] See Chapter 1.

[2] e.g. the pronouncements made at his accession (*HS* 99A.35b; *HFHD*, vol. III, p. 255) and the religious ceremonies started for the new dynastic house (*HS* 99B.4b; *HFHD*, vol. III, p. 274).   [3] i.e. *ming* and *shih*.

still many reasons for distrust by those who looked at recent developments critically.

The principle of imperial rule, based on the hereditary succession of the monarch, could be traced back with some uncertainty to the famous 'Three Dynasties'; but it had certainly been followed during the Han dynasty. How then had it come about that someone who was not a member of the Liu family had been enthroned as Emperor? And those who had a long memory for constitutional precedent may well have recalled the solemn oath that had been agreed between Liu Pang, the first Han Emperor, and his immediate followers at the outset of the dynasty. This had been designed to ensure that none save a member of the house of Liu should be appointed to be a king in one of the domains of the Empire;[4] surely it was all the more flagrant a breach of tradition if this principle had been abandoned in the case of the Emperor himself.

The claim that Wang Mang had been acting the part of a second Duke of Chou was almost certainly advanced with his connivance. But unfortunately herein lay another anomaly. For, as was told in the sacred writings, the Duke of Chou had lent his assistance nobly to an infant king and retired selflessly when the latter had attained the age of majority. It could hardly be claimed that Wang Mang's behaviour was comparable with this precedent. In the first place his origins came from a completely different family—indeed from one of the scorned and distrusted families of imperial consorts, who had before now embroiled the palace hideously in intrigue and dynastic plot; and, secondly, so far from effacing himself in order to preserve the continuity of the reigning house, Wang Mang had allowed himself to be persuaded to substitute the Wang family in place of the Liu family.

But, even granted that the new regime was modelled on the great house of Chou, was there any reason to suppose that it

[4] *SC* 9.10 and 9.23 (*MH*, vol. II, pp. 414 and 426); *SC* 17.3; *HS* 3.5b (*HFHD*, vol. I, p. 201); *HS* 18.1b.

had really adopted its principles and that it could flourish in the same magnificent way in which that kingdom was alleged to have prospered some thousand years previously? For it was said that the kings of Chou had ruled and possessed their moral authority thanks to the blessing of Heaven, and it could therefore be expected that if Wang Mang's regime was intended to resemble that of Chou, it too would receive such benefits. But was there any convincing evidence that this would be likely? Certainly the floods of the Yellow River which were to burst forth in two or three years' time could hardly argue that an era of cosmic harmony had dawned. And although Wang Mang had seen to it that a lot was made of the strange events that had been reported to the court, there was no definite certainty that they had taken place spontaneously. Indeed, there were some who questioned the truth of these events; for example of the stone said to have been engraved with characters in red that ordered Wang Mang to assume the imperial throne, or of the strange dream which had been reported to a member of the house of Liu. In that vision the dreamer had been informed of Wang Mang's accession and provided with corroborative proof.[5]

In addition, opinion was by no means clear as to the interpretation of these phenomena or omens; and you could never tell whether, after the passage of a few years, the same events would be said to have forecasted Wang Mang's success or his failure. Even more to the point, if Wang Mang had really been chosen to be Heaven's representative, one might at least expect that there was good reason why Heaven should desert Han after the two centuries in which it had chosen to bless the dynasty. No signs of such an abandonment had been vouchsafed, despite the abortive attempt to find them a few years previously (see Chapter 8).

[5] For the stone (AD 6), see *HS* 99A.25a (*HFHD*, vol. III, 218–19); for the dream and other portents (AD 9) see *HS* 99A.34a (*HFHD*, vol .III, p. 250).

Some people doubtless had a ready answer to this question, and would say that it was only recently that the government had finally decided to direct the cults of state towards Heaven and not towards the placation of other powers. It was true that it had only been since 31 BC that the house of Liu had come to worship Heaven formally and with the most solemn of services, and since then the religious devotions of the house had been anything but consistent or regular. Could one wonder, in such circumstances, that Heaven had bestowed its favours elsewhere, to one of its own known devotees?

Indeed the foundation of the Hsin dynasty had come about in a singularly peculiar way. As yet China's imperial history was short. Only two houses had claimed to rule as Emperors of all China, and there was no series of precedents which could be cited in favour of establishing a new regime or which showed how a defunct regime had justifiably fallen into ruin and merited replacement.

Wang Mang's rise to prominence had depended to some extent on the good fortune and high positions which had been enjoyed by his forbears in the fifty years which immediately preceded his accession. At the same time there were some remarkable similarities between the ways in which the Wang family had been able to further their fortunes and earlier examples. For there had been several occasions in which the family of an imperial consort had risen to the highest places in the state; and although the circumstances were somewhat different in each case there were certain features in common that could bear a grave interpretation.

Over two centuries previously, after the demise of the founder emperor, the Empress Dowager Lü had made a bid to win supreme power; she had started by being content to rule behind the scenes, while two infant Emperors had been nominally enthroned; and she had seen that some of her closest relations were appointed to the highest offices of state. Finally she had been able to assume imperial rule in her own person; and but for the eventual antagonism and resistance of the Liu family, she might well have succeeded in substituting the Lü for the Liu family.

Other examples could be quoted from the subsequent history of the dynasty. The family of Wu ti's Empress Wei had held senior positions and exercised considerable influence on the conduct of public affairs; but the debacle of 91 BC had effectively prevented them from seizing pride of place before the Emperor.[6] Later the Huo family had come near to exercising supreme power in the Empire;[7] Huo Kuang had been virtual dictator during the minority of the Emperors Chao ti and Hsüan ti, and these had been married to his granddaughter and daughter, respectively. Like Wang Mang, Huo Kuang had exercised his influence by virtue of his title of *Ta-ssu-ma* or Marshal of State; and it was just this title that had been held by four members of the Wang family before Wang Mang.[8] The strength of the latter had been built up, like that of Huo Kuang, during the minority of an emperor (P'ing ti), to whom he had married his daughter. But there was one important reason to differentiate between the two cases. This lay in the final step which Wang Mang had actually taken in AD 9, when he assumed the title of Emperor. And at that time there were doubtless some who remembered that the plot to instal Huo Kuang's son, Huo Yü, in that position had ended in the renewal of the strength of the Liu family and the utter ruin of the Huo family.[9]

To some it may have seemed that there were further reasons for bewilderment; for while Wang Mang was actively displaying characteristics or adopting modes of behaviour that were ascribed to the Duke of Chou, there were also those who saw him as a second Huo Kuang.[10] However, it needed only a

[6] See Chapter 2.   [7] See Chapter 4.
[8] See Chapter 5, p. 158, note 10.   [9] See Chapter 4.
[10] *HS* 99A.14b (*HFHD*, vol. III, p. 176).

moment's reflection to show that the political attitudes and fundamental principles of the Duke of Chou and Huo Kuang were utterly at variance. How could Wang Mang be likened both to the Duke, who was quoted as believing in the exercise of government by precept and ethical example, and to Huo Kuang, who had been praised for the initiative, expansion and positive methods of government?

Possibly this contradiction appears to be clearer now than it did at the time. For to the Chinese it was more important to preserve form than to adhere to accepted opinion. It was more important, if Wang Mang's claims to leadership were to be accepted, to show that his position and status were those that had been held honourably in the past; for this held greater significance than drawing a precise parallel with a single paragon of good conduct. It was necessary to compare Wang Mang with those who had deserved well of China by contributing to its tranquillity and welfare; and for this purpose it was perfectly possible to accord Wang Mang due praise for his appearance in the role of successful statesman who had held completely opposing views or advocated contradictory policies. The main point of the comparison lay in the positions of state that they held and their recognised part in the structure of government, and in this way excellent precedents were found for Wang Mang to follow, both in the Duke of Chou, as Regent, and in Huo Kuang, as Regent and Marshal of State.

There were those at court in AD 9 who had heard talk of dark deeds that had been perpetrated in the palace in the past so as to secure the dynastic succession for a son or to rob a rival family of this honour. It was well known that two sons of Ch'eng ti, borne of low class women, had been put to death, some said by the Emperor's own hand.[11] These crimes had been committed in 12 and 11 BC and they had been intended to placate one of Ch'eng ti's mistresses, the concubine Chao; but little good had come of this in the long run, so far as the Chao

[11] See *HFHD*, vol. II, pp. 369f.

family was concerned. For once Ai ti's reign was over and Wang Mang had regained a dominant place at court, he had lost no time in seeing that the two Chao sisters, one of them Ch'eng ti's Empress and the other his mistress, were degraded and removed from court;[12] later the Empress was forced to commit suicide. In addition there were ugly rumours circulating about the way in which P'ing ti had met his end, at a mere fourteen years of age;[13] none could be sure that Wang Mang had not had a hand in that. Similarly, one could not help wondering what had happened to the two-year-old infant who had been thrust forward at the time of P'ing ti's death in AD 6, and for whom Wang Mang had acted as regent.[14]

Probably there were some who genuinely welcomed Wang Mang's decisive actions as a determined effort to free the court of the pernicious rivalries and intrigues that had bedevilled it for so long; and they may have been willing to countenance some ruthless action in order to secure this end. In this way the posthumous degradation of the Ting and Fu empresses[15] may have been seen as an attempt to rid the court of malicious influences and to introduce a measure of stability. But it must have been difficult to sustain this charitable view of Wang Mang's behaviour when this extended to acts that were unethical, violent and criminal; and so it had fallen out with Wang Mang's treatment of P'ing ti's own mother and other members of the Wei family. Wang Mang started by doing his best to keep them away from the palace, but an attempt had

---

[12] See *HFHD*, vol. II, pp. 45–6 and *HS* 99A.4a (*HFHD*, vol. III, p. 137).

[13] See *HFHD*, vol. III, p. 57 for a consideration of this question. Dubs' conclusion, after examining the relevant passages and considering the motives, is that while there is not sufficient evidence to sustain a definite charge that Wang Mang had murdered P'ing ti, there is reason to acquit him of the allegation.

[14] i.e. Liu Ying, *HS* 99A.25a (*HFHD*, vol. III, p. 217); for his dismissal see *HS* 99B.1b (*HFHD*, vol. III, pp. 261–2); and for his subsequent isolation see *HS* 99B.2b (*HFHD*, vol. III, p. 264).

[15] *HFHD*, vol. III, pp. 45f.; see Chapter 8.

been made to resist this pressure, and he had reacted sharply and in a way which was by no means new to Han dynastic politics. To avoid the danger of dispute, Wang Mang had the Wei family eliminated, mainly by execution; and although the Empress' mother was herself left alive with the enjoyment of full honours, Wang Mang did not hesitate to have his own son executed; for he had been involved in a plot to re-instate the Wei family.[16]

It may be asked how Wang Mang's political principles were translated into practice and how far they affected the conduct of affairs, the measures of government and the lives of individuals. This question may be examined in connection with social distinctions, state institutions, land-tenure, the coinage and foreign affairs.

Han had inherited certain social distinctions from the Ch'in Empire. These had derived from the need of government to encourage service to the state, to spread the load of administrative duties among those who could undertake them, and to display the bounties of imperial government publicly. For these purposes the Ch'in Empire had devised, and the Han Empire inherited, a system of some twenty orders of honour, which conveyed to the recipient symbols of social status and privileges of a material nature, such as exemption from state service and relief from the most cruel punishments of state. The system had been operated in different ways during the Han dynasty and was distinct from the further mark of high honour and social status, the title of king, which was conferred on relatives of the emperor and held on an hereditary basis.[17]

These twenty orders of honour, of which the highest was that of the *hou* or nobility, were redolent of the aims of Modernist

---

[16] *HS* 97B.21b–22b; and *HS* 99A.16a (*HFHD*, vol. III, p. 180).

[17] See *Aristocratic Ranks*. It is to be noted that the Ch'in system comprised seventeen or eighteen ranks and the Han system twenty ranks, of which the highest (*hou*, nobility) was held on an hereditary basis.

government in so far as they derived from an attempt to make the state as strong and rich as possible, by offering effective rewards for services rendered; and under Wang Mang they were effectively replaced by a different set of formal distinctions of rank that had formed an element of the tradition of the kings of Chou. Even before P'ing ti's death, Wang Mang had himself received the title of An Han kung (AD 4),[18] and this had constituted a new departure in imperial practice, which had not hitherto used the expression *kung*. This deliberate resuscitation of a term which had featured in the history of China before the Ch'in era was followed in AD 8 by the institution of five ranks of nobility, which were claimed to have been in use under the kings of Chou.[19] Those who had held the nobilities of the Han Empire were given new titles, accordingly, while the title *kung* was reserved for exceptional cases only. The final step of abolishing the titles held by the kings of Han ensued in AD 9;[20] and until the Han dynasty was restored, there occurred no general conferment of the lower orders of honour such as had formed a notable feature of state occasions in the past.[21]

These actions may appear to be no more than formal changes, but in so far as they struck a keynote for contemporary government their symbolic effect may have been far greater than their practical significance. The same principle may apply to changes that were introduced in the nomenclature of some of the institutions of state. The terms adopted by Wang Mang as titles for the senior officials of the central government and the provin-

---

[18] *HS* 99A.17a–18a (*HFHD*, vol. III, pp. 185f.).

[19] i.e. *Kung, hou, po, tzu* and *nan*; see *HS* 99A.31a (*HFHD*, vol. III, p. 238). For further steps that were taken in AD 12, see *HS* 99B.19a (*HFHD*, vol. III, p. 321).

[20] *HS* 99B.4b (*HFHD*, vol. III, p. 274).

[21] See *Aristocratic Ranks*, p. 168. Along with other changes of AD 8, the title *Kuan-nei-hou* fell into disuse and was replaced by that of *Fu-ch'eng* (*HS* 99A.31b, 32a; *HFHD*, vol. III, p. 241).

cial government alike were largely taken from phrases that appear in the *Book of History* and in this way Wang Mang asserted his claim to be re-establishing the institutions of a glorious past.[22]

Reference has already been made[23] to the abortive proposals of Shih Tan to introduce restrictions on land holdings and slave-ownership; and despite political rivalries,[24] Wang Mang was likewise ready to suggest such changes; for like Shih Tan he was sponsoring Reformist policies, which, in this case, had first been voiced in Han by Tung Chung-shu.

As was usual Wang Mang's announcement of his plans[25] was framed in solemn terms that were designed to attract attention and to rally support from all sections of the community; and the terms of his announcement ran on lines with which Reformist propaganda was only too familiar. He praised the *ching-t'ien* system which had been practised under Yao, Shun and the Three Dynasties to the general well-being of the people of China. This claim was coupled with a strict censure of the immoral conduct of the Ch'in Emperor in increasing the rate of taxation solely to satisfy his own ambitions; and it was alleged that in the Han period such practices had led to the marked disparity between the great estates of the rich and the landless condition of the poor. Similarly the sale of slaves was castigated as running counter to the principles of Heaven and common humanity, and it was said that the heavy rate of taxation

---

[22] See *HFHD*, vol. III, p. 105. For changes in the offices of the central government (AD 1 and AD 9), see *HS* 99B.3b, 4a (*HFHD*, vol. III, pp. 269, 271); for the provincial offices and units (AD 14), see *HS* 99A.24a and *HS* 99B.24a (*HFHD*, vol. III, pp. 215f. and 338).

[23] See Chapter 8, pp. 267f..

[24] When Wang Mang was dismissed from the title of *Ta-ssu-ma*, at the beginning of Ai ti's reign, his place in high favour was taken by Shih Tan; see Chapter 8, p. 268.

[25] *HS* 99B.8a (*HFHD*, vol. III, pp. 284f.); see also C. M. Wilbur, *Slavery in China during the Former Han Dynasty* (Chicago, 1943), pp. 452f.

practised under Han, concealed though it may have been, had been one of the major causes of crime.

For these reasons Wang Mang sought to impose a ban on the sale and purchase of land and slaves; and small families owning large estates were required to surrender some of their holdings for distribution to those who had none. In practice the scheme proved impossible to operate; it disrupted the work of the farmers and commerce, and very large numbers became involved in judicial processes. However, both those who saw the dawn of a new era in the reforms and those who perceived a dire threat to their own well-being and wealth were to know before long that their hopes had been dupes and their fears liars. In AD 12[26] a courtier pointed out to Wang Mang that ancient practices could not necessarily suit contemporary expedient, and he even had a word of praise for the practices of Ch'in. Wang Mang was obliged to withdraw his proposals after a mere three years and to allow full recognition once more to the sale of land and slaves.

Another cause of general bewilderment and economic upset may be seen in the many changes which Wang Mang introduced in the coinage. As with the attempt at land reform, these measures were represented as being a return to ancient, pre-imperial practice; and despite the large number of variations and modifications, the proposals had no permanent effect and brought little material benefit.

Wang Mang's intention was to introduce a departure from the single standard cash coin whose form had been finalised and whose manufacture had been brought under the sole control of the state mints in 112 BC;[27] and in its place he wished to introduce a multi-denominational system. The situation was made more uneasy and complex by the frequent changes which pro-

[26] *HS* 99B.20a (*HFHD*, vol. III, pp. 323–4).

[27] *HS* 24B.16a (Swann, p. 293); for the history of Han coinage, see Swann, pp. 377f.

gressively reduced any confidence that an agricultural people may have had in the use of coinage as a means of exchange. In 7 AD three new coins, to the value of 50, 500 and 5,000 cash were introduced to circulate along with the single cash;[28] two years later the 500 and 5,000 pieces were withdrawn,[29] leaving the old single cash and the fifty cash piece in circulation; but in AD 10 a far more ambitious scheme was introduced[30] which was based on the use of other media than copper, in a highly systematic way. These included gold, silver, tortoise shell and cowries, and it could certainly be claimed for Wang Mang that he was reverting to articles of exchange that had featured in China's economy in the remote past. Unfortunately the political shape of China, the use of coins and the value of the media had all undergone a profound change in the meantime. Small units of gold had been used in the pre-imperial age within the southerly kingdom of Ch'u. Larger units, whose weight had been specified, had been used during the Han empire in place of 10,000 cash; but these bars of bullion had been limited to certain transactions only, and it could not be said that they had circulated freely as units of exchange. The other precious media on which Wang Mang called included the rare cowry shells such as had been used as articles of barter or exchange in the Shang-Yin period; and precious shells which had been accepted as articles of tax or tribute.

Wang Mang's adoption of these media in no less than twenty-eight denominations was highly perplexing and utterly impossible to maintain successfully; and the claim that the government was re-introducing ancient practices that had once been effective could hardly be substantiated in the context of a united Chinese empire. Further changes were soon to

[28] *HS* 99A.30a (*HFHD*, vol. III, p. 234); *HS* 24B.21a (Swann, p. 323).
[29] *HS* 99B.7a (*HFHD*, vol. III, p. 281).
[30] *HS* 99B.15a (*HFHD*, vol. III, p. 306).

follow, in AD 14 and 20;[31] and there ensued a marked increase in the common practice of minting the only coin in which any confidence was reposed, the old five-*shu* piece. This minting was accomplished without the permission of the government, and Wang Mang was soon forced to introduce stringent measures to restrict such practices by punishing the law-breakers; he tried in vain to stimulate the circulation of the new coins by artificial means.

A further feature of Wang Mang's dispensation which was difficult to comprehend, concerned his attitude towards foreign peoples. The saintly rulers of Chou, so one had been given to understand, had refrained from embarking on military expeditions; they had believed that the sovereignty of Chou would extend peacefully and naturally, in response to the welcome that foreign peoples would accord to the King's example of good government and benevolence; and they, or at least their advisers, disapproved of any active steps that were designed to extend their territories by force. Herein lay a marked contrast with the attitude of the Ch'in Empire and the Modernist statesmen who had successfully shaped foreign policy during Wu ti's reign; for it had been thanks to their initiative that Han territory had been increased by the foundation of eighteen new commanderies between 135 and *c.* 81 BC.

Now Wang Mang had made much of his claim to be following the principles of the kings of Chou; but when it came to practical matters of foreign policy, his attitude had appeared to be as active and aggressive as that of Wu ti's statesmen. Before he had become Emperor, but while he occupied a dominant position, the government had taken the gratuitous step of conferring honours on the descendants of men who had taken a leading part in Modernist policies. These included the descendants of Huo Kuang (honoured in AD 2), Wei Ch'ing, Chin Mi-

[31] *HS* 24B.26a *HFHD*, vol. III, p. 500 (Swann, p. 349f.); *HS* 99C.10a (*HFHD*, vol. III, p. 401).

ti and Fu Chieh-tzu (AD 4), and Kan Yen-shou and Ch'en T'ang
(AD 7); and they also included descendants of men such as
Cheng Chi and Chao Ch'ung-kuo, who had promoted policies
of colonial establishment rather than military advance (in AD 6
and 1–5 respectively).[32]

Once he had become Emperor, Wang Mang's attitude grew
even more positive and pronounced. The posture that he
adopted *vis-à-vis* the Hsiung-nu was anything but likely to
maintain friendly relations, and could be interpreted easily
enough as being aggressive. This attitude led to the abortive
despatch of military expeditions against the Hsiung-nu in 11
and 21;[33] but by the time that the second one was to be launched
it had already become apparent to the leaders of the states of
central Asia that China no longer commanded the strength that
it had enjoyed during the rule of the Han Emperors. It is not
altogether surprising to read that by the time of Wang Mang's
death (AD 23) the routes that led from China to the west had
been cut, and relations with the communities of central Asia
had been severed.[34]

The intellectual climate could certainly have been expected to
favour Wang Mang's cause in AD 9. Some twenty years previously two of the leading interpreters of phenomena, Ku Yung
and Tu Ch'in, had expressed views that were favourable both
to the Wang family and to the Reformist views that he claimed
to champion. Tu Ch'in, in particular, had had occasion to warn
his patron Wang Feng (Wang Mang's uncle) that he should
follow the example of the Duke of Chou.[35] Ku Yung had been
one of the clearest exponents of the theory of Heaven's warning

---

[32] *HS* 17.26a; *HS* 17.28a; *HS* 17.30a; *HS* 18.8a–8b; *HS* 18.11a; *HS*
69.16b; *HS* 70.19a.

[33] *HS* 99B.11a and 14a (*HFHD*, vol. III, pp. 295 and 304); see also
HFHD, vol. III, pp. 120–1.

[34] *HS* 96B.35b, 36a.

[35] *HS* 60.6b, *et seq.*, and *HS* 60.12b, *et seq.*; see Chapter 7, p. 246.

voice; he had not hesitated to apply this to the contemporary regime of Ch'eng ti's government, and Ch'eng ti himself had witheld his friendship from him as he was known to side with the Wang faction.[36] But both these men had died[37] before Wang Mang had taken the final step of assuming the imperial throne, and we cannot say what their attitude might have been had they witnessed those events.

Liu Hsiang, however, who died in the year preceding Wang Mang's assumption of the throne, was one of the few intellectuals who came out strongly and bitterly against him, despite his sympathy with many of the causes which Wang Mang claimed to support. Liu Hsiang had lived long enough to witness the growth of the Reformist movement, and he had worked with many of the statesmen who had been responsible for transforming China's policies from those of the Modernists. He had frequently expressed himself in favour of the practical aims of the new men, such as the elimination of contemporary abuses in government, the reduction of extravagant living in the palace and the undue influence that was being exercised by relatives of the Empress. Liu Hsiang laid considerable importance on the occurrence of phenomena and followed Tung Chung-shu's example of seeking an analogy between past and present so as to reach the correct interpretation of these strange events.

It has been observed above that Liu Hsiang did not hesitate to show an independence of mind when necessary, and that he would refuse to conform with established arguments if there was just cause for disagreement;[38] in his attitude to Wang Mang he exhibited the same degree of courage. Seeing the dangers that would beset the empire by the substitution of the Wang family in place of others who had been in favour hitherto,

[36] *HS* 85.18b.

[37] *HS* 19B.47b; *HS* 85.19a. Ku Yung was appointed *Ta-ssu-nung* in 9 B C; he resigned on the grounds of ill health in 8 B C and died shortly afterwards.

[38] For his views regarding Ch'en T'ang see Chapter 7, p. 240.

he did not forbear to describe the risks in his writings; and he must have been one of the very few men who dared to voice a comparison with past history when the court had come under the domination of the families Lü and Huo.[39]

We know something of the reactions of three other leading intellectuals who lived to see Wang Mang's accession. There are signs that two of them—Yang Hsiung and Huan T'an—suffered disillusion and disquiet after an initial sympathy with Wang Mang's cause; and that in the third case, of Liu Hsiang's son Liu Hsin, this unease was sufficiently strong to induce him to take a fearful risk and meet a violent end.

Like Liu Hsiang, the famous writer and philosopher Yang Hsiung (53 BC–AD 18) had not been shy of criticising the contemporary scene; and he called for active reforms to implement the results of official inspection and the discovery of abuses. His sympathy with Wang Mang was such that he had actually composed a prose essay in defence of his regime, at a date which cannot be precisely determined.[40] However, under Wang Mang's government, Yang Hsiung either refused or was never invited to accept high office; and in AD 11 he was implicated in a plot against Wang Mang and nearly arrested.

Huan T'an, another contemporary philosopher (43 BC–AD 28) who forms an important link in the growth of Wang Ch'ung's thought, was likewise sympathetic to the Reformist cause. But apparently he refrained from praising Wang Mang in public; and although he held office in Wang Mang's government, his duties were of a technical rather than a political nature. He was thus concerned with administrative problems such as the control of floods or the organisation of music for the new regime, and as far as we know he was not called upon to pronounce publicly on Wang Mang's authority to rule or the nature of his

---

[39] *HS* 36.25b, *et seq.*

[40] See *HFHD*, vol. III, p. 110; T. Pokora, 'The Life of Huan T'an' (*Archiv Orientální*, vol. 31, 1963, p. 72); *Wen-hsüan* (SPTK, ed.), 48.9a–20a; E. von Zach, *Die Chinesische Anthologie*, vol. II, pp. 898–905.

government. However, he criticised Wang Mang severely once his regime had fallen, and in view of Huan T'an's intellectual integrity it is difficult to dismiss his behaviour as that of a mere time-server.[41]

To demonstrate that his authority had been blessed by the supreme powers of the cosmos, Wang Mang invoked the evidence of phenomena and the sequence of the Five Elements; and it would have been impossible for him to do so with any conviction, but for the theories that had been put forward by Tung Chung-shu, Ku Yung, Tu Ch'in and Liu Hsiang. For these and other Reformist thinkers had shared the belief that Heaven takes a deliberate and decisive part in ordering the temporal government of man.

Reference has been made above[42] to some of the events which were said to presage Wang Mang's rise to become Emperor. Shortly after his accession (AD 9) he sent commissioners to proclaim throughout the Empire the list of favourable omens with which his regime had been blessed.[43] The document they bore was said to have extended to forty-two sections which included good auguries of Wang Mang's imperial character and power (five items); signs of the Heavenly mandate (twenty-five items); and auspices of good fortune (twelve items). This was designed to prove beyond any shadow of doubt that Wang Mang had been assigned to replace the Han dynasty and to take possession of the world; and a summary of the contents of the document alluded also to the sequence of the Five Elements, which led to the same conclusion.

Here, however, Wang Mang formally introduced a change in the state's theory of cosmic order, which may well have been somewhat puzzling at the time.[44] Under the Ch'in Empire and

---

[41] See Pokora, *op. cit.*, pp. 11, 48.
[42] See p. 288.
[43] *HS* 99B.9a (*HFHD*, vol. III, p. 288).
[44] *HFHD*, vol. III, p. 106; see Chapter 1, p. 29 and Chapter 8, p. 281.

according to the views of the Modernist statesmen of Han it had been held that the dominating power of the cosmos passed in turn from one element to another in so far as each one overcame its predecessor. In this way it could be shown that Han had been blessed initially by the power of Water, and from 104 BC by the power of Earth. Wang Mang, however, followed the lead of Tung Chung-shu and Liu Hsiang, who believed that the power of the cosmos passed from one element to the next in so far as each one gave rise to its successor. According to this theory it could be shown that the kings of Chou had been blessed by Wood and the Han emperors by Fire, and it could logically be expected that Wang Mang would flourish under the patronage of Earth. Such a theory could be substantiated in a number of ways, principally by the claim that Wang Mang had been descended from the 'Yellow Emperor' or the Power of Yellow, which was the colour associated with Earth. Evidence could also be found to suggest that Han had existed not, as had been maintained, under the patronage of Water and then of Earth but under that of Fire.[45]

These considerations may have had a practical bearing on changes in the protocol of the court and in the divisions of time whereby the day was reckoned; and they were in all probability in the forefront of Liu Hsin's mind when he introduced a new calendar.[46]

There were a number of reasons why the interests of Liu Hsin should coincide with those of Wang Mang. Both men had been out of favour during the reign of Ai ti; both supported the ideas of the Reformists, the one by reason of sincere intellectual conviction, the other perhaps because he could exploit those ideas to gain political support; and the accession of the infant, known later as P'ing ti, in the year before AD 1 afforded opportunity to both men to pursue their ambitions. Thus Liu Hsin could hope

[45] *HS* 25B.23b; see Chapter 8, p. 281.
[46] i.e. the *San-t'ung li* (*HS* 21A.32b).

that a new dispensation, in which Wang Mang was the dominant influence, would allow him to introduce certain books such as the *Tso-chuan* into the Canon, and to prescribe forms of worship and ceremonies which he believed to be in the true tradition of the kings of Chou. Liu Hsin had become familiar with ancient writings and traditional forms of protocol, which could now be put to political use, largely in the course of the work which he and his father had put in at the collation of literary texts and the arrangement of the imperial library.

Wang Mang would particularly welcome the support of Liu Hsin, both in so far as he was a well-known intellectual, and also because he was a member of the Han imperial family. He could hope that the new books and written authority which Liu Hsin sponsored would rally to his cause the solid support of the intellectual world and demonstrate to the court that his own exercise of temporal authority was legitimate and just.

Liu Hsin need have suffered no qualms of conscience in serving Wang Mang so long as a member of the house of Liu was seated on the throne; and during the reign of P'ing ti his relationship to Wang Mang may well have been so close that, when Wang Mang actually threw off the mask and assumed the imperial title, Liu Hsin could not have severed relations with him short of staging a rebellion. In addition the ties between the two men had been strengthened by the marriage of Wang Mang's son and Liu Hsin's daughter.[47] However, the friendship and alliance of the two men was soon to be transformed into bitter enmity. Two of Liu Hsin's sons were implicated in a plot against Wang Mang in AD 11[48] and were executed, and the same fate overtook one of Liu Hsin's daughters in 21.[49] The advance disclosure of a much more serious plot which was being hatched against Wang Mang in

---

[47] *HFHD*, vol. III, p. 57.   [48] *HS* 99B.16a (*HFHD*, vol. III, p. 310).
[49] *HS* 99C.11a (*HFHD*, vol. III, p. 404); see also *HFHD*, vol. III, p. 448, note 23.2.

23 led to the discovery and execution of the conspirators; and these included Liu Hsin.

A crucial consideration which many must have borne in mind in determining their attitude to Wang Mang lay in the reactions of the imperial Liu family to his behaviour, but unfortunately there was no clearly defined decision here. For it was one thing for statesmen, courtiers or officials to take active steps to show their support for Wang Mang, e.g. by reporting, or possibly fabricating, the occurrence of omens, or by submitting long documents in praise of Wang Mang's character and achievement.[50] Equally clear were the views and intentions of men such as Chai I, who were not members of the Liu family and had been ready to launch an open revolt against Wang Mang.[51] But what would weigh most heavily with those who were as yet uncommitted would be the view taken by members of the Liu family; and here if ever lay a house which was against itself divided.

At the time (AD 6) of Liu Ch'ung's attempt to oust Wang Mang, after his assumption of the regency, Wang Mang was supported by Liu Chia;[52] but Chai I's formidable revolt of AD 7 carried the hopes of other members of the Liu family in so far as the rebels intended to establish Liu Hsin on the throne.[53] Three plots which were launched against Wang Mang in AD 9 involved members of the Liu family, i.e. Liu Yü who, it was intended, should take the place of Wang Mang, Liu K'uai and Liu Tu; but the situation had been obscured by the action of Liu Yin, brother of Liu K'uai, who chose to side with Wang

[50] See *HS* 99A.17a and 23b (*HFHD*, vol. III, pp. 184 and 212) for the despatch of eight messengers and their glowing report (AD 4–5); *HS* 99a.10a and 27b; (*HFHD*, vol. III, pp. 162 and 226) for the adulatory addresses of Chang Sung in AD 3 and AD 6.

[51] *HS* 99A.30a (*HFHD*, vol. III, p. 235).

[52] *HS* 99A.27b (*HFHD*, vol. III, p. 226).

[53] Not to be confused with Liu Hsin son of Liu Hsiang: see *HS* 99A.30a (*HFHD*, vol. III, p. 235).

Mang.[54] In addition Wang Mang had in the meantime enjoyed the positive support of Liu Ching, who had written in encouraging Wang Mang to take the throne, and thus to respond to a lead provided by certain strange phenomena;[55] once the revolts of AD 9 had been crushed, no less than thirty-two members of the Liu family pledged their support for the new regime.[56]

Perhaps the most famous and most perplexing case was that of Liu Hsin (son of Liu Hsiang), who actively helped Wang Mang to take the throne but later forfeited his life in plotting against him; and in view of Liu Hsin's importance in the intellectual developments of the day, his influence must surely have been of prime consideration. It remains open to question wherein lay the dominant motives of the members of the Liu family at this juncture of Chinese history. Some were doubtless moved by a genuine faith in the character and achievements of the new leader; others were perhaps moved by personal ambitions; and some, while having lost their faith in the strength of their own family's heritage, may still have wondered whether the performance of China's new master would prove to be a more honest, effective and successful dispensation than that of their own forbears.

[54] *HS* 99A.35a; *HS* 99B.7b and 12b (*HFHD*, vol. III, pp. 253, 283, 299).
[55] *HS* 99A.34a (*HFHD*, vol. III, p. 250).
[56] *HS* 99B.14a (*HFHD*, vol. III, p. 304). The thirty-two men included Liu Chia, whose support had been given in the revolt of Liu Ch'ung (AD 6).

The Institutions of Han Government

Fuller accounts of the structure of Han government have been given by writers such as Chavannes (see *MH*, vol. II, pp. 513f.), Wang and Hulsewé (see *Remnants of Han Law*, pp. 14f.). The following brief summary is included here for ease of reference.

The government of the Empire was conducted by a hierarchy of officials who held posts in the central and provincial offices or as military officers. The most senior of these officials acted in effect as the emperor's most trusted counsellors and statesmen; the most junior held the humblest of posts as clerks or runners. The relative seniority of a post was determined by its place on a scale of stipends, which graded an official among his colleagues in the service. This scale was defined in terms of *shih*, i.e. the annual allowance of measures of grain, and the actual stipend was paid partly in kind and partly in cash. The scale comprised twenty (later sixteen) grades ranging from substantive 2000 *shih* to 100 *shih*.

The following scheme of the major offices of state is based on a formal ideal rather than on a realistic arrangement, and it is not known in practice to what extent all the posts which are listed were filled or in what way responsibilities were precisely allocated.[1] The institutions of government had been established

[1] See *HS* 19 for an introductory account of the principal offices of state and a chronological list of their incumbents.

both so as to distinguish between different specialist responsibilities and to prevent supreme powers falling into the hands of
a single high-ranking official. But it will be shown below that
as the dynasty proceeded means were developed whereby the
highest powers of decision could be wielded by the members
of an inner coterie or private secretariat (the *shang-shu*) rather
than by the most senior officers of the central government.

THE CENTRAL GOVERNMENT

The central government included, in descending order of importance and seniority (*a*) the senior statesmen, (*b*) the nine
ministers of state and (*c*) other high ranking officials who were
independent of (*b*).

(*a*) At the outset of the dynasty, senior statesmen were
appointed to be Chancellor (*ch'eng-hsiang*: Dubs—Lieutenant-
Chancellor), Imperial Counsellor (*Yü-shih ta-fu*: Dubs—
Imperial Clerk Grandee), and Supreme Commander (*t'ai-wei*:
Dubs—Grand Commandant). However from early on the
office of Supreme Commander was not filled regularly, and
from 139 BC it was suspended. Occasionally two Chancellors
were appointed, one of the right and one of the left. Towards
the end of the dynasty attempts were made to replace this
system by the establishment of three senior statesmen who bore
different titles and were supposedly ranking on a par (see
Chapter 8, pp. 257f.).

The Chancellor, who was assisted by two principal aides,
bore general responsibility to the Emperor for the administration of the realm and could exercise some check on the proposals submitted to the throne from other officials. The Imperial
Counsellor ranked immediately below the Chancellor, but the
functions of the two officials were to some extent comple-
mentary. The Imperial Counsellor was assisted by a number of
subordinates and was responsible for the issue of orders and

their distribution to junior officials, and for the performance of civil servants in their various capacities.

There were also a few other posts of an honorary rather than an executive nature to which senior officials were sometimes appointed. These included the posts of Senior Tutor (*t'ai-fu*: Dubs—Grand Tutor), Senior Teacher (*t'ai-shih*: Dubs—Grand Master); and Senior Protector (*t'ai-pao*: Dubs—Grand Guardian). The incumbents of these offices had advisory rather than administrative duties.

(*b*) The nine ministers of state comprised officials who bore departmental responsibilities for a particular aspect of government or of the affairs of the court. They ranked below the senior statesmen and they were supported by an assistant, together with the directors and assistants of subordinate agencies. Table 6 lists the titles which were adopted in 104 BC[2] and by which the nine ministers of state are usually known.

(*c*) The nine ministers of state who are listed in Table 6 were graded at the rank of 'substantive 2000 *shih*' (*chung erh ch'ien shih*). With the exception of the *chih-chin-wu*, who also received that stipend, other officials of the central government who bore independent responsibility for specific duties ranked at the next grade of 'two thousand *shih*' (*erh ch'ien shih*). These officials included the *Chih-chin-wu*, Superintendent of the Capital (bearer of the golden mace) who was responsible for the security of the capital city; the *t'ai-tzu t'ai-fu* and *t'ai-tzu shao-fu* (Senior and Junior Tutors to the heir apparent); the *chiang-tso ta-chiang*, Superintendent of Buildings (court architect); the *chan-shih*, Superintendents of the Households of the Empress and Crown Prince (Supplier); the *tien shu-kuo*, Superintendent of the Dependent States (Director of the Dependent States); the *shui-heng tu-wei*, Superintendent of Parks and Lakes (Chief

[2] For the significance of the change of terminology in the titles of officials at this time, see Chapter 1, p. 31.

Table 6. Titles of the Nine Ministers of State

Title	Rendering adopted here (Dubs)	Responsibilities	Subordinate officials or agencies*
T'ai-ch'ang	Superintendent of Ceremonial (Grand Master of Ceremonies)	Maintenance of religious cults of state	Agencies for music, prayer, sacrifice, astrology, divination, medicine
Kuang-lu-hsün	Superintendent of the Palace (Superintendent of the Imperial Household)	Control of counsellors, courtiers and those awaiting appointment	Gentlemen-at-arms and imperial escorts; various counsellors
Wei-wei	Superintendent of the Guards (Commandant of the Palace Guards)	Command of the security guards for the imperial palace	Various officers of the guard
T'ai-p'u	Superintendent of Transport (Grand Coachman)	Administration of transport for imperial use	Imperial stables and carriages
T'ing-wei	Superintendent of Trials (Commandant of Justice)	Conduct of legal processes	Inspectors and moderators of trials
Ta-hung-lu	Superintendent of State Visits (Grand Herald)	Receipt of foreign dignitaries	Interpreters, official lodges
Tsung-cheng	Superintendent of the Imperial Family (Superintendent of the Imperial Household)	Maintenance of orders of precedence within the imperial family	Officers of the inner apartments and of the households of the princesses
Ta-ssu-nung	Superintendent of Agriculture (Grand Minister of Agriculture)	Receipt of major revenues, payment of official stipends, provision of supplies, monopolies of state	Officers for granaries, distribution, price control, iron marketing
Shao-fu	Superintendent of the Lesser Treasury (Privy Treasurer)	Collection of minor dues; imperial workshops	The secretariat, offices of medicine, music, various crafts

* Only a selection of these officials or offices is given here. For a full list, see Chavannes in *MH, loc. cit.*

Commandant of Waters and Parks); and the governors of the three divisions of the metropolitan region, i.e. the *ching-chao-yin*, Metropolitan Superintendent of the Right (Governor of the Capital); the *tso-p'ing-i*, Metropolitan Superintendent of the Left (Eastern Supporter); and the *yu-fu-feng*, Superintendent of the West (Western Sustainer).

THE PROVINCES

Apart from the three divisions of the metropolitan region, the Han empire was organised administratively as kingdoms (*kuo*: Dubs—states) and commanderies (*chün*). The kingdoms were entrusted to close kinsmen of the Emperor and transmitted from father to son; and the government of these kings was organised as a small scale replica of the Emperor's central government, in which the central government retained some rights. At the beginning of the dynasty the ten kingdoms together stretched over a larger extent of territory than the fifteen commanderies whose administration was subordinated directly to the Emperor's own government. By the beginning of the first century BC, the size of the kingdoms and the powers of the kings had been reduced very substantially; and a number of new commanderies had been established, both by incorporating some of the territory of the kingdoms as such and as a result of the expansion of Han interests in the north, south and west. By now the commandery had become the standard and normal unit of administration, and the kingdoms survived in a minor capacity only. By the end of the western Han period there existed a total of eighty-three commanderies and twenty kingdoms.[3]

Commanderies were controlled by the Governor (*t'ai-shou*: Dubs—Grand Administrator) and the Commandant (*tu-wei*: Dubs—Chief Commandant). The governor, who ranked at

[3] For a list of these units and a map to show their approximate position, see *RHA*, vol. I, pp. 178–81.

2,000 *shih* was charged with the general care of the area and the commandant (sub-2,000 *shih*) bore responsibility for security and military matters. Both the commanderies and the kingdoms comprised smaller units which corresponded in size to English counties. These were the Prefectures (*hsien*: Dubs—Prefecture), Nobilities (*hou*: Dubs—Marquisate) Estates (*i*: Dubs—Estates), and Marches (*tao*: Dubs—March). Of these the prefectures were the standard and most numerous of the 1587 units which existed in AD 1-2; and they were governed by prefects who were appointed by the central government. Nobilities were areas wherein the nobles were entitled to collect taxation from a specified number of households and of which they retained a proportion for themselves; and the nobilities were held on an hereditary basis. The estates were small areas whose yield was made over for the upkeep of select female members of the imperial family; the marches existed in areas where the inhabitants were not assimilated to the Chinese way of life and rule.

These units were themselves sub-divided into districts (*hsiang*) which comprised villages or settlements (*li*); and the local officials who maintained order and supervised the administration at this level were appointed by the authorities of the commandery or the prefecture.

In 106 BC the government established a system of some thirteen Regional Inspectors (*tz'u-shih*: Dubs—Inspector of a Circuit) in order to tighten its control of the empire. These officials were appointed by the central government, and were responsible for inspecting the work of provincial officials and reporting directly to the central government if they observed cases of maladministration, corruption or oppression. The inspectors operated in both the kingdoms and the commanderies, and they ranked at a considerably lower grade than the governors of the commanderies. In addition in some cases the central government set up specialist agencies directly under its own control. These were responsible for, e.g. the iron and salt industries, control of traffic at the frontier, the promotion of sponsored colonies, the production of certain textiles.

MILITARY COMMANDS

The highest ranking military officers bore the title of General (*chiang-chün*: Dubs—General) and were responsible to the Emperor for the conduct of campaigns as ordered by the central government. It was usual Han practice to appoint several general officers concurrently, possibly in order to avoid the risk of investing control of the armed forces in the hands of a single man. Some posts for General existed fairly regularly throughout Western Han (e.g. *Tso* or *Yu chiang-chün*, Generals of the Left or Right). Other appointments were made for a particular campaign or task and the purpose of the appointment was sometimes incorporated in the officer's title (e.g. *Tu-Liao chiang-chün*, general of the Trans-Liao Command). Most of the generals' posts were graded at the same level, or slightly below, that of the nine ministers of state.

For the less important campaigns, colonels (*hsiao-wei*: Dubs—colonel) were appointed for short periods, and they were commissioned to act independently, like the generals. Some posts of colonel were established on a more regular basis, and their titles included an indication of their duties.

THE INNER COURT

In addition to the titles of the type that have been considered and which carried responsibility for specific duties within the regular hierarchy of the civil service, the Han government conferred certain extra titles which carried particular privileges such as that of entering the palace without the need of a special summons to do so. These non-substantive titles demanded no specified duties and carried no stipend. In some cases there was no limit to the number of men on whom they could be conferred, and they were often bestowed on men who held office in the regular organs that have been described. The titles included those of *Ta-ssu-ma* (Marshal of State: Dubs—Commander-in-Chief); *shih-chung* (Attendant at the Palace: Dubs—Palace Attendant); *chung-ch'ang-shih* (Regular Attendant at the Palace: Dubs—Regular Inner Palace Attendant); *chi-shih-chung* (Palace Servant: Dubs—serving within the palace). Officials who were singled out for these honours formed an inner group who attended the Emperor and proffered counsel and assistance as required.

On some occasions an official who was a member of this inner coterie was ordered to lead, control or supervise the business of the secretariat (*shang-shu*), which was one of the offices subordinated to the Lesser Treasury (see p. 310). It would then happen that effective control of government could pass from the duly constituted organs, which were known as the 'Outer Court' and over which the Chancellor presided, to the officials of the Inner Court, i.e. the members of the Secretariat, who enjoyed direct and immediate access to the Throne and whose positions had been honoured by the extra gift of one of the non-substantive titles. Thus, although the regular organs of government continued to exist, the control of the Empire would pass to men such as Huo Kuang or Wang Mang, who had received the additional title of *Ta-ssu-ma* and had been given specific orders to lead the secretariat. At times the secretariat was staffed by eunuchs.

Glossary of Chinese and Japanese Proper Names and Terms

Ai ti 哀帝
An Han kung 安漢公
An-shih fang-chung 安世房中
An-ting 安定

Chai Fang-chin 翟方進
Chai I 翟義
Chan-shih 詹事
Chang An-shih 張安世
Chang Ch'ang 張敞
Chang Ch'ien 張騫
Chang Ch'ien-ch'iu 張千秋
Chang-i 張掖
Chang Kan 章贛
Chang Kuang 張光
Chang Shuo 張朔
Chang Sung 張竦
Chang T'an 張譚
Chang Yen 張晏
Chang Yen-nien 張延年
Chang Yü 張禹
Ch'ang-an 長安
Ch'ang-ch'eng chün 昌成君
Ch'ang-hsin 長信
Ch'ang Hui 常惠
Ch'ang-i 昌邑
Ch'ang-lo 長樂
Chao 趙
Chao Chao-i 趙昭儀
Chao Chieh-yü 趙倢伃

Chao Ch'ung-kuo 趙充國
Chao Fei-yen 趙飛燕
Chao Hsüan 趙玄
Chao-i 昭儀
Chao Kao 趙高
Chao Kuang-han 趙廣漢
Chao Kuo 趙過
Chao P'o-nu 趙破奴
Chao t'ai 昭臺
Chao ti 昭帝
Ch'ao Ts'o 晁錯
Ch'e-hou 徹侯
Ch'en 陳
Ch'en Ch'ih-kung 陳持弓
Ch'en Hsien 陳咸
Ch'en Hui 陳惠
Ch'en Pao 陳寶
Ch'en Sheng Liu t'ai-p'ing huang-ti
　　陳聖劉太平皇帝
Ch'en T'ang 陳湯
Cheng 鄭
Cheng Chi 鄭吉
Cheng Hsüan 鄭玄
Ch'eng (assistant) 丞
Ch'eng (King of Chou) 成
Ch'eng-hsiang 丞相
Ch'eng-hsiang shih 丞相史
Ch'eng ti 成帝
Chi-fa 祭法
Chi-nan 濟南

Chi-pin 罽嬪

Chi-shih-chung 給事中

Chi-sun 季孫

Chi Yen 級黯

Ch'i 齊

Ch'i tu-wei 騎都尉

Chia I 賈誼

Chiang Ch'ung 江充

Chiang-chün 將軍

Chiang Nai-shih 江乃始

Chiang-tso ta-chiang 將作大匠

Chiang-tu 江都

Ch'iang 羌

Chiao (teaching) 效

Chiao (worship at the bounds) 郊

Chieh-yü 倢伃

Chien-chang 建章

Chien-p'ing 建平

Chien ta-fu 諫大夫

Chien-wei 犍爲

Ch'ien-jen 千人

Chih (magical plant) 芝

Chih (sacred site) 畤

Chih-chih 郅支

Chih-chin-wu 執金吾

Chih-su tu-wei 治粟都尉

Ch'ih ching tzu 赤精子

Ch'ih hsing 弛刑

Chin 金

Chin-ch'eng 金城

Chin Mi-ti 金日磾

Chin-t'i 金堤

Chin wen 今文

Ch'in 秦

Ching-chao yin 京兆尹

Ching chih 敬之

Ching ti 景帝

Ching t'ien 井田

Ching Wu 景武

Ch'ing 頃

Ch'ing-ho 清河

Chiu ch'ing 九卿

Chiu-ch'üan 酒泉

Ch'iu-tzu 龜茲

Ch'iung-ch'eng T'ai-hou 邛成太后

Cho-yeh 涿野

Chou 周

Chu An-shih 朱安世

Chu-hou 諸侯

Chu-hou-wang 諸侯王

Chu Hsi 朱熹

Chu-i 諸邑

Chu Po 朱博

Chu-tsu shang 祝詛上

Ch'u 楚

Ch'u Shao-sun 褚少孫

Chü 車

Chü-ch'i chiang-chün 車騎將軍

Chü-shih 車師

Chü-yen 居延

Ch'ü-li 渠犁

Chüan 卷

Chüan Pu-i 雋不疑

Chüeh 爵

Chün 郡

Chung ch'ang shih 中常侍

Chung erh ch'ien shih 中二千石

Chung-ho 重合

Chung lang chiang 中郎將

Chung-shan 中山

Chung-shu ling 中書令

Chung-wei 中尉

Êrh ch'ien shih 二千石

Fa 法

Fan Ming-yu 范明友
Fang-shih 方士
Fang Tsu-shen 方祖燊
Fei T'iao 非調
Fen-yin 汾陰
Feng (ceremony) 封
Feng (place) 豐
Feng Chao-i 馮昭儀
Feng Ch'ün 馮逡
Feng-chü tu-wei 奉車都尉
Feng Feng-shih 馮奉世
Feng Tzu-tu 馮子都
Fu (poetic form) 賦
Fu (surname) 傅
Fu-ch'eng 附城
Fu Chieh-tzu 傅介子
Fu Hsi 傅喜
Fu-jen 夫人
Fu-min 富民
Fu Shang 傅商
Fu Yen 傅晏
Fujikawa Masakazu 藤川正數

Han chiu i 漢舊儀
Han Hsing 韓興
Han Hsüan 韓宣
Han Li 韓立
Han shih yen-chiu 漢詩研究
Han-shu 漢書
Han Yüeh 漢說
Hao 鄗
Hao-men 浩亹
Heng-shan 衡山
Ho-chien 河間
Ho-ch'in 和親
Ho-p'ing 河平
Ho-tung 河東
Ho Wu 河武

Hou (captain, noble) 侯
Hou (empress) 后
Hou erh nien 後二年
Hou Han-shu 後漢書
Hou shen 侯神
Hou t'u 后土
Hou yüan erh nien 後元二年
Hsi-ho 西河
Hsia Ho-liang 夏賀良
Hsia-hou K'uan 夏侯寬
Hsiang 鄉
Hsiao Ho 蕭何
Hsiao Wang-chih 蕭望之
Hsiao-wei 效尉
Hsieh-lü tu-wei 協律都尉
Hsien (king's title) 獻
Hsien (prefecture) 縣
Hsien (river) 鮮
Hsien-lang 賢郎
Hsin 新
Hsin-yüan P'ing 新垣平
Hsiu-t'u 休屠
Hsiung-nu 匈奴
Hsü 許
Hsü Chia 許嘉
Hsü Fu 徐福
Hsü Han-shu 續漢書
Hsü Kuang-han 許廣漢
Hsü P'ing-chün 許平君
Hsü Po 許伯
Hsüan ti 宣帝
Hu 斛
Hu-han-hsieh 呼韓邪
Huai 槐
Huai-nan 淮南
Huai-yang 淮陽
Huan T'an 桓譚
Huang 湟

Huang-hou 皇后
Huang Hui 貢暉
Huang I 皇矣
Huang ti 黃帝
Huang Wen-pi 黃文弼
Hui ti 惠帝
Hung-fan 鴻範
Huo 霍
Huo Cheng-shih 霍徵史
Huo Ch'eng-chün 霍成君
Huo Ch'ü-ping 霍去病
Huo Chung-ju 霍中孺
Huo Hsien 霍顯
Huo Kuang 霍光
Huo Shan (brother of Huo Yün)
　霍山
Huo Shan (son of Huo Ch'ü-ping)
　霍嬗
Huo Yü 霍禹
Huo Yün 霍雲

I 邑
I Feng 翼奉
I-hai 乙亥
I ta chuan 易大傳
I-wei 乙未

Jen An 任安
Jen-shen 壬申
Jen Sheng 任勝
Jen-tzu 任子
Jen-yin 壬寅
Jih-chu 日逐
Ju-chia 儒家
Ju Hou 如侯
Ju-nan 汝南
Ju Shun 如淳

Kan-ch'üan 甘泉

Kan Chung-k'o 甘忠可
Kan dai ni okeru kokka zaisei to
teishitsu zaisei to no kubetsu narabi
ni teishitsu zaisei ippan
漢代に於ける國家
財政と帝室財政と
の區別並に帝室財政
一斑
Kan dai ni okeru rei gaku no kenkyū
漢代にあける禮學の
研究
K'ang-chü 康居
Kaoku 考古
Kao tsu 高祖
Katō Shigeshi 加藤繁
Keng Shou-ch'ang 耿壽昌
Ku 蠱
Ku Chi 谷吉
Ku Liang 穀梁
Ku-shih 姑師
Ku wen 古文
Ku Yung 谷永
Kuan-nei-hou 關內侯
Kuan-t'ao 館陶
Kuang-ch'uan 廣川
Kuang-han 廣漢
Kuang-ling 廣陵
Kuang-lu-hsün 光祿勳
Kuang-lu ta-fu 光祿大夫
Kuang-yang 廣陽
K'uang Ch'ang 匡昌
K'uang Heng 匡衡
Kuei-yang 桂陽
K'un-mi 昆彌
Kung 公
Kung-sun Ao 公孫敖
Kung-sun Ching-sheng 公孫敬
　聲

Kung-sun Ho 公孫賀
Kung-sun Hung 公孫弘
Kung t'ien 公田
Kung yang 公羊
Kung Yü 貢禹
K'ung An-kuo 孔安國
K'ung Kuang 孔光
Kuo 國
Kuo-feng 國風
Kuo Shun 郭舜

Lan-t'ien 藍田
Lang 郎
Lang-yeh 琅邪
Li (administrative division) 里
Li (family) 李
Li (propriety) 禮
Li Chi 李季
Li-chi (text) 禮記
Li Ch'ung 李崇
Li Fu-jen 李夫人
Li Hsün 李尋
Li I 李姬
Li Kuang-li 李廣利
Li Ling 李陵
Li Wei 李微
Li Yen-nien 李延年
Liang-fu 梁父
Liao 遼
Lien Pao 廉襃
Lin 麟
Lin-ch'iang 臨羌
Ling-hu Mao 令狐茂
Ling-ling 零陵
Liu Ao 劉驁
Liu Ch'e 劉徹
Liu Chi-tzu 劉箕子
Liu Ch'i 劉啓

Liu Chia 劉嘉
Liu Chiao 劉交
Liu Ching 劉京
Liu Ch'u-li 劉屈氂
Liu Chü 劉據
Liu Ch'ung 劉崇
Liu Fu-ling 劉弗陵
Liu Heng 劉恒
Liu Ho 劉賀
Liu Hsiang 劉向
Liu Hsin (set up as emperor AD 7) 劉信
Liu Hsin (Ai ti) 劉欣
Liu Hsin (son of Liu Hsiang) 劉歆
Liu Hsing 劉興
Liu Hsü 劉胥
Liu Hung 劉閎
Liu K'ang 劉康
Liu K'uai 劉快
Liu Pang 劉邦
Liu P'eng-tsu 劉彭祖
Liu Ping-i 劉病巳
Liu Po 劉髆
Liu Shih 劉奭
Liu Tan 劉丹
Liu Tse 劉澤
Liu Tu 劉都
Liu Yin 劉殷
Liu Ying (Hui ti) 劉盈
Liu Ying (infant emperor AD 6) 劉嬰
Liu Yü 劉紆
Lo 雒
Lo-pu-nao-erh k'ao-ku-chi 羅布淖爾考古記
Lo-yang 洛陽
Lou-lan 樓蘭
Lu 魯

Lü hou 呂后

Luan Ta 欒大

Lun-heng 論衡

Lun-t'ai 輪臺

Lung-hsi 隴西

Ma Ho-luo 馬何羅

Ma T'ung 馬通

Man-ch'eng 滿城

Mang 莽

Mao-ling 茂陵

Min-yüeh 閩粵

Ming chu 明主

Ming-t'ang 明堂

Mu (shepherd) 牧

Mu (unit of measurement) 畝

Nan 男

Nei-shih 內史

Nung tu-wei 農都尉

O-i 鄂邑

Pa 霸

Pan Chieh-yü 班倢伃

Pao Shēng-chih 暴勝之

Pao yüan t'ai p'ing ching 包元太平經

P'ei 沛

Pen ming 本命

P'eng-lai 蓬萊

P'ien 篇

Ping Chi 丙 or 邴吉

P'ing Tang 平當

P'ing ti 平帝

Po 伯

Po hu t'ung 白虎通

Po-shih 博士

P'o Yen-shou 繁延壽

Pu-ching 不敬

San chi 散騎

San kung 三公

Sang Hung-yang 桑弘羊

Shan-shan 鄯善

Shan-yü 單于

Shang-ch'iu Ch'eng 商丘成

Shang chün 上郡

Shang-kuan An 上官安

Shang-kuan Chieh 上官桀

Shang-lin 上林

Shang-shu 尚書

Shang-shu ling 尚書令

Shang ti 上帝

Shang Yang 商鞅

Shang-yin 商殷

Shao-fu 少府

Shao Hsin-ch'en 召信臣

Shao-kao 召誥

Shao Weng 少翁

Shen Pu-hai 申不害

Shih 石

Shih che 使者

Shi-chi 史記

Shih-chung 侍中

Shih Hsien 石顯

Shih Huang-sun 史皇孫

Shih Kao 史高

Shih Tan (courtier of Yüan ti) 史丹

Shih Tan (marshal of state 7 BC) 師丹

Shih Te 石德

Shih-yüan 始元

Shiki kaichū kōshō 史記會注考證

Shina keizai shi kōshō 支那經濟史考證

Shou 守

Shu (commandery) 蜀

Shu (method) 術

Shu (unit of weight) 銖

Shu-shih 庶 氏

Shui-heng tu-wei 水 衡 都 尉

Shun 舜

Shuo-wen 說 文

So-chü 莎 車

So-yin 索 引

Sou-shen chi 搜 神 記

Sou-shen hou chi 搜 神 後 記

Sou-su tu-wei 搜 粟 都 尉

Ssu-li hsiao-wei 司 隸 校 尉

Ssu-ma 司 馬

Ssu-ma Ch'ien 司 馬 遷

Ssu-ma Hsiang-ju 司 馬 相 如

Ssu-ma Kuang 司 馬 光

Ssu-tzu 思 子

Su Wen 蘇 文

Su Wu 蘇 武

Su Yü 蘇 輿

Sui-ho 綏 和

Sun Chien 孫 建

Sung (poems) 頌

Sung (state) 宋

Sung-shu 宋 書

Ta-chiang-chün 大 將 軍

Ta-fu 大 夫

Ta-hsing-ling 大 行 令

Ta-hung-lu 大 鴻 臚

Ta-ni wu-tao 大 逆 無 道

Ta-ssu-k'ung 大 司 空

Ta-ssu-ma 大 司 馬

Ta-ssu-nung 大 司 農

Ta-ssu-t'u 大 司 徒

Ta Tai li chi 大 戴 禮 記

Ta-yüan 大 宛

T'ai 泰

T'ai-ch'ang 太 常

T'ai-chu 太 祝

T'ai-ch'u yüan-chiang 太 初 元 將

T'ai-fu 太 傅

T'ai i 泰 一

T'ai-pao 太 保

T'ai-p'u 太 僕

T'ai-shih 太 師

T'ai-shih-ling 太 史 令

T'ai-shou 太 守

T'ai-tzu 太 子

T'ai-tzu shao-fu 太 子 少 傅

T'ai-tzu t'ai-fu 太 子 太 傅

T'ai-wei 太 尉

T'ai-yüeh-ling 太 樂 令

Takigawa Kametarō 瀧 川 龜 太 郎

Tan 旦

Tan Ch'in 但 欽

Tao 道

T'ao-Ch'ien 陶 潛

Te 德

Teng Kuang-han 鄧 廣 漢

Ti (earth) 地

Ti (emperor, power) 帝

Ti chih 地 祇

Ti chu 地 主

Tien-k'o 典 客

Tien-shu-kuo 典 屬 國

T'ien 天

T'ien Ch'ien-ch'iu 田 千 秋

T'ien-kuan 田 官

T'ien-shui 天 水

T'ien tao 天 道

T'ien ti 天 帝

T'ien Yen-nien 田 延 年

Ting I 丁姬
Ting Man 丁滿
Ting Ming 丁明
Ting-ssu 丁巳
Ting-t'ao 定陶
Ting Wai-jen 丁外人
T'ing-wei 廷尉
Ts'ao Ts'an 曹參
Tso chiang-chün 左將軍
Tso chuan 左傳
Tso-p'ing-i 左馮翊
Tsou Yen 騶衍
Tsung-cheng 宗正
Tsung-p'iao 從票
Ts'ung-shu chi-ch'eng 叢書集成
Tu Ch'in 杜欽
Tu Chou 杜周
Tu-hu 都護
Tu-Liao chiang-chün 度遼將軍
Tu T'o 杜佗
Tu-wei 都尉
Tu Yeh 杜鄴
Tu Yen-nien 杜延年
Tuan Hui-tsung 段會宗
Tun-huang 敦煌
Tun shih ho 屯氏河
T'un-t'ien hsiao-wei 屯田校尉
Tung Chung-shu 董仲舒
Tung Hsien 董賢
Tzu 子
Tzu-chih-t'ung-chien (k'ao-i) 資
　治通鑑 (考異)
Tzu-t'an 紫壇
Tz'u-shih 刺史

Wang Cheng-chün 王政君
Wang Chi 王吉
Wang Chin 王禁

Wang Ch'ung 王充
Wang Feng 王鳳
Wang Fu-jen 王夫人
Wang Han 王漢
Wang Hsien-ch'ien 王先謙
Wang Hung 王閎
Wang Ken 王根
Wang Li-ch'i 王利器
Wang Man 王曼
Wang Mang 王莽
Wang Shang 王商
Wang Shun 王舜
Wang Yen-shih 王延世
Wang Yin 王音
Wang Yü 王宇
Wei (consort, state) 衛
Wei (girth) 圍
Wei Ch'ang-chün 衛長君
Wei chiang-chün 衛將軍
Wei Ch'ing 衛青
Wei Chün-ju 衛君孺
Wei Hsiang 魏相
Wei Hsien 韋賢
Wei Hsüan-ch'eng 韋玄成
Wei Hung 衛宏
Wei I 衛姬
Wei K'ang 衛伉
Wei Pu-kuang 衛步廣
Wei Shao-erh 衛少兒
Wei Tzu-fu 衛子夫
Wei-wei 衛尉
Wei-yang 未央
Wen hsüan 文選
Wen-hsüeh 文學
Wen-hua ta ko-ming ch'i-chien ch'u-
　t'u wen-wu 文化大革命期
　間出土文物
Wen ti 文帝

Wen-wu 文物
Wo-wei 渥洼
Wu, Chi 戊己
Wu-hsing chih 五行志
Wu-huan 烏桓
Wu-ku 巫蠱
Wu-lei 烏壘
Wu-shan 巫山
Wu-sun 烏孫
Wu ti 武帝
Wu-tu 武都
Wu-wei 武威

Ya 雅
Yang Ch'ang 楊敞
Yang Hsiung 揚雄
Yang-shih 陽石
Yang-wu 陽武
Yang Yün 楊惲
Yao 堯

Yen 燕
Yen-ch'i 焉耆
Yen Shih-ku 顏師古
Yen ti 炎帝
Yen-t'ieh lun chiao chu 鹽鐵
　論校注
Yin 殷
Yin Chieh-yü 尹偨伃
Yin Chung 尹忠
Yin yang 陰陽
Yu-fu-feng 右扶風
Yu nei-shih 右內史
Yü-shih ta-fu 御史大夫
Yü-wu 余吾
Yüan ti 元帝
Yüeh-fu yin chien 樂府音監
Yüeh-fu yu chiao 樂府游徼
Yün-yang 雲陽
Yung 雍

Index

DATE DUE

OCT 0 9 2002

APR 1 8 2012

95562

95562

951
L82